Successful Failure

SUCCESSFUL FAILURE

The School America Builds

Hervé Varenne and Ray McDermott

*with Shelley Goldman, Merry Naddeo,
and Rosemarie Rizzo-Tolk*

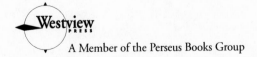

Westview
PRESS

A Member of the Perseus Books Group

To our fathers

Copyright © 1998 by Westview Press, A Member of the Perseus Books Group

Published in 1998 in the United States of America by Westview Press, 5500 Central Avenue, Boulder, Colorado 80301-2877, and in the United Kingdom by Westview Press, 12 Hid's Copse Road, Cumnor Hill, Oxford OX2 9JJ

Library of Congress Cataloging-in-Publication Data
Varenne, Hervé, 1948–
   Sucessful failure : the school America builds / Hervé Varenne and
Ray McDermott with Shelley Goldman, Merry Naddeo, and Rosemarie
Rizzo-Tolk.
      p.   cm.
   Includes bibliographical references and index.
   ISBN 0-8133-3165-X (hardcover) — ISBN 0-8133-9129-6 (paperback)
   1. Education—United States—Evaluation—Case studies.   2. School
failure—United States—Case studies.   3. Education—Social aspects—
United States—Case studies.   4. Educational anthropology—United
States—Case studies.   I. McDermott, Ray.   II. Title.
LA217.2.V37   1998
370'.971—dc21   97-43850
                                                                                                              CIP

The paper used in this publication meets the requirements of the American National Standard for Permanence of Paper for Printed Library Materials Z39.48-1984.

PERSEUS
POD
ON DEMAND   10   9   8   7   6   5   4

Contents

PART TWO
Education and the Making of Cultural Facts

Figures

Preface

It is easy to identify and criticize the American school preoccupation with failure, for the evidence is abundant that too many people leave school scarred. The more difficult task is to come to a point where one can think about education and schooling without necessarily thinking about failure or success as categories for the identification of children. In this book we show how limiting these categories are, and we build the case for a new way of thinking about education and schooling.

Somehow the people of the United States have organized a terrible problem for themselves: They have made individual learning and school performance the institutional site where members of each new generation are measured and then assigned a place in the social structure based on this measurement. Learning has become an instrument for so much else than education that the vocabulary commonsensically used to talk about learning and education cannot be trusted. It is a vocabulary of individuals succeeding and failing that continues to hide the common situation. It takes hard intellectual work to clear the decks for only a moment. This is the task we pick up in this book.

In this preface, we state the case against the language of success and failure and then confront the difficulty involved in building a new language for talking about children, education, and schooling. The same rhythm appears through the book. We ask readers to visit almost any scene in the United States where what is commonly known as "education" is to be found. There they will find people busily doing this or that but almost always doing one fateful thing: determining who is the most successful. Sometimes the emphasis on relative success is intense, and the competition for grades or other rewards is ubiquitous. Elsewhere, particularly in settings where many have had a long history of designated failure, the search for relative success may be muted or hidden. In either case, there are always students worried about how they are doing relative to others. There are always parents and teachers worrying about students worrying. And there are always professional educators and researchers worried about the adequacy of the testing and its effect on everyone. Worriers worrying about the worries of others. There have been easier worlds in which to be either a student or an educator.

The measurement of individuals in competition with other individuals is an essential part of life in American culture. It is a source of entertainment on television quiz shows and sporting events, but mostly it is a source of worry, particularly around everything that has to do with schooling, most particularly at times of major transition, from entry into preschool to the search for a "top" graduate or professional school sixteen years later. At its best, competition allows people to perform at an intense level before winners and losers take their crowns only long enough to begin the next game. At its worst, competition produces losers who are then pushed out of the game. Academic competition in the United States is competition at its worst. Many are out of the game by the first grade or the fifth or the ninth. Eventually nearly everyone will be found wanting, having to accept the place an evaluator assigned as "their" place. So it is no surprise that children and parents should worry about individual school evaluations, teachers about their classes, principals about their schools, and policymakers about overall rates of success and failure. It is no surprise that all should struggle against these evaluations and, sometimes, cheat at what is never quite a game. This is the world people in America face. It has been this way for a long time, and it has been difficult to talk about education and institutionalize schools in ways that are not embedded in this worry about success and failure. There is no evidence it *must* be this way.

This book was written to show how much work is necessary for the American world to be reconstructed in the everyday life of everyone. Our hope is that this demonstration will suggest ways to transform this work. What human beings build, they can modify if they understand the context and mechanisms involved. There is good news here—but not easy news: The American patterns are much too powerfully inscribed on the social landscape to be simply wished away.

The good news must be stated often. In Chapters 1 to 4, we look at students officially identified as failing and we show them to be amazingly complex and ingenious in their responses to the pressures of their conditions. In the process we expand our lead question from "how are they doing on this or that little task" to a more difficult one that moves us radically away from personal performance into a crowded social thicket: How will they be identified by others in the social distance? As soon as this is done, the picture changes as we show how failure is reasserted even by those who say they wish to help. And so, our good news must be tempered: Handling school tasks is usually easy, but handling them while managing an environment filled with others ready to notice what is wrong is something else altogether. Students in various educational settings—at an after-school club, at home doing homework, at a home for runaways, and in a school for dropouts—are in much better shape than they would appear through the usual institutional lens. But our recognition of their successes is not consequential if schools have only so much success to give.

Similarly, when we look carefully at children performing well in a prosperous suburban middle school, there is a surprising story to tell (Chapter 5). For the most part, successful children are rarely more than one step ahead of failure: A quiz here or there, a bad day on the SATs, a behavioral blemish on their record—just about anything can knock them off their chosen paths, or at least that is what they are constantly told. There is rarely a moment for them to let down their guard. Failure is always possible, always imminent, always immediately around the corner. They are rarely allowed to forget failure, and they work hard avoiding it. Still, their repeated failures may not be too consequential either, since there are others, in other classes and other schools, who will be known as having failed worse.

Having presented chapters about the ingenuity of those who fail and the worries of those on the road to success, our book can address its central question: How are we, as researchers, to write so as not to reproduce the very conditions of the worries and the distorting efforts at mitigating the effects of failure? How are we all to escape both success and failure?

These are not usual questions, and the social sciences are badly equipped to ask them. Mostly, researchers let themselves be caught by parents and politicians who want to know why particular children, and particular kinds of children at that, fail more often than others. The answers that make sense to those who ask the questions range from theories of inherent intelligence to theories of political injustice. The theories are different in emphasis, but they mostly work with the given categories and thus reconstruct a world in which success and failure remain a fact of life and in which whatever else may happen, whatever programs may be implemented, however much money is spent, children will be identified as having succeeded or failed. We wish to back out of the dead end by refusing to answer any questions that would focus our attention on a Johnny who can't read or a Sheila who can. Our task is to focus attention on the questions themselves and on those who ask them.

Instead of searching for better ways to explain success and failure, we document the intellectual foundations of the interpretative scheme by which success and failure are constantly reproduced as analytic and political categories even by those most dedicated to building the intellectual foundations of a better world. We hope to show that school success and failure are not simple consequences of the way the human world must be. It is a cultural mock-up, what we call a cultural fact. The success and failure system, as a cultural fact, is real in its connections to the political economy, exquisitely detailed in its connections with the everyday behavior of the people who make up the system, and in both these ways massively consequential in the lives of all. Yet it does not have to be this way, and if everyone stopped measuring, explaining, and remediating, school success and failure would in a significant sense disappear. Other ways to stratify would soon evolve, but this evolution would have the virtue of separating education from resource allocation.

Demonstrating the cultural facticity of success and failure is a relatively easy task. More difficult is the attempt to reformulate the conceptual materials from which the categories are fashioned. If we are right that success and failure are arbitrary categories America has naturalized as ways of talking about the characteristics of individual children, then noting the *success in failure* and the *failure in success* has us in a battle with the conceptual foundations of American culture, including American social science and education. Words that come easily to American readers, words such as individual, identity, skill, ability, disability, intelligence, competence, proficiency, achievement, motivation, self-esteem, objective test, grade level, and so on are screeching fingernails on the theoretical chalkboard for us. We know what they mean and why people use them, for we are full partners in the culture that makes these words so commonsensical. They are sometimes useful, and we use them all too often in our description of colleagues, friends, and students. We have also become aware of the institutional contexts in which their use can be lethal not just to those who are labeled failures but to those who share the goals of democratic education for all.

In 1991, we set out to write a simple and direct book. By mixing a few new papers with already published ones, we intended to say once and for all what we had been trying to say in our separate ways for the previous fifteen years. Failure is a dangerous category, easy to overuse institutionally and terribly unfair to young children who are increasingly subject to classification before their potentials are meaningfully explored. Culture is more than ideas and symbols—it is the human construction that resists human action. There, we said it; but it is not enough. That we as anthropologists can dismiss failure as a cultural trap or that we as citizens can confront failure as an unnecessary version of social inequality does not make failure go away. More important, it leaves untouched the conceptual and political foundations that have made failure such an integral part of schooling. These latter forces are so potent that we cannot afford to ignore them in our own lives; as parents, for example, it is difficult to give up on the effort to have one's own children avoiding failure at all costs. As researchers, we must also realize we are not free to write as if these forces were just a figment of the collective imagination. They are facts that stand in our way.

After five years of trying, we have not written a simple book. The old essays had to be reshaped and rewritten from scratch, and the new essays took us in directions we did not expect. Our dedication to understanding everyone in terms of the work they do with the thickly textured culture that constrains their learning—their intelligence, their ideas, curiosities, wishes, and dreams—has put us in opposition with the interpretive habits of American education. In "the school America builds," to use the words of our subtitle, it is common sense to assume that the most important thing to know about a child's performance in school is what was placed into the child's inner self, into the psychological core. In the school we would make, no one would quite care about measuring how much went there–and no one would keep track of it institutionally. It is not that we deny the importance of early experience or personality. Instead we affirm that one's past must be maintained and actively re-created in the present and that this is always done with many others—many of whom we do not know. In American theories of school failure, children are understood apart from a full account of their cultural present as if discounting the present as it has evolved from the past is the only way to respect the individuality of the child. We want to restore the balance, and we focus on the activity of those who are identified as failures as an opportunity to see them heroically managing their culture. Above all we want to show them as actors facing facts and thereby to affirm their freedom from a world that may break them but never quite makes them.

An account showing we all are engaged in a spectacularly successful failure is not easy to write. At every turn in the argument, an extra interpretive effort is necessary. We think it is well worth the effort.

Hervé Varenne and Ray McDermott
New York and Palo Alto

Acknowledgments

If a child cannot fail or succeed at school without many others lending a hand, how much more so for the authors of a book. We must acknowledge first the traditions that have nurtured conversation over the last twenty years: the French structuralism of Ferdinand de Saussure, Marcel Mauss, Claude Levi-Strauss, and Louis Dumont; the ethnomethodology of Harold Garfinkel, Harvey Sacks, and Emanuel Schegloff; the cognitive anthropology of Charles Frake and Harold Conklin; the semiotic anthropology of David Schneider, Clifford Geertz, Robert Murphy, and Milton Singer; the linguistic and literary wisdom of Mikhail Bakhtin, Roman Jakobson, Dell Hymes, and Alton Becker; the literary Marxism of Raymond Williams and the psychological Marxism of Lev Vygotsky; the educational anthropology of Jules Henry and George Spindler; the kinesics of Ray Birdwhistell, Albert Scheflen, and Adam Kendon; and the multidisciplinary wisdom of Gregory Bateson and Paul Byers. Before there was postmodernism, there were many other upstarts who fought off received categories without forgetting that the world can be interrogated systematically.

Each of these traditions has given rise to a new generation of powerful intellectuals who have kept the field moving. We have worked with many of them directly and we want to thank them for challenging us: Keith Basso, John Baugh, Jack Bilmes, Richard Blot, George Bond, James Boon, John Broughton, Michael Brown, Eric Bredo, Michael Cole, Concha Delgato-Gaitan, John Dore, Lee Drummond, Frederick Erickson, Richard Frankel, Perry Gilmore, Charles Goodwin, Margaret Goodwin, James Greeno, Peg Griffin, Grey Gundaker, Clifford Hill, Joel Kuipers, Jean Lave, Charlotte Linde, Hugh Mehan, William Peter Murphy, Reba Page, Susan Philips, David Smith, Lucy Suchman, Deborah Tannen, Henry Tylbor, Naoki Ueno, Philip Wexler, and D. Lawrence Wieder.

In no human world can one make something for others without institutional help. Many have done so in various ways and at various stages of our research: The National Institute of Education, the Elbenwood Center for the Study of the Family as Educator at Teachers College, Columbia University, the Spencer Foundation, the Laboratory of Comparative Human Cognition at the University of California at San Diego. We also want to thank all the individuals who let us enter their lives for research purposes. We cannot name them but they know how profound is our recognition of their contribution.

We have known each other for twenty years, and for ten of them we worked in the same department and lived in the same building. Along with Paul Byers, we shared hundreds of students and sat together on more than one hundred dissertations. We also shared families and watched each other raise six children. Susan Varenne and Shelley Goldman lived the home show with us and made it meaningful while somehow finding the time to work on the details of their own careers. One of us lost a father right before the start of the book, the other right at the end, and we miss them both.

Once upon a time, we both had a dissertation committee, and our debt to those who brought us into the field cannot be acknowledged enough. Thanks again to Harumi Befu, Charles Frake, Milton Singer, and George Spindler. Through it all Ray McDermott has had a shadow committee made up of his three brothers: Robert, Joe, and John McDermott.

A handful of people have read and commented on various chapters, and we wish to thank them for their critiques: Reba Page gave detailed written accounts for the first six chapters; Eric Bredo, Mary Cotter, Grey Gundaker, Laura Kerr, Ellen Lagemann, Sherry Ortner, D.C. Phillips, Tina Syer, had much to say about early versions of various chapters; and Chapter 6 received careful scrutiny in a reading group made up of Mizuko Ito, Joan Fujimura, Susan Newman, and Lucy Suchman. Allison Stratton helped us with final editing tasks. We are also thankful for the help from past and present crews at Westview: Dean Birkenkamp, Cathy Pusateri, and Melanie Stafford.

Having recognized our debt, it is also customary to state the not-so-obvious: What is to be found in these pages is what we have made with all that all these people have given us. It would not have been what it is without them. But it is not quite what any, including either one of us separately, might have expected it would be.

H.V. and R.M.

Introduction
Hervé Varenne and
Ray McDermott

In a way, culture substitutes itself to life, in another way culture uses and transforms life to realize a synthesis of higher order.

—Claude Lévi-Strauss,
The Elementary Structures of Kinship ([1949] 1969: 4)

In a famous account of growing up in America, Maxine Hong Kingston tells of her sister's silence when, for the first time, the two of them had to act in a setting ruled by English and the School. She tells of her own inability to speak the character "I":

> It was when I found out I had to talk that school became a misery, that the silence became a misery. I did not speak and felt bad each time I did not speak. I read aloud in first grade, though, and heard the barest whisper with little squeaks come out of my throat. "Louder," said the teacher, who scared the voice away again. The other Chinese girls did not talk either, so I knew the silence had to do with being a Chinese girl.
>
> Reading out loud was easier than speaking because we did not have to make up what to say, but I stopped often, and the teacher would think I'd gone quiet again. I could not understand "I." The Chinese "I" has seven strokes, intricacies. How could the American "I," assuredly wearing a hat like the Chinese, have only three strokes, the middle so straight? Was it out of politeness that this writer left off strokes the way a Chinese has to write her own name small and crooked? No, it was not politeness: "I" is a capital and "you" is lower case. I stared at that middle line and waited so long for its black center to resolve into tight strokes and dots that I forgot to pronounce it. (1975: 166–167)

Kingston grew up to become a master of the American "I." She has written one of the great educational autobiographies of the twentieth century, and she has been duly celebrated for it.

As educators and scientists concerned with action, we[1] are looking for ways to understand the conditions of such achievements. What makes reading "I" easy or difficult? What makes a famous author? What does it take to write an autobiography? Would Maxine Hong Kingston have ever written such a text had her mother stayed in China (or American industry not needed cheap labor to build railroads and clean clothes)? What did Maxine Hong Kingston do that is her own? What is she responsible for?

1

These are the questions we ask of various lives conducted in and around American schools—the lives of children, teachers, parents, and educational researchers. As cultural anthropologists, we ask these questions of people acting with others and performing various tasks in settings where issues generally thought relevant to education get raised: reading, cooking, doing homework, singing, discussing social issues, taking tests. The questions have a set of easy commonsense answers: People do well or badly "because" something is right or wrong with them or their lives. But we are not satisfied with such answers. What is more, we refuse to be caught by the logic of the questions. We go in a different direction and show that these questions and their commonsense answers are aspects of one encompassing discourse. We refer to this discourse as that of the "School" in "America." We capitalize "School" to indicate we are not referring to any particular school, and we use "America" to indicate that we are interested in particular ways of talking about, and doing, education that no one in the United States can escape—whatever the community, ethnic group, race, class, or gender affiliation. This is the institutionalized framework that must be carefully described if anyone, whether concerned with research, policy, or practice, is to understand the situation of the persons they hope to help. It is a framework that was built over generations—thus our concern with culture.

It is certainly reasonable to focus on Maxine Hong Kingston as an independent, indeed heroic, agent. Few would object if we talked about her personal strength in the face of adversity or about other qualities that eventually allowed her a successful career in schools. Any mention of her talent in weaving a gripping story would make sense. An audience in America would probably accept the need to wonder what might have happened if she had grown up elsewhere, and it would recognize that we should consider the political, economic, and symbolic conditions that pushed and pulled emigrants to California in the first half of the twentieth century. By the dictates of the discourse, it would make sense to mention poverty and exploitation in China, wars and revolutions in Europe, railroads and robber barons in the United States, all conditions that somehow shaped a place for the Chinese who crossed the Pacific.

The political and economic questions are less commonsense questions than the ones about talent and fortitude, but they can lead to new questions we have only recently learned to ask about the role of language, symbolism, and textuality in the shaping of human life. The new questions would have us focus on the very act of Kingston *writing*, in *English*, an *autobiography*, for *publication* and encourage us to talk about the evolution of literary genres and rhetorical forms. We might then mention the *Confessions* of St. Augustine and the texts produced by many others from Benjamin Franklin to Malcolm X, tales of difficult origins, struggles, and eventual success, many of them European tales built on earlier cultural forms and then transformed in the ideological context of the United States, what we call America. This line of inquiry could lead to talk about publishing houses and distribution systems, vast complexes of bureaucracies and technologies that make some personal acts available to a large audience through particular symbolic means. We could then talk about those who read *Woman Warrior* and are moved by it, asking the same questions of them that we asked of Maxine Hong Kingston, and we could analyze the institutions that shape a literate audience, train it to respond to confessional tales, and make it eager to read more.

We use insights from all these traditions to answer what is, fundamentally, one encompassing question: When we celebrate *Woman Warrior*, whom do we celebrate, Maxine Hong Kingston, her readers, or America?

This question must be asked of any act performed by any person alive in the United States: Who and what are involved in reading aloud to an audience the symbol "I" on a page? Or, to illustrate from the case studies we present in this book, who is responsible for a child being teased for saying "pisghetti" when all his peers can say "spaghetti"? What is involved in working-class families with similar demographic profiles helping their children with homework and making different places for their children's identification, one as successful and the other as a failure? What difference does it make in the unfolding of lives at the bottom of New York City's social rankings if it can be shown that young adults in a homeless shelter or an alternative remedial high school can perform together complex social tasks that demonstrate care for each other and a complex understanding of their situation? What is the implication, for both theory and practice, of the evidence we present that "who people are," in some kind of abstract psychological space, and even "what people do," as it can be documented through careful description, may be quite irrelevant in guiding the response of the rest of the world to what they do? We can show failed children succeeding at school tasks and successful children failing at similar tasks. And we can show how such performances are sequenced with other performances by other people in such a way that they are dismissed, co-opted, and reinterpreted. Throughout the case studies we show how many people are involved, even in the most local scenes, in establishing the consequences of what happened.

This book is an investigation of who and what are involved in the eventual evaluation of a life as a success or failure in school terms. Who is responsible, and whom, or what, should we celebrate, or blame? Eventually, we come back to celebrating and blaming "America"—not as an abstract system but as the product of what people continually construct with what they find *always already there* around them. To make this point, we follow a consistent path. Where others focus on school success, we could just as easily focus on failure. And thus we highlight the arbitrary and limiting nature of the categories "success" and "failure." They are not categories that can ever capture the good sense of what children do. They directly conspire to prevent all of us from understanding the conditions within which the child's life is constructed (America). This is the paradoxical result of American interpretations that supposedly focus attention on the individual child but do so, mostly, by examining that child and then labeling him or her, thereby stopping the analysis where we think it should begin. Where we begin, always, is with Maxine Hong Kingston as an actor involved in building something. This moves us, always, to a search both for the other actors— the builders—in the constant presence of whom she is acting and for the tools they all find around them. The human world is made up of the remnants of everyone else's activities. It is an artifact or, in words we like to use, a *cultural fact,* something that was *facted* (from the Latin past participle of the verb "to make"). It is always made and always about to be remade.

Schooling and Cultural Fact

Let us start again with our questions about Maxine Hong Kingston but ask them of the sister she mentions, about whom she says little. This sister, and her silence, can stand for the many who never become famous authors or who, to invoke the more usual standard, do not take the road to a comfortable, middle-class life.

As a personal and institutional success, Kingston could be held up as an exemplar of the ways American institutions, including the schools she attended, whatever their problems, allowed her to express her individual, unique self. The apologists of America have indeed made this case with great persuasion over the past 200 years: America is the field so organized that individuals can shine. Even as we criticize particular practices, the general argument is hard to contradict. The problem, of course, is that not all individuals in the United States get to go where some others go: Everyone can race; only one can win. The problem of relative success is most powerfully etched when we wonder about the fate of the Hong family's silent sister and the many others who never move to something their teachers celebrate. Who is responsible for identified failures? The child? The parents, teachers, social workers, and therapists who have responsibility for the child? Or the peculiar constructions that have been built over the past 350 years in what has become "America"?

Our focus on the difficulties that continue to plague schooling is necessary for moral reasons. Success, the flash of genius that temporarily blinds us and eventually reveals a person's particular glory, is not problematic. Only failure is. It is not by chance the fundamental question in educational research is phrased negatively: Why can't Johnny read? In a later chapter, we play at raising the reverse issue: Why can Sheila read? Our question of Sheila is a variation on the questions we asked of Maxine Hong Kingston, but our goal is not to answer the questions. Our goal is to understand the imperative that makes educational research always start with a hunt for the causes of success and, more poignantly, failure. Given the need to understand education as a broad social process that involves much more than schooling, the puzzle is why the question about Johnny should be made the most pressing. For us, the problem American schooling faces as both a political and a scientific activity is the success/failure system. For journalists and politicians to celebrate those who are "above average," many must be known as "below average." The first are dependent on the latter. Success and failure are the products of the same America. Failure allows for the definition of success, and together they frame everyone: children, teachers, parents, and researchers in the United States (and other parts of the world caught by the schooling system that evolved in Europe).

By the same logic, an understanding of the failure of urban schools requires an understanding of the success of suburban schools. Inner city and suburb do not belong to different worlds. They belong to the same differentiated world. Our task as social scientists is to analyze this differentiation and to highlight what it offers to human action and how it constrains or expands possibilities. To do this, we must struggle with the analytic tools given by the tradition that produced the cultural facts of success and failure in the first place, tools such as standardized tests that measure and identify people as failures or successes. We must confront this tradition and its tools if we are to understand its products. We must focus on the institutions that do the characterizations: Who decides who is a success or failure; when and how is the identification done and in what terms, under what circumstances, and—above all—with what legitimate consequences?

To accomplish the shift in the unit of analysis from the identified individual to the set of individuals working together on their common circumstances, we must return to the original moment when a child who was not quite yet Maxine Hong Kingston, the famous author, confronted "I" on a page in the midst of a classroom filled with children and a teacher in the context of a school filled with still more children and teachers, along with administrators and other adults, in the context of a school bureaucracy in a large city and so forth.

> At that moment, everything is in suspension.
> Nothing has happened.
> And then, the child's delay is *noticed*.

It is noticed by another human being, but not just any human being in a neutral setting. It is noticed by *a teacher* (not a janitor), *in a school* (and not at home), *during classtime* (and not on the playground). Suddenly, the difference between performance and the teacher's expectations has been made into a difference that can make a difference in the biography of the child. The delay has become a "failure" in need of explanation, evaluation, and remediation. The child's act (in this case, the nonact) has been recognized and identified as a particular kind of act that must lead to further actions by possibly a host of other people. In certain schools but not in others, the act-made-into-an-instance-of-school-failure can itself be used as a token justifying an even more consequential identification. The particular act is taken as exemplary of the kind of acts performed by this kind of person; it is now the child, rather than the act, that is identified as a success or failure. The act may be used as a token justifying the identification of the school as a whole; there are successful and failing schools. This can be extended to characterize a group with whom the person is identified. On this basis, arguments are made comparing the success of recent immigrants from the Caribbean to that of native African Americans. In the process, a child's paradoxical "I" disappears behind a "me," behind a persona in a cultural drama that others have constructed with what the child has accomplished.

The process we have just outlined is fundamental to our approach. No person is self-made. We take George Herbert Mead seriously when he states that "the others and the self arise in the social act together" ([1926] 1964: 169).[2] All persons-as-known are eventually made through the interaction of the actor and millions of relevant others, most of whom the actor has not met face-to-face. In describing a handful of lives from Japan, David Plath phrased a similar understanding about the interplay between individual biography and its use in the social world:

> Culture, character, and consociates weave a complicated fabric of biography. The process is not only lifelong; it is longer than life. Consociates begin to shape our personal course even before we are born, and may continue to renegotiate the meaning of our life long after we are dead. To this extent, a person is a collective product. We all must "author" our own biographies, using the idiom of our heritage, but our biographies must be "authorized" by those who live them with us. (1980: 7)

More formally, we assume any act by an authorial "I" must be approached as a moment in a complex sequence involving at least three steps, or three positions in a minimal social system. First, a child reads; second, someone else gives this reading a place within a particular symbolic system that transforms the original act into a "success" or a "failure"; third, someone else delivers the consequences of the placement. For Maxine Hong Kingston, reading "I" in school involves her as the student to be evaluated, the teacher as evaluator, and groups that take the evaluation into account (say, parents, administrators, employers, educational researchers, etc.) for their own purposes. Years later, she participates in another version of the sequence: She writes a manuscript, then someone publishes it, and finally the book is celebrated.

Each step is a complex setting where human beings work together and, eventually, achieve something, a "thing" that is recognized as having happened and stands as the fact on which further history can be made. Think, for example, of two strangers meeting on a city street: One asks for the time, the other gives it, the first thanks the other, and they go their separate ways, having asked for and having given the time.[3] Now think of a teacher and a student who know each other well for having spent many months in the same second-grade schoolroom. They may start with the same words as our two strangers, but they can end in a quite different place, the child having been tested for and having failed/succeeded in demonstrating the knowledge to tell time. The same question about the time can, in different settings, play to a quite different purpose: different settings, different struggles, different outcomes, that are made to fit into different systems of consequences.

In the latter stages of most any sequence of activity called educational in America, success and failure are major symbols. The same behavior, knowing what time it is, for example, in a nonschool context likely serves another purpose, and it is unlikely to be evaluated as a success or failure. Even in the second grade at the initial moment of the teacher's asking for the time, neither success nor failure nor even their absence were necessarily relevant. The teacher, momentarily without a watch, may have simply wanted to know the time, in which case it made no difference who answered the question; or the teacher may have been driven to find out who knew how to tell the time, and individual and documentable success or failure became the issue at hand.

Knowing the time becomes an instance of success or failure when the actors are related institutionally to a wider set of persons with an interest in documenting who knows what.

In organizing a cultural analysis of schooling, we need a general framework that preserves the independence of both the person and the person's activities from the systems (economic, political, symbolic, etc.) that provided the resources for the person's activities and made sense of the activities by providing still other persons with the resources for plausible identifications and further actions. All acts, initially, are not part of the system that may eventually acquire them even though it is likely they are already sensitive to that system. "All action," warned John Dewey, "is an invasion of the future, of the unknown. Conflict and uncertainty are ultimate traits" (1922: 12). All actors, initially, are not particular kinds of persons even though they always have at their disposal the resources of the personae others let them claim. The qualities of acts and persons are not intrinsic to the act or person. They belong rather to the sequence of acts, and to the group of persons, within which acts and persons are found. One must thus move from local, fleeting moments when someone like Kingston is confronted by an "I" on the printed page or other moments when, much later, she writes the same "I" with ease and in ways that please her audience to the moments when people concerned with her for some reason (teachers, editors, literary critics) place her act in their own history. At the same time, one must remember Kingston always is fully involved as an active participant struggling with "I," with her teacher and mother, with her publishers and editors. Still, she remains caught in a web of constructions and identifications she cannot escape. The one thing she cannot do is enforce a substitution of the Chinese 我 for the American "I."[4] Even if she had tried to make the substitution as an intellectual game to challenge her teacher into a consciousness of other possibilities, the difference it would have made to the teacher would have been inexorably different from the difference (or its absence) it might have made to her mother. Kingston, like us, inhabits America.

Culture in Question

In the fragment we quoted earlier, Kingston writes, "I knew the silence had to do with being a Chinese girl." In the process she offers an interpretation of "the" silence. We must confront this interpretation. As far as we are concerned, Chinese girlishness is not a state of being.[5] Not talking is not a trait, among others, that Chinese girls possess more than people born to parents who came to the United States from other parts of the world. It is something that happens to some girls in American classrooms, something that is identified with China and then used as an explanation for the particular biographies of the people who have been so identified. It is an *American* cultural fact, one that is specific only in the peculiar house that dominates the human landscape in the United States.

Our point is complex, and we address it throughout the book and particularly in Part 2. At this stage, we simply want to sketch the problem in its relation to general

political discussions about schooling. In the process, we introduce, first, the understanding of "culture" that we inherit from the anthropological tradition on which we
build and, second, our position with regard to the interplay of culture with education broadly conceived. A concern with culture is nothing new, certainly not in the
field of education. John Dewey, in *Democracy and Education* ([1916] 1966), was
aware of the multiplicity of human societies and of the ways in which participation
in various societies transformed the lives of people who were born into them. The
first generations of anthropologists, from Franz Boas (1928) to Margaret Mead
(1928), had an abiding interest in education in both social scientific and political
terms. Psychology has lagged behind in its use of the term "culture", although with
the rise of cultural deprivation theories of school failure (Deutsch 1967), it has been
invoked repeatedly in any effort to explain the fate of the poor in the United States.
It seemed good common sense and altogether liberal to expect people to adapt themselves to their conditions, including poverty, to develop "cultures" that responded to
their needs and then to pass the cultures along to their children. Although a radical
critique revealed the severe limitations of the analysis, it has nonetheless remained a
plausible account of the behavior of the disenfranchised. It regularly reappears in educational research, and we must deal with it repeatedly throughout this book.

Among anthropologists and many other educational researchers, "cultural deprivation" and "the culture of poverty" explanations dropped out of favor, and starting
in the 1970s, particularly through the work of sociolinguists, alternate explanations
of school failure among the poor were offered. Researchers began to focus on the linguistic, ethnic, and racial differences that appear to have a profound impact on
American classrooms. From the sociolinguistic point of view, the harsh conditions to
which people had adapted by developing a "deprived" culture were not so much the
product of poverty within the United States as they were the products of historical
processes by which industrialized societies invaded and colonized. People pushed out
of their areas of origin and pulled to major industrial centers gave their children
something of their past that did not fit in classrooms organized on different ("dominant," "hegemonic," "middle class," "American") principles. It seemed obvious that
this process would lead to miscommunication and other kinds of trouble.

By implication at least, Maxine Hong Kingston appears to have been operating
with what is now called the "difference" theory of trouble in School. She and her
peers were silent "because" they were Chinese, children of immigrants from China
with different understandings of proper behavior in schools not adapted to them.
She was also a precursor of a movement in educational policy that has its roots in the
intellectual argument about difference but that simplifies the anthropological understanding of culture. Culture, in classical anthropology, is about borrowing, transmission, learning, and transformation. The "difference" analysis, by contrast, emphasizes the unchangeable self as constructed in early childhood. Given such an analysis,
it makes sense to call for the development of special programs to train teachers and
students to learn each other's ways and perhaps reach some kind of middle ground.
In recent years, a more extreme and essentialist theory has been argued under the la-

bel of "multiculturalism." It may be less a theory than a political cry for the good society, but it is too close to our interests for us to ignore it. In most versions, multiculturalism starts with the same assumption of difference in historical origin and evolution that anthropological understandings of culture have developed. Popular multiculturalism overrides good sense in arguing that every group has a definite membership of persons who have been made, through birth and early socialization, both the same as each other and different from others. At its worst, multiculturalism implies that every person has but one true or legitimate culture (Kingston is first and foremost "Chinese"), that the legitimacy of the claim is based on lines of descent (Kingston is Chinese because her parents are Chinese), and that the claim is about the ownership of a culture by its members (being Chinese is Kingston's own culture; it is "her" culture).

Anthropologists, since Boas's (1938) struggles against nineteenth-century racial theories of humanity, have protested loudly against theories of culture that emphasize descent and ascribed membership. Even those who stressed early enculturation operated with a theory perhaps best summarized by Margaret Mead ([1942] 1965) when she asserted that any human infant, whatever its background, can become a full participant of any group, however different the groups may be. Claude Lévi-Strauss ([1955] 1963c) went further in claiming that all personality types were possible in all cultures if only because anyone can reject the local cultural imperatives of the places where they were born. A person has no choice about living with these imperatives but can nonetheless confront them on every detail. A human being is never frozen in a particular pattern. Human beings learn, and they never stop learning. Being Chinese is not a matter of being but of becoming. Being Chinese is not a matter of identity but of identification, as a person's work is recast by the person's consociates as a particular kind of work. When one is born in the United States of parents who migrated from China, "being Chinese" is not a fate; it is an achievement. Being Chinese American is something that is worked on by a child in relation to parents, school, neighbors, detractors, and crosstown bigots. It is an achievement fashioned out of material bequeathed the whole population by America.

This way of thinking about culture recaptures what has always been powerful about the concept and has established its place in the social sciences. There is something specific about any arrangement of human beings. On the basis of a universal biological constitution, human groups always elaborate new ways of organizing themselves that must take into account both their biological constitution and, more important, the human history of the group, including its many and continuing contacts with other groups. This is the import of the statement by Lévi-Strauss that we use as an epigraph. In history something is made that then forms the world newcomers, whether infants or immigrants, have to inhabit. Kingston's mother came to California, where she found the category "Chinese," and she had to struggle with the identifications those already in California proposed for her. In the same manner, the surviving Amerindians, the Mexicans, and the newly arriving Europeans had to reconstruct "China" through their encounter with these other immigrants. A genera-

10 *Hervé Varenne and Ray McDermott*

tion later, Kingston entered school and its evolved identifications for Chinese children, including probably the identification of Chineseness with "silence." Was that identification self-generated by the Chinese, as Kingston, along with most readers of her book, might assume, or was it jointly produced by them and their non-Chinese contemporaries, as we suspect? Was it a quality of Maxine Hong Kingston, or was it something she and her teachers constructed together? Was it a cultural fact?

A classic case of systematic silence developed from the study of black children in school.[6] As was demonstrated repeatedly by William Labov (1972), this silence was situation-specific, and extraordinary fluency could be found in nonschool settings (see Gilmore 1985 for an exemplary study). Black children are not silent as a trait of their personality or even their culture. Silence is not their identity. They *appeared* quiet-in-school-with-white-teachers. To claim silence as a personality trait is different from claiming silence as a situated accomplishment. The institutionalized existence of the linguistically deprived, silent black child says more about educational stereotypes than about black children. Since the stereotype was disallowed by sociolinguistic research thirty years ago, we have been forced to watch an amazing shift in identification as black children have gotten to be known as precisely not silent but violently aggressive. Blacks are not now, and never have been, acquiescing and simple-minded Uncle Toms. Nor are they, not now, not ever, not only, not simply, the scary rap singers adopted and demonized by the media (Giroux 1996). Still, and whatever the behavioral facts, all blacks in the United States, along with all whites, native born and newcomer, do have to struggle today with the images and the performances that Uncle Tom and Ice-T are made to suggest. What no one can do in the United States is to act as if the pieces that make American culture are not there. Uncle Tom and Ice-T are cultural facts.[7] As cultural facts, they are constructions with more solidity perhaps than the cities, suburbs, and highways that make up the landscape.

Success and failure, like dangerous black maleness, silent Chinese girlishness, and so on and so forth, are categories, scripts, and stage directions that frame joint human action. These labels do not exist for their accuracy but for their powers of evocation, and they must not be confused with the people for whom they may at times be used. From our perspective, black maleness is not a property of black males but of American culture. It is not that black maleness exists outside of the people who together perform it for each other. It is rather that black maleness may be scripted more by white males, and black and white females, than by black males alone. Conversely, what is to count as "white" has been continually transformed by the Africans have who had to deal with those who brought them to the Americas and by their descendants who continue to resist their conditions. Together Europeans, Africans, Asians, and Amerindians have produced something unique in the world: an America that does not belong to any one of them. Some of their descendants may have more power in shaping America than others, but all have participated, if only through passive resistance and the fact of their presence. For those who begin life in the United States, whether child or immigrant, America is the fact they inherited, and it will frame them for the rest of their lives.

Culture and Context

Culture has little to do with the habits parents train their children to have; it has everything to do with the environments parents build for their children to inhabit. These environments, houses with their many rooms, including the classrooms and homes that concern us in this book, are usually talked about as the "contexts" in which particular traits, such as silence or aggressivity, become visible. This phrasing assumes the independent consequentiality of the trait: a Learning Disabled child is, inherently, learning disabled even though the disability may show or may be consequential only "in certain contexts." Indeed, most specialists in such matters, assume that a special disability, wherever it comes from, whether from genetic defects or a difficult early socialization, must somehow be hardwired in the body of the child.

We take a different position, grounded in an old intuition in sociology and anthropology. From Émile Durkheim ([1897] 1951), we accept the idea that "deviance" is constituted by what is made normal. And we follow Ruth Benedict's (1934) suggestion that particular cultural patterns might generate particular problems for particular people. Most starkly, Learning Disability (LD) may be a *product* of America, not something that is *revealed in* America. LD is a room well stocked with all that it takes for some children to be demonstrated as carriers—whether they are carriers or not, whether there is such a thing as LD for any human being to carry, whether LD would make a difference for anything if there were no rooms for its identification, and whether special treatments are required once it has become common sense that it is an affliction that a proper democracy should take into account. From this perspective, one concentrates on all the activities performed around a child, activities that identify the child as Learning Disabled, and make contexts for still others to act in terms of the identification. LD is a room that constrains not only the children made to stand inside but all the other children and adults who visit the room and keep it alive. The idea here may be explicated through various metaphors, each of which highlight one property of our model. Birdwhistell (in McDermott 1980) once explained "context" using the analogy of a rope: "I like to think of it as a rope. The fibers that make up the rope are discontinuous; when you twist them together, you don't make them continuous, you make the thread continuous. . . . The thread has no fibers in it, but, if you break up the thread, you can find the fibers again. So that, even though it may look in a thread as though each of those particles is going all through it, that isn't the case. That's essentially the descriptive model."[8]

Out of multiple discontinuities, threads, or persons, an event of a new order is built; ropes or LD become facts. The fibers do not make the rope. A mass of fibers is not a rope. An aggregate of persons in a crowd does not make a cultural institution. But once fibers are made into a rope or a crowd into an institution, something new has happened for all those who encounter it and cannot ignore it or escape from it. The rope needs fiber. LD needs children and teachers. A child's life will evolve differently whether he is "acquired by LD" or escapes it. But LD itself is not produced by the child. Our interest in this book is LD as an institution and the American School as the even thicker rope of which LD is but a strand. Much has been done on the impact of institutions on persons. Comparatively less analytic attention has been given to the daily workings of institutions, particularly with a culture theory not caught in the tangles of representing culture primarily as something having to do with learning. This is what we want to develop.

Institutions, of course, are not literally ropes, and the metaphor can go only so far. We also want to highlight how self-evident and inescapable a constructed world can become. The problem for children identified with LD or any other kind of school failure is that the diagnosis appears so commonsensical. This issue of perception invites another analogy. In 1908, Fraser discussed what he called the "twisted rope illusion" (see Figure I.1). It is a set of black and white geometrical shapes so organized that they do two things. On the one hand, they give the overwhelming impression, to a commonsense observer, of *one*, *spiraling*, black and white, twisted cord. On the other hand, from the point of view of an analyst, the same shapes can be said to be the representation of a *series* of twisted cords arranged in a set of *concentric circles*. The effect is strong enough that if one is asked to follow any of the circles, one's finger easily follows the eye into the center of the circle; one must work hard to resist one's senses enough to trace concentric circles (one trick is to place a circular mask such as a small coin at the center of the figure). The difficult point is that there is no rope on the paper, just alternating streaks of black and their apparent absence, the latter made significant by contrast to both the black streaks and the black squares. It is not just that the rope "fibers" are analytically unavailable when one looks at parts of the design, it is rather that half the fibers have no representation except in contrast to other fibers and other parts of the background Still, the rope and its fibers remain overwhelming events on observers caught by the design and unable to escape something that was made for them.[9]

From Benedict to Lévi-Strauss and Birdwhistell, anthropologists have found a figure-ground argument congenial to their understanding of what happens in culture when individual traits begin to have institutional consequences in particular localities or, to use the more traditional language, when traits are "incorporated into a culture." The same intuition is often summarized with statements that go something like "All parts of any system define all other parts of the system." The point is that the elements that together make a pattern, much like the black markings on Figure I.1, gain their particular power to move people in particular directions because of the ways they are arranged with other elements, not because of their own properties. When a child who may find it difficult to do certain things at certain times enters those settings in school where LD is going to show up, it is not so much that the child changes as that those around the child change the way they respond and thereby (temporarily) construct the child as a particular, LD, kind of person.

The rope metaphor highlights how higher-order events appear in the history of humanity as cultural facts for all to take into account. The twisted-cord illusion highlights how the individual pieces that appear to make these cultural facts are themselves "made" by the pattern, not perhaps in their physical substance but cer-

FIGURE I.1
The Twisted Rope Illusion

SOURCE: (Fraser 1908: 325).

tainly in their social consequences. Still, these metaphors do not highlight a central theme of our own understanding of culture: Fibers in ropes, black stains on white paper, all are static objects dependent on the activity of some observer to activate their potentiality. The twisted-rope image is an illusion to the extent that it produces various effects on observers (including the designer of the image), but it is the observer who is active, whereas the image itself does not move. In culture, the situation is quite different. The fibers are alive and active, taking into account that they are made to be in a rope they do not control.

The first two metaphors focus our attention on the fact that children, teachers, parents and administrators, as "children," "teachers," "parents" and "administrators," do not "exist" independently of the School that defines them all for each other in their particular school qualities. There can be no "students" if there are no "teachers," and no "success" in the absence of "failure." This is not to say there are no human beings there. It is to say that they are hard at work taking into account, whether they are reconstructing or demolishing, the particular position that has acquired them or that they have inherited. These positions and the properties, rights, and privileges attached to them are utterly without power in the absence of all the other categories. The properties of the cultural pattern are maintained by the activity of the people who are caught within it. In the School, it is people, active single biological agents, that hold each other accountable to being what they must be to each other, that is, teachers, students, and administrators. In any school, the successful and the failed are the specific products of long interactional sequences involving much work by many people. The successful and the failed do not originate all made up in their particular qualities. They are slowly fashioned until the overall picture looks right enough that other active powers do not get upset by what was done, or not done, more locally. The people are all together, entwined with each other, one rope, one culture of consequence for all.

To state the general point we are making about culture, we can use still another metaphor, that of the house. For us, *culture has less to do with the habits we acquire than with the houses we inhabit.*[10] Culture is certainly about construction, though more about the houses that are *always already there* when people get born than about those they may try to build during their lives. Culture is about the words people use, the clothes (in French, *habits*) they wear. It is also about rooms in the sprawling mansions, along with the servant quarters, that history has built. This is the metaphor that is implied in our subtitle: This book is about "the School America builds" with its many rooms, positions like success and failure, Learning Disability and talent, positions that eventually get filled generation after generation with the people who are at any time required to fill them. There would be no schools or families, successes or failures, if no one performed what needed to be performed for the event to have happened.

It is certain people do change the rooms in which they are placed. We document many such changes. Families in similar conditions may arrange different local worlds for their members to inhabit. Teachers may implement programs far from stereotypic school tasks. But such changes can go only so long before neighbors, administrators, competitors, near and far get concerned. All human action is joint, partially under the control of many "significant" others—interpreters and enforcers with the power or authority to reconstruct the walls that local activity always damages. Eventually, as each person checks the closest others, as each small group checks other small groups in the neighborhood, the culture into which they were all born or recruited gets reconstructed, though perhaps not exactly in the same shape as it was. We do not believe there are actual plans to the house America builds or an actual architect. Analytically, the School escapes everyone, and particularly the many who think they are in charge of it. A first step in reorganizing this unplanned but ever present and ever changing house is to take its power into account.

We use five case studies to illustrate the usefulness of such an approach. Above all, we explore the implication for research of looking at success and failure as two rooms within the *same* house that many people inhabit and are at work maintaining, reconstructing, and, it is hoped, remodeling.

Adam, Sheila, Joe, and Others at Cultural Work

We started with the emblematic figure of Maxine Hong Kingston to introduce our interest in the cultural construction of schooling and its consequences for all who live in the United States. We can now proceed with the particular versions of this question raised by each of our ethnographic reports. In the first, we offer the LD story we have already started to tell: When we are informed that Adam, the child who appears in Chapter 1, is Learning Disabled, what do we see? Is it Adam, the Learning Disabled child? Or is it LD, the cultural fact? If it is the latter, as we are quite convinced it is, what about him and the other people at work with him? And how does LD fit within the broader American landscape? As we begin answering these questions, new areas of investigation begin to emerge. In the next four chapters of Part 1, we show in turn how small groups can transform their local conditions; how relative strangers can get involved in a complex, focused activity; how activities can be reconstructed as they get noticed and replaced within broader social sequences; and how local performances are made to fit within the broader canvas.

We do all this by looking carefully at fleeting moments in the everyday life of various people when, together, they construct something the School would recognize as educational. We look at children cooking in an after-school club (Chapter 1). We look at other children and their parents doing homework together (Chapter 2). We look at young men and women singing in a choir (Chapter 3). We look at adolescents performing a teacher-initiated task in an alternative urban high school (Chapter 4). We look at other adolescents endlessly competing with each other in an upper-middle-class junior high school (Chapter 5). In each setting, we focus on a few seconds or minutes to be constantly reminded of the activity of the people about whom we write. They are not automatons somehow determined by the system of which they are a part. In each setting we focus on a few seconds or minutes in order to be continually reminded that the people about whom we write are not enacting dumbly a script they do not understand. People are active, at work, and the culture that came before them would not remain alive without their activity. In the detail of their local practices, we can see people struggling, and we can see the conditions against which they struggle. This type of intense gaze on what people do in the detail of their everyday life is what we understand as ethnography, a mode of investigation that is particularly well suited to bringing out aspects of the human condition that the human condition itself always conspires to hide. Where people will be found, we have learned, can never be fully predicted from a knowledge of their initial conditions. Even initial conditions are hard to account for, since most of the descriptions we have of them say both more and less than what needs to be said. Usually the most significant features of their conditions, those with the most consequences on future action, are least available to common sense. One hundred years of ethnography has confirmed the usefulness, indeed the absolute necessity, of inductive searches carefully tracing what people do in specific places and at specific times, what they take into account and what they may be making for themselves and their consociates.

To develop analytic categories true to the ongoing, sensuous engagement of people building their lives together, we often vary the lenses we use.[11] Sometimes we focus in detail on the moment-to-moment unfolding of a single interactional sequence. At other times, we summarize many such sequences and trace their connections over a range of persons and events. In all cases, we are interested in seeing how the participants themselves reveal, *in their very behavior,* that which they cannot escape in a particular setting, that which is *always already there* when they start and remains when they end. At the same time, these lenses allow us to notice the many ways in which the people do not quite do what they might be expected to do, the ways in which they do more or do something else—at the very same time they take into account that which others have made for them.

The case studies we present in the body of this work were conducted over the past twenty years in different contexts. In each case, we have asked the same fundamental question about the conditions of personal action, and we answer it by engaging the conditions guiding personal action in the most local circumstances.

We start with Adam in Chapter 1. Something in his activity as it is sequenced with the activities of others around him makes him salient and problematic in certain settings. What and who makes Adam's activity "special"? We continue with Sheila and Joe in Chapter 2. What is it exactly Sheila and her parents do to make it appear that doing homework (and succeeding in school) is easy for them, whereas it is difficult for Joe and his mother? Next, in Chapter 3, we look at a group of late adolescents famous for their low self-esteem and inability to work together: How did they perform a complex and novel task directed by a person with little personal experience with their social and cultural background? We then move to the schools because in America, they are the legitimate grounds for the determination of success and failure. In Chapter 4, we show how an innovative program in an alternative high school can appear to be both a success and a failure. In Chapter 5, we end the ethnographic part of the book with an account of the activity of a whole school and community, and we wonder how one should understand the constant testing, quizzes, and competitions among students who are virtually fated to succeed on sociodemographic criteria alone. What is behind their parents' anguish and frantic activity to train them ever more rigorously for these competitions?

These questions are variations on our original question about Maxine Hong Kingston's puzzle when confronted with the printed "I." Our questions keep us puzzled at precisely the same point. What is it that makes this "I," and the individual to which it points, the center not only of political legitimacy but of research into human processes?

Although Chapter 1 starts as if it were the story of Adam, it quickly turns into a chapter on the four Adams that the people in his life constructed for various purposes in different settings. The case study is based on work Michael Cole, Lois Hood, Ray McDermott, and Kenneth Traupmann conducted in the late 1970s. They started looking for Adam as a person with qualities. Adam, it was officially said, was Learning Disabled. And yet the more they looked for Adam as he acted in concert with others, the less they saw "Adam." What they saw, eventually, were people making certain qualities salient at certain times but not others. These qualities were sometimes performed by Adam, and those who looked at him were sometimes justified in their identification of his LD qualities. Still, each identification made a difference in interaction only at certain times. At other times, the Learning Disability disappeared for all practical purposes. At still other times—particularly when major decisions about his future placement in schools were being made—the disability was all there was.

Learning Disabilities of all types (whether grounded in biology, emotional traumas, or cultural difference) are consequential only to the extent that they are made to fit within a cultural system that identifies them. The inability to read fluently is a problem only if it is noticed at particular times by particular people who must mete out the consequences of having been noticed as not being able to read. In the early 1980s, Hervé Varenne, Ray McDermott, Hope Leichter, Vera Hamid-Buglione, and Ann Morison looked at familial literacy, focusing eventually on two closely matched working-class families of Irish descent in the same, mostly Polish, neighborhood of New York City (Chapter 2). In one family, the child of focus was known as doing well in school, in the other, as not doing well. The identification of Sheila's and Joe's qualities were the product of the families' own symbolic system. No school professional was involved—actually both children were doing moderately well by the standards of diagnostic tests—but the process was the same. At particular moments within more broadly defined settings, Joe's symbolic identification was not only affirmed by what the people said about him but was specifically performed as an occasion for celebration or degradation.

Particularly striking is that the symbolic identification of a child with a quality is performed by the same persons who, a few minutes later, may not make this identification as they let the same behavior they earlier noticed pass as irrelevant. Thus it is not because Adam had to act in concert with particular teachers and psychologists that he was identified as Learning Disabled. These very teachers and psychologists, as soon as they shifted out of the positions where the disability was visible, lost the ability to see it. What they could do had changed. They, like Adam, were multiple. "Being a teacher" is not a quality of a human being. It is a quality of a culture that requires at certain times, and not at others, that "teacherliness" be displayed, a display that involves making success and failure visible and documentable. We show how this "teacherliness" can be performed in family groups and how it can be sequenced with other activities, some of which have to do with being in a family together and others which have to do with what other institutions (particularly the School) require of a family. In the process we continue the demonstration that "culture," as a pattern of interaction among certain people, is itself not a property of persons and thus must be investigated by looking directly at interaction. It is interaction that makes people visible as particular types of people, not the other way around.

The third case study (Chapter 3) is about a group of late adolescents in an agency for "street kids" in New York City. For a few months, they came together around a music teacher and choir director who had no previous experience with this population. The original study by Merry Naddeo (1991) focuses specifically on a rehearsal to demonstrate the close and effortless meshing of each person's activity within the rehearsal. The tasks accomplished were complex and subtle, and they were hidden by glossing the activity as "singing." Singing in a choir involves beginning and ending together, doing transitions from one song to the next, handling time-outs for directions, and so on. In the choir, the participants even had to deal with new members who had to be taught how things were done without actually interrupting rehearsal. They did this for close to half an hour while being challenged by people attempting to organize a competing activity in the same room. Throughout, one voice was heard. No one stood out. All were invisible, or perhaps equally visible as a group of amateurs doing music together. For a while the commonsense labels we could use to classify them (such as African American, Hispanic, Lutheran, Italian, pimp, prostitute, student at Columbia University, late adolescent, middle-aged, or people who might test low or high on various scales of self-esteem, emotional stability, schooling, or intelligence) became irrelevant and inconsequential. The social organization of a particular type of musical performance took over and redefined participants as tenors, sopranos, director, and accompanist.

As the choir gave way to other activities, the spell was broken. Individual voices attempted to make themselves heard: "Can you teach me the piano?" "Do you know anyone in the music business who can get me an audition at the Apollo?" The issues became questions of individual "talent" (as questions of individual merit are talked about in the artistic world). Like questions of intelligence or its euphemisms in the world of the School, these are questions that imply the ever-present possibility of a negative answer: "You do not have the drive and application to learn the piano." "You have a good voice, but no better than hundreds of others, and you have no chance of making it in the music business."

The next case study (Chapter 4) reports on life in an alternative high school where Rizzo-Tolk (1990) studied a small group of students involved in an experimental project. We show how the students perform just the right sequence at the right time for evaluators to identify possible success as evident failure. The point again is not to blame teachers or administrators for failing to recognize "real" success (as a property of the students involved). Rather it is to show how the students can perform just what it takes for the teachers to produce a legitimate evaluation that itself justifies the existence of the school as a special school for students who fail regular programs.

The final case study (Chapter 5) is based on work by Shelley Goldman (1982). In many ways, it is the reverse of the preceding case in focusing on the paradoxical concerns of those who are most likely to succeed with altogether inconsequential competitions. It is the story of a school and a community at intense work constructing competitions. Continual quizzes, tests, exams, special projects, sports events, and so on produce complex rankings that are displayed in plaques, trophies, special citations. Individual qualities become public events, but the public itself, the community that is both audience and performers of a kind of suburban deep play, disappears.

The actual competition, of course, is to be found between this community and the communities represented by the Sheilas, Joes, and others whom we have seen at work earlier. But this competition is hidden. The salient competition is between essential equals, hypertrained athletes of the body or the brain who vie among each other for symbolic rewards. The other struggle, the one between "good" and "bad" schools, between suburb and inner city, even if momentarily invisible, is never irrelevant. Although our own research has not explored settings where one might find evidence of competition across communities, there is evidence that it exists. Ortner (1993), for example, has been bringing to light the anguish of parents who are ready to sacrifice enormous portions of their resources to ensure that their children will be raised in localities with "good" schools. When this is done, they continue to worry about their children scoring below 1200 on the SATs when the neighbors' children scored 1350. And they are willing to spend more resources to gain a marginal increase that may, it is hoped against much evidence, tip the balance when prestigious college admissions and scholarships are being awarded. At such moments, it is as if the street kids in the choir or the dropouts of the West Side do not exist. If they appear, they do so as irrelevant strangers from another world. But the gap between these worlds is itself constructed by parents of Hamden Heights worrying about their children. Their activities ensure that the performance of the kids from Manhattan Valley will not be a factor as the children of Hamden Heights are placed where they can be acquired by favorable positions in the social structure. The very existence of this deliberate activity reveals that the parents, and children, of Hamden Heights are sensitive to their actual condition: They are in competition with the parents and children of Manhattan Valley. This is what allows us to say that the culture of education in suburban New Jersey is the same culture as that found in the schools and agencies of the most urban areas of New York City. This culture organizes interpersonal relations at the local level (in both geographic and temporal terms) that we examine in each of our case studies. It also organizes the relations among localities, communities, and groups. This is America.

Education in America

The statement "This is America" brings us back to our questions about personal action and historical setting, personal responsibility, and cultural fact. The simple answer to our general question about how to weigh self- and other determination in human action is obviously that both must be taken into account when celebrating or mourning particular accomplishments. Still, we must explore theoretically what "taking into account" must mean. The three chapters of Part 2 of the book address this through a discussion of the use of the terms "culture" and "construction" in recent research on educational issues and concludes with the problem of understanding education in the United States as specifically American. In Chapter 6, we generalize the case studies of Part 1 and expand on our point that culture is as much a mechanism for disabling possibilities as for enabling them. We start with the argu-

ment that in educational research, the most common theories of culture disable both
the people they are used to understand *and* the researchers who use them. In Chapter 7, we show that this is less a product of personal misunderstandings than of the
rhetorical tools, metaphors, and research methodologies most commonly available
"in America." In Chapter 8, we explore in detail the "construction" metaphor
through a reanalysis of a well-studied case. The construction metaphor has been successful recently, and it is not surprising it should prove dangerous when used imprecisely. When it is used carefully, a proper understanding of the place of agency in the
most highly constrained of settings becomes possible. We conclude with a call for a
more carefully grounded theory of culture.

Ultimately, we believe that advances in general understanding must spring from
direct observation of what human beings do, observations guided by theories continually examined for the ways in which they might blind us to what is happening
around us and, worse perhaps, for all the ways through which they might produce
objects, that is, cultural facts, that are so absolutely real we cannot escape them even
when we experience the pains they may produce. It is only by doing this critical
work, systematically and painstakingly, that the questions we ask of ourselves can be
answered, albeit temporarily, and, more important, transformed. In the routine performance of their everyday life, people seldom answer directly questions about the
wide-scale constraints on their lives. Rather, they point at those aspects of their environment that at a particular moment are most salient to what they must be doing.
By struggling always to look more carefully at what people point to, we indeed have
a chance to transform our understanding and our efforts at reform.

NOTES

1. For various reasons we clarify throughout the book, "we" points first and foremost to the
joint authors, Varenne and McDermott, as persons in particular positions. It can also index
those who participated in our research. "We" also belong to a tradition of intellectuals, educators, and social scientists to which we want to contribute. In certain limited contexts, "we" indexes this tradition.

2. Our approach is related to G. H. Mead's overall discussion of conduct and the self
(1934, 1964). There is a problem in phrasing the distinction between actors and their identification with various social positions through first-person pronouns. Kingston's own experience is a graphic reminder that the "I" itself is more than a grammatical category unproblem-
atically shifting our attention to a speaker. It is also a powerful cultural category with
particular qualities that may hide, rather than reveal, the ultimate separateness of the actor. A
long tradition, from Tocqueville ([1848] 1969) to L. Dumont (1980), including anthropologists such as Hsu (1983), have made similar points. Varenne has discussed this in more detail
elsewhere (1977, 1983, 1984).

3. Variations in the "What time is it?" question have been explored for education by Sinclair and Coulthard (1975), Humphrey (1980), and Mehan (1979). Voloshinov ([1929]
1973) may have been the first to use it to illustrate the tie between context and meaning.

4. We will use the Chinese character usually translated as "I" to symbolize our struggle
against an individualistic culture that substantializes the "I" of any person. We do want to em-

phasize that we are not arguing, as per some deconstructionist philosophizing, that there is nothing but words and other cultural symbols at the center of a person's will to live—the center that is the issue of philosophy. This personal, distinct "I" may not be directly accessible even to introspection; it may not be describable or otherwise capturable in any particular language or symbolic system. Given this recognition of the limitations of these means for knowledge, we assume the personal center is not "empty." It is active.

5. There is considerable critical debate over Kingston's representation of the Chinese in the United States (see Wong 1992 and 1993 for a summary and discussion).

6. The other well-documented example is of Native Americans. See the discussions by Basso (1970, 1979), R. Dumont (1972), Philips (1972, 1983) and F. Erickson and Mohatt (1982). Boggs (1972) and Au (1980) propose a similar situation for native Hawaiians in school.

7. Not only do African Americans not have to perform in stereotypical fashion to have the stereotypes applied to them, it is not clear even that they have to exist. Contemporary European states can still generate a wave of anti-Semitism virtually without Jews in residence; even Japan, with little access to either Jews or Blacks, can nonetheless generate long cultural traditions of racism (Silverman 1989).

8. Birdwhistell's (1970; McDermott 1980) is a key formulation of context because the tradition of which he is a part, including the work of G. Bateson (1972), Scheflen (1973), and Kendon (1982, 1990), has been principled in the use of the term. Compatible ideas (cited throughout this volume) are available in Soviet activity theory, American ethnomethodology, and some cognitive anthropology. For example, compare the similarities in Birdwhistell's formulation of context with the following quote from Schegloff: "Taking sentences in isolation is not just a matter of taking such sentences that might appear in a context; but that the very composition, construction, assemblage of the sentences is predicated by their speakers on the place in which it is being produced, and it is through that a sentence is context-bound, rather than possibly independent sentences being different intact objects in and out of context" (1984: 52). What is true here of sentences is true of any behavior we might want to use as a unit of analysis.

9. Such images have been used extensively in gestalt psychology to illustrate issues in perception, particularly how figure and ground are constructed by the brain as it attempts to transform the ensemble of the visual cues it receives into objects it can distinguish and recognize. For a psychology founded on the possibility such "illusions" are the key to the ways we perceive the most mundane aspects of the world, see Köhler (1947, 1969); in the same mold, Lewin's (1935) paper on the feebleminded makes a number of points relevant to our argument here.

10. Bourdieu ([1970] 1977) has made much of the *habitus* built into persons by their culture; we prefer to stress the ongoing relations between persons and the environments they build for each other, their modes of inhabitation.

11. We are following here an analogy proposed by James Peacock (1986) to explain the nature of the ethnographic gaze: "harsh light, soft focus" in the hope of gaining the greatest possible depth of field, one that would even include the photographer, done to gain a better handle on all that is relevant to a particular event. In this book, mostly, we have chosen a lens and a light that allows for a much narrower focus, on the well-grounded belief such a gaze can reveal much of what Peacock and all anthropologists are looking for.

Part One

The Makings of Some Educational Facts

1 Adam, Adam, Adam, and Adam: The Cultural Construction of a Learning Disability

Ray McDermott
and Hervé Varenne

If maturity and development mean attunement to context, then . . . evaluation can be done only by the grandchildren of our grandchildren.
—A. L. Becker, *Writing on the Tongue* (1989)

When Adam started school he had a difficult time reading the same three-stroke "I" that made life difficult for Maxine Hong Kingston. There was no confusion with the seven-stroke Chinese character or with the demands of a culture that made "I"— every individual's very own "I"—a constant focus of conversation. Adam was born and raised in a well-to-do family. He had no trouble with America, at least in the all-important sense that he was comfortable with the details of American culture. When not reading and writing, he seemed perfectly competent in handling the minutiae of everyday life. In the first grade, he had trouble only with reading and writing. By age eight, he had been fully documented, by test after test, as having a severe Learning Disability (LD). Also by age eight, the problem was leaking into other areas of his life.

Just about the time Adam was turning nine, we gathered together the seventeen children in Adam's classroom and interviewed them for their opinions on various moral issues.[1] They were given a story about a boy who was sent to camp, couldn't swim, and was teased by the other children. They were asked if this was right or wrong. They responded with the expected options: It was not right to tease because teasing would make the boy feel bad; it was OK to tease because it would motivate him to learn to swim so well that he could return and tease everyone else. Most of the children were heard from, but Adam was silent. From teasing, our discussion went to a second dilemma story and a third, again with Adam remaining quiet. Finally, Adam raised his hand and said, "Remember the boy who couldn't swim and everybody was teasing him. Well, they shouldn't do that, cause sometimes, if you try harder and harder, it will just get worser and worser." Not knowing how to read and write is one kind of problem; looking at life as if everything is about to get "worser and worser" is another. Adam's problem with reading was spreading to other areas of life; he was becoming a well-defined Learning Disabled child.

By the common sense of all those around him, Adam's problem seemed inherently psychological: When faced with the task of taking print from a page or writing even a simple word, his brain did not seem to work up to par. In any comparison of individuals by competence in reading and writing, Adam would perform at the bottom of his class. The verdict was unanimous: Because of a serious problem with the mental machinery he brought to the task, Adam could not learn to read or write with the speed or skill of others his age.

By the standards of this book, Adam had a cultural problem. The details differed, certainly, from the problems faced by Maxine Hong Kingston or the other students discussed in the chapters that follow, but he had a cultural problem nonetheless. He was not alone with it: His parents suffered his pain, and so did the reading specialist who seemed to inflict it, the teachers who tried to work around it, and the children in his class who grappled with understanding it or sometimes used it to soothe them in their own difficulties. Simply because others experienced his problem and responded to it, we can say that Adam's problem was cultural, and even in this weak sense of the term we could demonstrate that Adam's problem was more than a mishap in his cognitive development. But we are struggling toward a stronger sense of "culture." Culture has to do with fabrication and artifice. It has been characterized by Plath (1980) as a "parliament of prodigals" to emphasize the multiplicity of those involved in the evolution of its institutions and the florescence of what they make together. Murphy and Murphy (1974) talk about culture as of a "collective illusion," and many talk about the "arbitrariness" of cultural forms. What is sure is that the prodigal parliamentarians of America can make of LD a fact that is totally real in its consequences. We could say they collude in keeping its institutions alive even as they try, or worse precisely because they try, to alleviate the suffering of the children labeled Learning Disabled (McDermott and Tylbor 1983; McDermott and Varenne 1995). We are trying to capture this by showing how many persons struggled to develop sophisticated, replicable, and consequential ways to establish that Adam could not read. We are trying to demonstrate how sensitive Adam himself was to the cultural demand that he surrender himself as not knowing how to read (if only by attempting, for example, to escape being caught and called Learning Disabled).

Adam could not be disabled on his own. He needed others to recognize, document, and remediate a disability that had to be made "his." More important, without a culturally well-organized apparatus identifying a certain percentage of American children as officially Learning Disabled, Adam could simply have been what he was, namely, a person who learned differently or on a different schedule than others.

The term "culture" traditionally refers to concepts, symbols, and beliefs found among a people, but we insist that an adequate cultural description must show such concepts, symbols, and beliefs in use and legitimately enforced in local situations populated by real people. America was ready for Adam to be Learning Disabled.

Maxine Hong Kingston was given a complex cultural menu: Chinese, American, and Chinese American, each according to a schedule organized in great part by those around her. Adam was confronted by a related cultural menu, and one option was that he could be identified as Learning Disabled. Other options were even less kind, for example, retarded, emotionally disturbed, or brain damaged (for the social history of these terms, see Coles 1987; Sarason and Doris 1979). Since World War II, there has been an onslaught of special education designations for children in American schools, and it is Adam's fate to be acquired by one of them. In a previous generation, he might have been called stupid for his slow pace, and he would have been finished with schooling early in life. Learning Disabled may be a better label than stupid, and there is the hope that with an appropriately protective education, those called Learning Disabled might be able to stay for the full duration of school and perform, however differently or belatedly, on a par with others (Rawson 1968). This fervent hope can be no better than the cultural framework in which it both emerges and must be put into action.

Adam a generation ago, Adam now, and Adam a generation from now each encounters a quite different set of pressures and designations with which a life must be shaped. We cannot observe Adam at work in the past or the future. We cannot observe him alive in the world of poor whites in Appalachia or in an aristocratic family in England. Nonetheless, we are quite sure the seemingly biological problem that made it difficult for him to read would have had different consequences for his life in other circumstances.

Guesswork about faraway times and places aside, we were able to observe Adam in different moments of his everyday life as a student in a liberal Manhattan private school. To extend the metaphor we introduced earlier, we can say that we looked at Adam in four of the rooms he occupied: in settings around New York City unmarked for any particular activity, in a weekly after-school cooking club, in various classroom lessons, and finally, in a one-to-one testing environment. Adam's behavior varied remarkably across the four settings, and so did the behavior of those around him. Adam, we might just as well say, appeared as four different people: Adam, Adam, Adam, and Adam, as we suggest in our title. More commonsensically, we might have said that he was a single person in varying contexts. We suspect that it would be more helpful to think of him as a radical 我 who, like the rest of us, was viewed through multiple lenses, each making something different of him and thus preventing him, as 我, from ever being directly accessible. When taken together, these four versions of Adam tell us less about him than about the patterning of the diverse positions available to persons reading and writing in America. To the extent that Adam's problems with print varied with his circumstances, we can talk about the interactional organization of his disability, and to the extent that his circumstances were well-structured versions of each other, we can talk about the cultural organization of his disability.

Three Accounts of the House Adam Inhabits

In unmarked moments of his everyday life, Adam was quite invisible as a child with problems. If he needed information, he asked for it. If he needed to read or write, he could do a little on his own, and whether he did it well seemed to be of little concern to him or to those around him. If the task was beyond what he could do, he simply organized others to do the job; nothing seemed to lead to an evaluation of his intelligence or competence in the way such issues showed up in the more school-based settings. Adam was a great storyteller, and he was a popular raconteur in his mixed third- and fourth-grade classroom. Time spent with Adam outside of school showed only the Adam the other children adored. In addition to being the classroom bard, he was a good drummer, and he had started to use his big size to gain some respect at basketball. If he had problems learning how to read and write, they were not to be found in the daily round outside of school.

Away from everyday life, at the opposite end of a continuum of freedom and school-induced constraint, was Adam in the testing environment. We gave the children tests to learn how they performed on traditional tasks of the type used in experimental cognitive psychology. We hoped the test results would give us a base to compare how the children handled analogous tasks in more spontaneous settings, such as cooking clubs, where tasks were defined and redefined from one moment to the next in situ and without the illusion of experimental control. If psychological studies were filled with accounts of the importance of children attending, remembering, and problem solving, we should have been able to find something like those activities while the children were making cakes. To compare cooking-club thinking practices with more-controlled laboratory performances, we brought each child to a one-on-one testing environment where he or she was administered questions from IQ tests and some more interesting probes we had taken from the experimental literature.[2] Because we were too close to the children to take an objectivist stand, we hired a professional tester to administer the tasks. Most of the children did well on the tests, and many seemed to enjoy being asked to do hard things without recourse to adult help.

It was in this situation of individual child against a well-defined task that Adam most often displayed his differences. The tasks were designed to show individual differences, and they did their job well. Adam performed miserably, almost randomly, as if he were wildly guessing at answers without giving them any thought. A careful look at the videotapes indicated that he was thinking a great deal, although mostly about matters only tangentially related to the tasks presented. Mostly Adam was searching for ways to get the answer from the tester, a well-documented strategy among children expecting to get too many questions wrong when left to only their own thoughts (Cicourel 1974; Thomas et al. 1971). The tester was professionally nonreactive, but Adam would diligently wait on the tiniest cue.

One question had only two possible answers: cup or spoon. It was an easy question with a limited range of answers, and all the other children had picked the right answer. As the tester finished presenting the situation, Adam threw his head back and said "Oh! That's easy." We were relieved when we watched the tape, and even the tester reported she was looking forward to him feeling good about one task. After a closer look, it was not even clear Adam had heard the content of the question. He followed with the beginning of the wrong answer, found the smallest twitch in the behavior of the tester, and then changed his answer: "Cu-uhm-spoon." In this case, Adam primed the environment for the "right" answer. Other questions were less amenable, and the tester worked hard not to give away crucial hints. Adam struggled most painfully with the test of digit-span memory, a hallmark of Learning Disabled children, getting at most a string of four, whereas others in his class were handling six and seven digits.

There is a paradox hiding in this rather commonsense account: The formal organization of the testing session was designed to produce the most neutral and objective circumstances for Adam to reveal his true unique individual self, the culture's "objective" version of Adam's 我. Ironically, the test used the most artificial and inflexible circumstances to deliver its portrait of Adam. It was a setting that framed tightly what the two protagonists could do. Tests leave little room for negotiation, play, resistance, or transformation. Rather, any evidence of attempts to negotiate, play, resist, or transform can be taken as prima facie data for only one kind of evaluation, the specialized one for which the test situation was designed. Everything is scripted by a long tradition of professional development by culturally designated specialists: testers, counselors, social workers, and therapists who can find in almost anyone's behavior evidence of the kinds of problems they know how to look for and record in ways that still others can use (Becker, H. 1963; Cicourel and Kitsuse 1963; Wieder 1974; Pollner 1978). While Adam was in the test setting, all behavior was relevant to only one thing: the revelation of whether he was Learning Disabled. All other possibilities opened in Adam were canceled and thus, from our point of view, his 我 escaped, as it must always do in any culturally constructed attempts at capturing it.

On its own, the test setting revealed little about the full complexity of Adam's life, but it did use his behavior to highlight the specifics relevant to a cultural portrait of disability. To this extent, it is our point that the trait Learning Disabled was not his; it belonged to the test, its developers and interpreters, and the school systems that had little choice but to take it seriously.[3] Adam "borrowed" the trait or, rather, since we cannot assume that he did it willingly, Adam was acquired by those in charge of preserving the facticity of LD.

It is not enough to say we saw different Adams in the four different settings. We must also give an account of the organization of these settings. One account is all too familiar: Everyday life is "easier" than tests, and the continuum from everyday life through clubs and classrooms to testing settings is to be understood in terms of cognitive difficulty. There are other possibilities we must explore. The continuum can also be conceived in terms of constraint, from the apparent freedom of everyday life

FIGURE 1.1
A Continuum of Settings and Three Ways of Thinking About Them

Everyday life	*After-school clubs*	*Classroom work groups*	*One-to-one tests*

Increase in cognitive difficulty,

Increase in special constraints, and/or

Increase in institutional visibility and individual vulnerability

to the specialized, artificial, strongly framed, or scripted constraints of the test setting. Finally, the continuum can also be understood in terms of institutional visibility and thus in terms of individual vulnerability to being intelligible only in terms of
the setting at hand. Figure 1.1 offers a view of the continuum of settings for Adam
to be Adam, Adam, Adam, and Adam and three ways of thinking about how he
could have been so different across the settings. The three different ways of thinking
about the continuum, namely, increase in difficulty, constraint, and vulnerability,
have different implications for how we think about Adam. As the world got harder,
more artificial, or socially threatening, the less well Adam performed and the more
he was noticed, documented, and remediated. It makes a difference which version of
the continuum one takes most seriously.

If the continuum captures cognitive difficulty, then the tasks require more mental
effort and ingenuity as one moves from the ease of everyday life to the taxing questions of the psychometric test. Most psychologies of cognition are united in assuming that everyday life is simple and that it is necessary to press subjects with difficult
questions to locate the structure and limits of their competencies.[4]

The continuum can capture specialized constraints in the sense that in much of
everyday life, one has access to whatever can be used to get a job done, but at the
other end of the continuum, on tests, one is severely limited (with classrooms and after-school clubs, depending on the moment, taking up the middle ground). In everyday life, if one needs to remember a phone number, it is possible to memorize it,
work out a mnemonic, look for a pattern in the touch-tone number display, or simply
look it up in the phone book; on a digit-span test, however, no aids are allowed. In
everyday life, the task is to have the number when it is needed in whatever way is convenient; on a test, the task is to show off what one can do without resources, and the
alternative is called cheating. Although gaining control of a seven-digit string could
be an example of a cognitively well-defined task, socially, whether one does it to get
done a job or simply to show off how a job might get done makes a great difference.
Adam performed well in everyday life; he handled the tasks that came his way. He did
not perform well when he was limited by a social script that said he had to handle the
task by himself in a specific way with no help from his friends.

The continuum could also capture *social visibility* and *vulnerability* in the sense
that as one moves from everyday life and after-school recreational clubs to school
and diagnostic psychological tests, there is a marked increase in what can go wrong

and may even be noted legitimately in the permanent history of a person. There is a marked increase in the attention others give to the form of one's action and in the severity of the consequences such notice may trigger. It is of course possible to get things wrong in everyday life and to be laughed at to boot, but most failings last little longer than the next task to be done. It is as if the everyday world does not have time for documenting every slip, as if it is simply more important to perform the basic tasks of life than to notice how well one has performed them and then to record an evaluation for further use. Some people are better cooks, basketball players, or calligraphers than others, but there is rarely a price to pay or gain for doing these jobs badly or well—unless one is applying for a job as a cook or a basketball player. School tests, in contrast, are organized for the purpose of documenting who is doing better than whom, and a point this way or that can make for a quite different institutional biography.

The children in Adam's class noticed that there were school-relevant things he could and could not do. Sometimes they made sport of him for his shortcomings, but these difficult moments were not generally turned into barriers in his institutional life. Passing insults are not to be confused with full "status degradation ceremonies," in which a whole person is compared negatively to what an institution requires (Garfinkel 1946, 1956; Pollner 1978). A passing insult leaves fleeting memories, whereas a written, official school record leaves not enough passing children (Goldman 1982; Oakes 1987).

Not unlike many children, Adam could not say the word "spaghetti" and would instead say "pisghetti." Apparently, he was the last child in the class to make the transition. During cooking club early in the year, the kids started singing a song about foods that they liked. Adam sang along. When they got to the word "spaghetti," they all stopped while Adam, much to everyone's delight, continued to sing on with the mispronounced word; on the next chorus, Adam was sharp enough to stop when everyone else stopped, but without relief, for everyone asked him why he didn't sing the next word. Later, in the cooking club, Adam made a green cranberry bread, a possibility if one puts the ingredients in exactly the wrong order into an aluminum bowl. Everyone gathered around to laugh, but Adam confronted them directly: "So I made a goddamn mistake. So what?" Neither the mistake in singing nor the mistake in cooking kept Adam from continuing to participate in these activities.

However painful the scenes from everyday life or the after-school club might be momentarily, they paled before the struggles in more classroom and testlike environments. We watched a fifteen-minute reading workbook lesson in the classroom. Adam was asked to match pictures with words: "race" with a runner, "face" with a face, "rake" with a rake. This was a tortuous task for Adam and for anyone who dealt with him. He read "face" as "flake," a troublesome mishap. Phonics is not easy for children, even for those who already know how to read. In this case, there was the hard "c" and the soft "c," and the confusing entry of the "l." Nor was it clear that Adam understood what he was supposed to do even if he could read the word, for there are many ways to relate words to pictures. The teacher was making the rounds among tables of focused children. Adam got her attention, and after a few minutes of instruction, Adam seemed to know what to do. The other children monitored his development carefully but worried mostly about their own work. The teacher went off to work with other children, but Adam called her back. They had to start at the beginning, but again they made headway. The teacher left again, but when she returned, Adam said, "But what's a flake?" A few minutes later, with the teacher working with someone else, he tearfully pushed his book away and said: "It's too hard." The other children watched him carefully, and he did not return to a work focus.

The work may indeed have been too hard for Adam. But what made it even harder, although not intrinsic to reading as a task, was the fact reading was used as an occasion for Adam to be made visible as a particular kind of person, the kind of person-who-fails-because-he-is-Learning-Disabled. Instead of being made visible as easy or hard for individual readers, reading could have a quite different social function. Historically, reading has often been important only to the extent it was in the service of prayer. We would not expect an LD classification to emerge in such a setting any more than we would find a classification of "singing disabled" in contemporary churches. Not so long ago, the high aristocracy of Europe was not expected to know how to read but was expected to know how to dance and, in the case of boys, how to fence (Darnton 1985). Getting things wrong while making a cake in one's kitchen or even in a cooking club is one thing; getting things wrong in school or on tests is a different matter.

What is involved in taking an ordinary problem (not reading or even not singing well) and turning it into a Disability (McDermott and Varenne 1995; Murphy, R. 1987)? How many people have to be involved, in what order, and with what long-term arrangements among them for ordinary tasks like learning to read and write to become a social problem as well? These are questions many in anthropology and sociology have been trying to answer. In successive quarters of this century, Émile Durkheim ([1897] 1951), Ruth Benedict (1934), and Claude Lévi-Strauss ([1958] 1963a) have each offered general statements that we can use. We are trying a more delicate version in the traditions of Gregory Bateson ([1936] 1958, 1972) and Harold Garfinkel (1967), a version that is sensitive to the power of the words we, as analysts, must use, words that threaten our own articulateness. We are trying to steer between two bad choices; we can make common sense by working within received categories, or we can lapse into obscurity as we try to suggest something else than the common sense. How, in other words, should we summarize our concerns with Adam? Should we write:

We want to display how Adam's Learning Disability makes a difference.

No, because this would suggest that Adam's difficulties as interpreted exist independent of his circumstances. It might be better to write:

We want to display how Adam's Learning Disability is organized to make a difference.

This is better but still may lead a reader to assume that Learning Disabilities are there to be organized before anyone comes along to identify them. We don't want to imply that Learning Disabilities aren't there, of course, only that whenever we get to see them, the institutional world that makes us look for them and find them has always preceded us to the scene. Let's try again:

> *We want to display how people use institutional (cultural) resources to build scenes in which Adam can be shown to be a classic case of Learning Disability.*

This may be as close as we can get to a proper formulation for a book that focuses attention on resources and on people as actors making things visible. We can now proceed to look in further detail at two days of the cooking club, the day the children made banana bread and the day we, the educators and researchers, made the IQ bee. On these days, in quite different ways, as if out of nowhere but precisely not out of nowhere, as if no one could have known in advance that it would happen, Learning Disability moments were built for all to notice Adam as a problem and thus give Adam a problem he experienced keenly, as we also did. We might just as well say that *these are the moments when Learning Disability acquired Adam.*

Making Banana Bread and Other Troubles

We knew the children in Adam's class for about two months before we started the after-school clubs. Adam and seven other children were assigned to the cooking club, where in the course of making cakes and the like, we thought the children would have to read, plan, pay attention, solve problems, and remember, all in concert with each other and therefore in ways we could study. Not particularly noticeable to us in our time in the classroom or on overnight trips to the school farm, Adam came very much to our attention in the first two meetings of the club. He seemed possessed, jumped around the room, knocked over our equipment, and was, we thought, unable to focus on anything. By the third week, he calmed down, and unless we went looking to see how he was doing, we noticed him as only occasionally different. By the third week, Adam had figured out that in the cooking club, pairs of children were supposed to work together, and he took on a partner. Together, they were a perfect pair. Peter was shy and wore a baseball cap over his eyes, but he was a great reader. Adam was gregarious, ready always to do the social work necessary to getting a cup of milk from the one container that the four pairs of children had to share, but he had a difficult time with reading the recipe. Adam and Peter were constant partners in the cooking club. Peter would read the recipe, Adam would get and measure the milk, Peter would pour it into the bowls, and Adam would pick up the recipe and triumphantly read what they had accomplished.

On a few occasions, the adults designated cooking pairs, and the children resisted mightily. One day, the children gathered around the table to get started. They were in pairs of their own choosing: A with B, C with D, E with F, and G, whose partner was ill, was by himself. We organized them differently: A with F, B with C, and so on. They protested, but we insisted on our order. They started to make their cakes but seemed to have a hard time getting organized. Fifteen minutes later, a calm came over the room. We were amazed to see that they had arranged to be back in their original order: A with B, C with D, E with F, and G working with an adult. One pair had protested loud enough to get the adult to allow a change, another pair had fought with each other enough to force the adult hand, and a third pair sent one member to the bathroom long enough to bring about a rearrangement. We didn't know what hit us. Over that fifteen minutes, the pairs made some progress cooking; each pair had one child working on the cake and one child working on the reorganization. Amazingly, at key points in the cake making, the reorganization person would suddenly attend to the cooking, and at key points in the reorganization work, the cooking person would be attentive to the social situation. Attention always ran on two tracks, the social and the one prescribed by adults. Adam and Peter divided the work a little bit differently than might a pair with two shy good readers or two outgoing nonreaders, but there was nonetheless a definite social arrangement to the work that had to get done. When Adam and Peter worked together, the social work was almost invisible, and they quietly went about their cooking. When Adam and Peter were separated, they had to rearrange both the intellectual and the social work agenda.

All work pairs of their own choosing were gendered, boys with boys and girls with girls. When we tried to mix them, Adam wound up with Dawn, who refused to work with a boy. Adam might have read the recipe on his own, but this was treacherous. Instead he neatly rearranged the situation. First, he asked Dawn for help with no results. Then he pleaded for help, again with no results. Finally he stood over her and explained that he had an allergy to butter and that it made him vomit. Dawn joined the work team, and Adam had a pathway through a potentially difficult day.

The day of the banana bread was more difficult. Adam and Peter entered the room, as they always did, arm-in-arm. We were months into the cooking club, and they had the routine down. The adult would show them how to make the bread, they would watch, and then they would do it themselves under the guidance of the ever-helpful adult. This day was different. The adult gave a quick lesson on banana bread, but no one watched. Adam and Peter played football on the side of the room before turning to the center table to make "uhm, uh, banana bread?" Peter announced that he was allergic to bananas. The adult was furious about the football game, decided not to help anyone with cooking, and went off to a corner to play a board game with Peter. Adam was left alone with the recipe.

Not because we were bad people but because we had simply photocopied a recipe and some instructions from a cookbook for banana bread, Adam faced a difficult road: The instructions were on the right side of the page, and he started with the ingredients on the left, thereby doing most things in the wrong order. This did not have to be a problem, but almost anything can become a problem in a competitive setting. We also gave the students, stupidly we realized later, a two-cup cup. In addition, for Adam, there was the added excitement of sorting out teaspoon from tablespoon and baking soda from baking powder.

Adam needed some allies. Reggie and Rikki were available. Reggie was the only other boy in the group, and he had been locked out of the Adam-Peter dyad all year. He apparently took this to be a time for revenge. Adam called the group to order: "Let's get started, wouldjya." He had the recipe in hand, up to his face. No one came forward. Adam headed to the adult for help, but Reggie interrupted with a promise of help: "Give it here." Adam returned and handed the paper to Reggie, who did not take it; instead, in typical Reggie fashion, while Adam was holding out the recipe for Reggie to read, Reggie managed to hold Adam accountable: "Well, why don't you give it to me?" This pretty much characterizes what Reggie did with Adam. He would offer help but not give it, leaving Adam dangling in need of help, and publicly so.

Adam's other candidate for help was Rikki, who had had an argument with her partner and wandered around the room for about ten minutes before they patched up their relationship enough to start their own banana bread. During those ten minutes, Rikki followed Adam around, never quite helping, never quite joining the Adam and Reggie pair but always carefully watching their progress. At one point when Adam was having a difficult time getting information about what he should be doing, Rikki followed Adam across the room to the adult, stopped suddenly, stamped her foot, and screamed for all to hear, "Oh! Why can't you read?"

Over the next ten minutes, Adam made twelve stops for help. It wasn't just that he had a hard time reading. In fact, he barely looked at the recipe long enough to read. Even if he had the right information from the page, he had problems with trusting the information. He had problems measuring 1 3/4 cups of flour, particularly with the two-cup cup, and he had problems with putting the ingredients into the bowls in a particular order. He had problems with the others around him: with the adult who didn't want to help and recommended, "Figure it out for yourself, Adam. You weren't interested in watching before"; with Reggie, who seemed to enjoy making a spectacle of Adam's problem; and with the group of girls next to him, who wanted to make a better banana bread than Adam—and faster, too.

Amazingly, while handling all these problems, Adam still found time while he was sifting the flour to engage in social banter. Helene, fresh from the argument that kept her from working with Rikki, refused to join the rest of the group; instead, she settled on the floor to play a game of cards. Adam interrupted and told her to "go make a cake." She pouted, and he responded by calling her, sing-song, "a little baby boo boo, a little baby boo boo." Helene's friend Dawn jumped in and told Adam, "You just born." Reggie joined Adam's side: "You never will be born." Dawn again: "Better not be born than to see your face." And finally Adam capped off the exchange: "You just my imagination, Dawn." With that, Adam finished the sifting—actually he called it "shifting"—and had to focus on the problem of deciding what "1 3/4 cups" might be.

It took Adam a few minutes to finish with the flour. The adult formulations about how to get a proper measurement seemed not to help him much. So he filled the two-cup cup near to the top and returned to the adult, who then had only to point at the right line for Adam to understand. He went back to the table, singing a circus warm-up tune, and said, "Finally" as he scraped out the excess flour.

Adam's next move was lethal. In the list of ingredients, the second item after flour was yogurt. In the list of instructions, yogurt was fourth, after bananas. If Adam was ready to use the yogurt, he would have been a step ahead of Nadine's group, which was up to bananas (number three in the instructions list) and well on the way, as always, to finishing first at all costs in all categories. Adam looked around the table and said, "Where's the yogurt?" Nadine oriented immediately: "You're up to yogurt already?" He was not, of course, up to yogurt on the list of instructions, and worse, he didn't know there was a list of instructions as different from a list of ingredients. Nadine and Lucy had to set him straight, and they did it with a vengeance:

(The girls are screaming and Adam, whimpering. The double vowels in Lucy's talk are chosen to show that she is reading to Adam as one would read to a child in a phonics lesson. The scene opens with Adam returning from the adult with the sense that he knows what to do next.)

Adam: Finally! Where's the yogurt? Oh (reaches for yogurt).
Nadine: You're UP to yogurt already?
Adam: Yeah.
Nadine: Where's the bananas?
Adam: We, uhm, they didn't give us bananas yet.
Nadine: Well, go get 'em.
Adult: The bananas are here on the shelf.
Adam: But this is our second page.
Lucy: That is a teaspoon. That is a tablespoon.
Adam: This is a teaspoon, and it says . . .
Lucy: It says tablespoons, twoo taablespooons.
Adam: We're right here, Lucy. Lucy, we're right here.
Lucy:[Thatquoteright]s—
Nadine: That's the ingredients, not the instructions.
Lucy: That's baakiing powowder.
Adam: What do you mean, baking powder?
Nadine: You go in this order.
Adam: (Oh my god). What do you mean, in what order?
Nadine: Look! This is the instructions. That's what you need to do all this.
Adam: Ai yai yai. One . . . Cup . . . Mashed . . . Fresh (in a staccato mock reading).

(Everyone looks away, and Adam returns to the adult for more advice.)

Adam led a difficult life at competitive moments. He was making his banana bread against considerable odds. No one else was doing it alone, and no one else was being hassled by Reggie or actively ignored by the adult. Adam might have gotten the cake done, but the rest of the world seemed to insist on interfering.

Adam was experienced with this kind of problem. He knew how to handle it, albeit at a cost. He went looking for some help, but this time he was crying as he flopped, back first, onto the adult. He got some confirmation that he could proceed as he had planned, and because he was as much a member of the culture as Nadine, he headed back to the table claiming that he was right all along; actually he said to no one in particular, "I was right, stupid." No one responded until he tearfully yelled at Reggie, "Ah, c'mon Reggie, wouldjya?" Reggie said, "Crying?" and then softly added, "Here. I'll help you." Together they made their banana bread just as successfully as everyone else: Not a single one of them was edible.

Note the complexity of the "problems." There was the pathos of Adam crying. There was the chill produced by noticing how each individual in the room added a stone to the wall that eventually so boxed Adam he had to cry to escape it. It did not have to be this way. The construction of this particular kind of box is not driven by a human genome that organizes even little children. This box is a cultural one, and its construction is driven by a particular historical need to assert who can do certain specific things better or worse than others. Most other cultures are not organized around a needless competition of all against all, and even ruthlessly competitive cultures, contemporary Japan being a good example (Rohlen 1980, 1983), can leave the acquisition of literacy outside the competitive arena.

If nothing else, culture is relentlessly specific. Life in any culture engages participants in the technical problem of everyone learning to see coordination in the actions of many and well enough to produce and reproduce culturally identifiable scenes. The "child-who-cannot-read-tries-not-to-get-caught" and "the child-who-fails-gets-to-cry" are two such recognizable scenes. If Adam's cooking club had been a ballet, we would have marveled at its coordination. Throughout this book, we point to how exquisite such coordination can be. We also point to how seldom the coordination of everyday life scenes is appreciated by people in the culture or even by participants in the scene. In the case of Adam's cooking club, the coordination among the participants was made irrelevant to the total cultural fact that the point of the ballet was to hide itself in order to highlight the performance of one very talented or very untalented, even Learning Disabled, person.

Adam had a problem that invites pathos, and this, more than anything else perhaps, may be what ensures that future children will find themselves struggling pathetically in the same situations. His situation invites our sympathy, and such descriptions as we have just given are generally used to move readers to some action. In many ways, this is our goal too. The problem, our problem as educators of educators, lies in determining the direction of the movement. In response to the pathos of the ever increasing number of culturally well-identified failing children, a host of educational and developmental theories have evolved over the past half-century that proclaim they "focus on the needs of individual children so that they can become all they can be." This is a noble but easily misguided sentiment, and all the more so because a critique of the direction taken is often interpreted as a critique of the need to move. When we are concerned with all Adam-like children, we must never forget to worry about the steps taken to identify them as being in need of our help or about our definitions of the "all" in "all that they can be." As we work at identifying someone as a child in need, as we develop means to help others identify him, it is easy to stop considering the actual, active, alive child who handles his problem resourcefully, even in crying. The more pathetic someone like Adam is made to be, the more people get concerned with him and the more they may efface him. In institutional America, the only tasks professionals may, indeed must, perform as professionals given specific authority by the State is to document what is wrong with Adam. This is their job and responsibility. They may, in other settings and wearing other hats, protest a world that forces them to "be" these implacable evaluators of Adam's own incompetence. At the appointed times, and even at other apparently more benign times, they must, no matter what, perform the evaluation. It took us a long time to wonder why the adult tried to motivate the cooking club by announcing that he wanted to know who could make the best banana bread without adult help. Making banana bread had become another test. But of what? Bread making? But why? Who cares?

The pathos in any Adam's situation comes from the fact that "his" problem is precisely not his. Thus any attempt at helping him with it must not focus on him. The focus must be put on the institutions that make people (organizers, fellow students, researchers) care about how well and how fast Adam is, for example, baking bread. Eventually, in fact, this Adam made the bread. He always got his job done. Others might have hidden. He always tried. He kept going. He was always willing to ask for help and to return something for the help he received. But it takes three to establish a gift exchange: two protagonists and the crowd providing them with the gifts and fixing their value.[5] On another day, when he was again on his own trying to cook something, Adam asked Helene for information. She put her arm around him and steered him away from the cooking table while saying she would help him; about four feet from the table, she used both hands to push him away from the group and said, "And don't come back!" Adam's problem was that he was performing in a world in which "competition" (a particular type of ritual drama we discuss in detail in Chapter 5) ruled. In this drama, making bread was secondary to making the better bread or making it faster. The final bread in our scenario may have been inedible, but some children nonetheless showed themselves better and some worse at it. Once again, a school-related event had generated a clear demarcation between those who could and those who could not. Adam's problem was less in his head than in the people around him. This became clear to us on a personal level when we organized the IQ bee.

Making IQs in Public

About eight months into our year of work with Adam's class, we had a growing sense of the social and institutional constraints on the cognitive lives of the children. Better phrased, we had a sense of the ritual organization of behavioral displays that forcefully pointed, through certain institutional lenses, to the cognitive skills of the various children. We thought we knew, for example, that some kids simply knew how to look like they were learning, that others knew how to hide from getting caught not knowing something, and that still others could spend their day picking their spots and strategizing when they should take risks with the cultural currency of the classroom and when not. The cultural currency of the classroom, of course, grades children by how much they look smart or dumb. We also had a growing sense that when the children were not overwhelmed by these strategic concerns, they seemed to be much more accomplished and happier people.

We knew all this, in one way, because we had long years of experience in America. We knew it, in a different way, because we had been watching the children situate themselves in relation to the gains and losses that come with life in an American classroom. But there was also a way in which we did not at all understand the pressures on the children, so much so that we organized a competitive setting that gave Adam a terrible day. We did not mean to cause suffering. Our goal was to show how much smarter kids were when they were working with each other than when they had to work alone or, worse, when they were pitted against each other in a norm-referenced war of all against all. What better symbol of that war than the IQ test, and what better way to tackle the misuse of that test than to have the children show us that the test questions were uninteresting, ambiguous, and no match for the multiple and complex ways children might interpret them.

So we gave the children an IQ test that pitted teams of children against each other. Individuals were given questions, but if they were unsure of the answer, they could give their question to another child on their team. If one team couldn't arrive at an answer, the other team could have a try. Individuals and teams were both awarded points. Some managed more points than others, and some suffered more than others. Adam's difficulty became more obvious as the game went on, and we wondered how we could have ever organized such an event. Now years later, as cultural analysts, we have the same concern with an added question about the resources we had available for constructing such a scene. It was so easy to do, so in the matter of course, so—paradoxically—"natural." The children were from a highly successful interracial, interclass private school that charged tuition based on parental income. With an ideology based on John Dewey and Martin Luther King, the school offered the children both an environment in which they did not experience much competitive pressure and a challenging intellectual menu complete with tests and competitive games. Team competition is fun, particularly when it does not quite count, and we thought a great afternoon would be had by all.

When the children entered the room, they showed themselves to be ready to meet the demands of their culture. If we could set it up, they could respond accordingly. They immediately recognized from the single stool at the head of tables in a V shape that they were to have a quiz show or some kind of competition. Reggie yelled, "Hey, we gonna have a good day today. Anyone who wants to have a good day today, say 'Aye.'" Most of the kids yelled, "Aye." Then Adam made a more modest proposal: "Anybody who wants to *try* to make it a good day today, say 'Aye'" (Adam's emphasis). Only a few kids answered, halfheartedly.

Adam's first try during the IQ bee did not go well. He was the first to get something wrong, and he did so just as the other kids were talking about how easy all the questions were. As is the accepted practice with IQ tests, the questions got progressively more difficult as one moved through the test. As was the adaptive practice with Adam, he watched others handle the first few questions before he would venture to try one on his own, a sensible way to handle most situations but a lethal practice on a test in which the items get increasingly more difficult, more arbitrary, or more designed to show someone being wrong. With each new set of questions, Adam got the last and most difficult. Adam successfully avoided the easy questions about what animal bacon comes from and instead got the group's most difficult question on how many pounds are in a ton. Not only did Adam get it wrong, so did everyone else. Adam was the only one, however, to act as if he had been made smaller by the event. He covered his face with his hands and slowly slid down in his chair. He got smaller.

For his second question, which was about where the sun sets, Adam was urged on by his teammates to hand over his turn to someone else. "It's hard for him," they said, and "Remember, he can't guess." Adam got it wrong—"In the ocean?"—and so did his teammates before the other team gathered in a point with the right answer. The children noted that they covered all four directional possibilities in their guessing. Despite everyone getting it wrong, Adam continued to stand out, for only Adam had no points next to his name. He slunk down further in his chair. He was getting smaller as his problem got larger.

The third round of questions took up digit-span memory. The first question dealt with only three digits, and the children celebrated how easy the questions were. Gradually, they realized that each question upped the ante. Peter quickly told the story about his mother's friend who was "in school to be a test teacher." She practiced her tests on Peter, and he knew they could get difficult. We could also hear a whispered complaint from Adam that these questions were hard. Reggie got a question with five digits, and he slowly delivered the answer one digit and a pause at a time; everyone laughed and repeated his performance. Rikki got six digits in her question and missed one of them in her answer. By this time, Adam's turn was coming up. He had grown still smaller, sitting low in his seat, his hands over his face. Apparently, he was crying, and an adult asked, "Is this one too tough for you, Adam?" We were all beginning to squirm; this was not what we had had in mind.

By Adam's turn, he could expect seven digits. In addition to his having no points, his team was losing badly and his teammates could not afford his getting another answer wrong. Helene asked him to give her his turn, just as she had done on his previous turn, and he again declined. Adam may or may not have suffered, but he always tried and often cried. Nadine said that he should do it himself, an encouraging sentiment if Nadine hadn't been on the opposing team. Helene asked him why he was crying. Others answered that it was hard for him, and an adult suggested that he pass it by. Adam again claimed his turn even though, as one adult said, "Everybody misses some of them." A silence overtook the room as the tester directed attention to

Adam. He was asked to remember only four digits. He did it. Everyone cheered, even the children on the opposing team.

> Helene: Will you pass it to me, Adam?
> Tester: OK, Adam, is it your turn now?
> Adam: I'm not passing it to anybody.
> Helene: Oh-h boy (in a resigned voice).
> Tester: It's your turn now, Adam, right?
> Helene: Why are you crying, Adam?
> Lucy: Cause it's hard. It's hard for him.
> Scorekeeper): Well, just pass it by, that's all.
> It's no big deal.
> Helene: I'll do it for you, Adam, please?
> Reggie: You want.
> Adam: No, I don't want to pass it by (low and strained).
> Nadine: No, let him do it himself.
> Peter: He wants to answer questions, but they're hard.
> Tester: He can try it.
> Scorekeeper: Everybody misses some of them.
> (Uh-hums of agreement from several children)
> Tester: OK, Adam, you're ready?
> (Adam's hands remain in front of his face.)
> 6,1,5,8.
> Reggie: Ah!
> Adam: 6,1,5,8?
> (The children, except for Rikki and Adam, cheer, "Yea!")
> Reggie: Gimme five Adam! (holding out his palm)
> (Adam still has his head in his hands.)
> Please?

(Adam shakes his head no, and the children laugh.)

Adam had tried to make it a good day, and for a while, it had not worked out that way. He was the one who had said that "if you try harder and harder, it will it just get worser and worser." This may apply to us all as we try to make our schools more palatable. Happily, things turned around in the next part of the test, which involved storytelling, Adam's specialty. He won a prize for the most points for the day, and a full year later when we had the children back for a discussion of the previous year's after-school club, his favorite memory was that he won the day when we had "that, you know, quiz show thing." He had had a good day (Hood, McDermott, and Cole 1980).

Since that time, with the help of a fully protective and expensive education, Adam has graduated from college. He has outlived his classification as a Learning Disabled child. Away from the environment that was so well organized to find him not knowing something, he can get on with the tasks that come his way. It is likely that in the work world he does not have to spend his day as he did in the third grade, arranging to not get caught not knowing something. It is unlikely he has to spend his day not getting acquired by a Learning Disability.

The Cultural Construction of Learning Disabilities

The preceding case was meant to illuminate our point: There may have been something different about Adam, but this difference was not the source of the practical problems he encountered at times in his life. The problem did not consist in *his* "being" Learning Disabled as much as in his living *in a world* well organized to label and disable him. We do not claim to know what his difference, assuming there was one, consisted of, but we suspect that the search for the "it" of his difference has been quite dangerous to him. We do claim that the problem for him, for us as educators, and for us as analysts lies in the factuality of LD as a set of cultural and institutionally consequential practices that lead people with various degrees of authority or power to look for children to identify as Learning Disabled. Take away the institutions or limit their sphere of relevance and the "problem" disappears even if the difference does not.

Being different in the way, say, a severely dyslexic child is different does not make a Learning Disabled child in the cultural sense. Being acquired culturally by a Learning Disability does not make a child a Learning Disabled child in any neurological way. Our position, we insist throughout this book, does not require a theory of internalization, enculturation, or any other kind of "acceptance" by any person of the point of view of the other. We talk of Adam's sensitivity to his conditions, but we do not talk about his accepting the definitions that others suggest. His conditions were factual, culturally factual, as much a set of facts as the walls that surrounded the rooms in which our observations took place. No one could fail to feel pain when running into the walls, when being teased and otherwise identified even in the most benign ways as somehow unable to do something. Sensitivity to and practical consciousness of actual difficulties were not signs of Adam's self. Different children react differently to such pain. But sensitivity to personal pain must not hide the culture that constructs such painful conditions. Adam persisted in spite of the pain, and his having been born into a family that could afford the school he attended, it turned out eventually that his identification as Learning Disabled did not make much difference in his career. Other children might have been crushed. Still others might have veered into the defiant resistance of dropouts, street toughs, and motorcycle gangs (e.g., Willis 1977; MacLeod 1994). Learning Disability is not a destiny, but it is one of the roads open to children. Worse, now that it has become institutionalized, the livelihood of many well-educated people is dependent on a goodly number of children walking down this road.

Learning Disability, in our words, is a property of America, ideologically, legitimately, institutionally, and even economically. How this became the case is mostly outside the purview of this book, though we suggest the presence of a cultural imperative that has driven the evolution of the category over the past century. Ideologically, LD appears as a noncultural category that refers to an inner property of the child (whether genetic or internalized through various processes). As educational psychologists put forward a case for their skill at diagnosing LD and reformers made the case for the moral need for political institutions to legitimate the work of the psychologists, the diagnosis entered the institutional world. Administrators formulated regulations, teachers were required to follow them, and specialists were defined, trained, and put to work doing what they must legitimately do. This long historical process made the LD identification both morally good and commonsensically natural. If we searched for the earlier roots, we could probably show how the process is somehow related to industrialization, capitalism, and other aspects of the economic structure of modern societies. It is also related to the ideological individualism of Euro-American societies and to the liberal protest against capitalism and industrialization. After all, by the standards of modern democracy, if it makes sense to argue that all children are in some ways "different" from each other, then it is appropriate to construct institutions to identify these differences to ensure that each child is treated differently.

NOTES

As mentioned in the introduction, Adam's story was gathered during an interdisciplinary research project in the late 1970s when Michael Cole and the Laboratory of Comparative Human Cognition were at the Rockefeller University in Manhattan. The project was focused on the problem of ecological validity in psychological research, and as part of our effort to identify the various contexts in which different cognitive skills were made manifest, the performances of individual children, Adam included, became a way to organize our data. Different combinations of us have written the Adam story for various theoretical purposes. Although written from scratch, the present account borrows arguments and transcripts from Cole and Traupmann (1981); Hood, McDermott, and Cole (1980); McDermott (1993); and Newman, F. and Holzman (1993).

1. Joseph Reimer conducted the interview, using the Kolhberg moral dilemma stories as an eliciting device. In his dissertation, Reimer (1977) had shown that in a real-life group setting, children could often raise their level of moral reasoning over what they would display in a one-to-one interview. Because we knew the children of Adam's class well, because we had watched them on a daily basis handling moral dilemmas such as how much to tease one another, we were anxious to interview them with the details of their own lives at hand.

2. By a commonsense reading of experimental psychology, we should have been able to find some relation between what children were asked to do in the laboratory and what they found necessary to do in the real world, but we were able to describe little in everyday life that looked like what psychologists modeled and measured; on the implications of this negative finding for the ways we normally think about cognition and learning, see Cole, Hood, and McDermott (1978), Newman, D., Griffin, and Cole (1989), McDermott and Hood (1982) and the summary appendix in McDermott (1993).

3. A New York Times (April 8, 1994) report shows the result of having money available for a "careful" screening program for Learning Disabilities in a school for overachievers. The pres-

tigious Dalton School screened all its children and classified 36 percent of its first-graders as at risk, this despite a very high IQ average and an SES range at the top of all scales. On the politics underlying such madness, see Coles (1987).

4. The sociohistorical school of Vygotsky (1978, 1986) and his followers is an exception, and they have helped to remind us that a full account of the complexities of everyday life would overwhelm any account of what an individual subject might be up to at any given time. Fortunately, linguists, conversation analysts, and kinesicists have been describing the interactional world in enough detail to give body to claims about the ingenuity required of people in everyday life.

5. Arensberg (1982) once noted that a psychological analysis requires only one person behaving, a social analysis requires two people interacting, and a cultural analysis requires three people, two interacting and one interpreting the interaction. Our point, as Arensberg would agree, is that even a psychological analysis of Adam, if it is not to distort him by ignoring his circumstances, requires an account of him in interaction with others in ongoing institutional arrangements across scenes.

2 The Farrells and the Kinneys at Home: Literacies in Action

Hervé Varenne and Ray McDermott

In the introduction, we used the metaphor of culture as a house, a mansion really, in a village of houses into which one gets born and on which one is continually at work. This is a crowded village where many others are also at work both demolishing and reconstructing the collective dwelling with the tools and leftover material found in the various rooms. According to the logic of this metaphor, one could think of Adam (and all the other participants) as moving from room to room and in each being noticed, labeled, and treated as a different kind of person with different (dis)abilities.

Different things could be done in each of the rooms with different consequences for all involved. The metaphor might help us understand the historical details organizing what Adam and his consociates did while cooking bread or playing at being tested. The shape of the rooms in which we watched Adam were the product of an institution, the School, that none of the people involved could be said in any way to control. None of them had participated in the construction of the School, although a few had helped shape the particular school Adam found himself in. A few participants hoped they were working at altering a Testing institution that the researchers directly opposed but with which all were struggling. Adam himself was certainly unaware of the educational theories and their developers, who were somehow present when he asked for help at a time when it was relevant for him to be noticed as Learning Disabled. As researchers into the processes of the School, we must seek a systematic awareness that is difficult to achieve when we find ourselves in the same rooms Adam occupied.

Starting in this fashion allowed us to escape the temptation to blame Adam's peers, teachers, or school as the proximate participants who made difficulties for him. The pathos in Adam's situation was not misunderstanding or misdiagnosis but the blinding evidence that things were just the way they must be. Over the next few chapters, we explore the implications of this stance. One power of the house-with-rooms metaphor is that it allows us continually to be reminded of the movement possible within the walls of any room, including movement that can damage the walls between rooms or even remove them altogether. We pointed at this obliquely when we talked about Adam's school as a "private, liberal" school (and thus not a "conservative, military" school). Those who built this school carved or bounded a space within the School to make something that all (including the state boards that certified it) would recognize both as a proper school and as a "different" school. The very fact that such a difference was noticeable demonstrates that people in particular rooms (situations within large, complex, culturally organized fields for joint action) are not determined or even absolutely constrained by their conditions. People are always active, always transforming, if ever so slightly, their most local conditions without abolishing the more general constraints. In some cases, as we illustrate in this chapter, this activity produces new spaces, rooms for small groups (in this case, households) to inhabit and thereby to be enabled or disabled in new and more specific ways. In other cases, as we illustrate in the following two chapters, this activity produces a fleeting moment of success that no one notices or that gets specifically misunderstood.

To address these issues in more detail, we report on an ethnographic study of two children as they, their families, and their communities wove literacy into their daily lives. In the process they help us show how "actual" literacy, that is, literacy "in action," cannot be treated as a simple personal skill anymore than LD can be treated simply as a matter of individual handicap. Actual literacy is a product of cultural evolution both at the national level, where major institutions such as the School or Medicine define what must be known, and at the local level, where immediate consociates make this definition even more complex and immediately consequential. To understand reading, one must understand the social organization that allows and invites people to read. At the very least, for a reading to happen, it is necessary for people around a reader to organize reading materials as well as the time and space for the reading. Even the stereotypical "lonely" reading act, reading a novel in an armchair in front of a fire, requires massive social structures to organize many people to print the book, to furnish the economic means to deliver it to the reader, and then to leave the reader alone to read without interruption. As those of us who have tried to read the newspaper in a room with a small child present will testify, there is nothing "natural" in all this: If those around the reader do not cooperate, precious little reading gets done.

The central analytic question that should be asked of any act of reading is not one of skill (is the person able to read?) but of legitimacy (is the person allowed to read?) and authority (is the person's reading consequential for future action?). When an act of reading is performed in a group, both the identification of the reader and the authority of the reading are matters of serious social concern (Shuman 1986; Street 1984). In many instances, who may read can be quite restricted: Only particular adults may read with effect in schools, hospitals, or churches, and the restrictions are sometimes manifested in rules and regulations. In a Catholic mass, only the priest may read the words that consecrate the host and *have them count*. In a medical setting only physicians may read books listing diagnoses or medication and have it count—literally so in the case of insurance reimbursement. In families, this organization is often more implicit, but it can still be observed.

This organization is never purely under local temporal or spacial control. Those who hold people accountable for proper performance do not have to be present to be powerful. In America, literacy and the knowledge it makes accessible are too important politically for people not to be held accountable for performing the relevant acts practically in their everyday lives. Sick children must be brought to the attention of medical specialists, and uneducated children must be brought to the attention of educational specialists. Performances related to sickness and performances related to education are under different but similarly nonlocal control. By the same token, to the very extent that the overall organization is practically performed in local interaction, the actual performance can also reveal the operation of other, locally generated, patterns. And thus we can recognize neighboring families of the same class, ethnicity, and so on as somehow different from each other.

In order to make our argument about the relationship between structure and indeterminacy in the practice of familial literacy, we first focus on three kinds of literacy we found in the houses of two closely matched families. First, we look at "familial" literacy, that is, literacy used in passing through the daily round of life at home. This is the literacy that does not reveal itself as a topic for evaluation. Second, we look at the symbolic power of "special" kinds of literacy in the two families. These are literacies that are highly marked symbolically, though again not as a topic of evaluation. The special language of medicine, for example, has a power over the lives of the people that is quite different from the power of their own language. Although related to the language of the school, the language of medicine does not raise issues of school evaluation.

This brief look at two types—familial and special—of nonschool literacy leads us to a more detailed look at a third type, one we understand as controlled by the School, namely, homework. We examine this home-school interface initially in terms of what the families do not control, specifically, the cultural forms that make an activity homework rather than, say, curing an ailing child. We suggest how the family members involved in the homework hold each other accountable for maintaining the School frame. Then, we look at *variations in the doing of homework* to suggest how families can differ in organizing what they control while still being controlled by the school structure.

Sheila and Joe

In the shadow of cosmopolitan Manhattan, "Kingsland" is one of those areas of New York City that preserves the provincial atmosphere of a small town: narrow streets, low clapboard houses, and neighbors a parent can rely on to keep track of the little ones. It is a working-class, white, ethnic enclave that is best understood in terms of its borders (see Susser 1982; Suttles 1972). The area is small, and given local prejudices, the racially different people who surround the neighborhood dwarf it into defensiveness. Natives think of it as a great place to have grown up, but each generation yearns to move on. The road to success and the road out are parallel, and education is essential to both. Those who have made it have taken their degrees, moved to the suburbs, and return on holidays to visit the older generation. Those who stay behind are understood to have in some way failed.

Both Sheila Farrell (age ten) and Joe Kinney (age nine) lived in Kingsland. Both their families thought of themselves as "Irish" and drew on Irish ancestors to make their case. This did not prevent them from dating and marrying "outside" their group (Polish and Hispanic). The Farrells and the Kinneys were inserted into their neighborhood in quite different ways. Mr. Farrell was a truck driver. Mrs. Farrell held various jobs until the birth of her second child. Afterward she stayed at home near the center of a large group of close kin; her parents and six siblings lived in three nearby houses. At another extreme was Mrs. Kinney, who was the only one of her siblings to have stayed on the block of their youth. She had been separated from Joe's father, a salesman, for two years. She had to spend most of her day outside the neighborhood as a clerk in a government bureaucracy. Her family circle was expanded only to her mother, who took care of the children from the time they got out of school to the time she returned from her work. At that point she was by herself with Joe and his sister.

Sheila and Joe lived only a few blocks from each other and went to the same Catholic school a year apart, but they did not know each other. Neither of them was remarkable among the students of their school. They were chosen initially because their parents told us that Sheila was "doing well" in school and Joe was "not doing too well." We must emphasize that the contrast lay in the parents' evaluation. It is interesting as evidence that the parents were in the business of evaluation.[1] As a matter of fact, it soon became clear that the formal contrast (as "objective measures" could determine) was not great. Initially, it was perhaps easier to characterize both children as typical preteenagers from a working-class, American-ethnic neighborhood. This erased many of the differences that did exist between them and their parents. Even if Sheila and Joe were unique in the details of their lives, they can still be interesting to us as tokens of a type.

Familial Literacy

Both the Farrells and the Kinneys were literate in the broad sense that literacy was not a practical problem in either family. They could read what they needed to read to conduct the life to which they had been accustomed. This does not mean that all the members of each family read the same kind of materials with the same kind of ease or enthusiasm. There was much variation between individual members in formal level and actual use of school instruction. A few rarely read much more than the sports page of the newspaper, and others had gone to college. Some preferred to have recipes explained to them rather than read a cookbook, and others kept up extensive bulletin boards of familial events. Both families expected the children to possess an unspecified but well-bounded level of familial literacy. When Sheila was asked to set the coffee machine on perk, she was fully expected to be able to read the switches and, of course, she could. Similarly, whatever opinion Mrs. Kinney may have had of her son's lack of success in school, she too relied on Joe's literacy for the performance of many familial tasks that required specific, though perhaps limited, acts of reading. Both Sheila and Joe possessed all the literacy they needed to participate in family life within the social structure of their community. Indeed, it seemed to us that they already had the literacy needed to occupy the type of working-class occupations their parents held.

We are making a general though perhaps difficult point. The literacy of the Farrells and the Kinneys was a systemic literacy, not a personal one. It was not one for which the members were accountable in the same way as one is accountable for one's literacy in a second- or third-grade classroom. One does not "fail" familial literacy. Indeed, everyday literacy is all but invisible in the family.[2] It is embedded in other tasks: getting the right thing at the store, writing a card to a relative, or letting the children know where everyone is with a note on the refrigerator door. At such times, literacy as such is not highlighted. At other times, it is. There are ritual forms of familial reading such as "bedtime reading." In some families, though not among the Farrells and Kinneys, moments of reading may have religious, ideological, or ethnic value. There are still other ways of embedding actual reading in a familial scene. Most important for our purposes, reading is often marked for political and authoritative issues that eclipse the skill-based issues. Let us look at an example.

The Eye Ointment Scene

The Farrell's baby had contracted conjunctivitis. After considerable consultation among the women in the extended family, it was decided that the infection could be treated at home with the eye ointment Mrs. Farrell had in the medicine cabinet. The field worker wrote down the scene as follows:

> Mrs. Farrell brought out a small bottle of ointment on which was written "Ophthalmic Ointment." She proceeded to read the small print on the label to see if it contained the ingredients that she remembered were usually found in such medicines from her previous experience with conjunctivitis. She was not totally convinced. She turned to Vera [the fieldworker] and asked her opinion. Vera read the label, said that it was probably alright but that she did not feel comfortable taking chances with medicines. Mrs. Farrell agreed and turned to her husband, asking him to phone the pharmacy to ask the pharmacist's opinion. Mr. Farrell asked her why she didn't phone herself, to which she confessed she felt embarrassed. Mr. Farrell called the pharmacist and read aloud the information on the label. At almost every point of his explanation and reading, Mrs. Farrell interrupted to correct both his inaccuracies in pronunciation and in points of fact. He was visibly irritated, but nevertheless changed his words to accommodate her criticisms. Eventually, it was established that the ointment was the correct one.

This incident is paradigmatic of scenes in which literacy is used in such families as the Farrells and the Kinneys. Something happens: A baby is sick and all are involved. All must perform something relevant to the event but not necessarily, indeed probably not, the same thing. Some, such as Sheila, the elder sibling but medically still a child, must remain silent on the sidelines. Of more concern to us here, several must read. Mrs. Farrell read, the fieldworker read, and Mr. Farrell read. Their reading had different practical consequences. Mrs. Farrell found partial confirmation of her reading in the fieldworker's own. It was not sufficient. They had to confirm it with a specialist (the pharmacist). Mrs. Farrell did not make the call herself even though she was the better reader in the sense that she corrected Mr. Farrell and he accepted her correcting. In the process, every person's position within this complex social system was indexed and perhaps reproduced, though we should not fail to notice the various hesitations. Things were not absolutely clear. The conditions were not so overwhelmingly determinant that one could simply follow the prescriptions.

Analytically, the ointment scene reveals the practical achievement of family life in the face of conversational indeterminacy (Varenne 1992). At the end of the sequence, the participants were not where they were at the beginning. Something had happened. What had happened was the product of smaller-scale sequences that particular people occupying particular positions performed in particular ways that had a particular power over future sequences. This improvisational process made for a unique event that was from then on going to be part of the family's history. The event itself remained controlled by what had been and remained *always already there*, namely, the set of definitions and rules of relationship that organized who could do what, when, how, and with what kind of effect.

Our focus on all behavior as relational should serve as a basis for differentiating the structural from the indeterminate in familial literacy. Clearly, the eye infection is something that must be handled socially. In a family like the Farrells, many people are involved, and they must deal with each other. But even in more isolated conditions, we would see that it takes many people and many conversations to deal with something like an infection. In the modern United States, one must deal with experts. One must deal with a drug company. One may also have to deal with those who criticize and variously resist what may then be derisively referred to as "the medical establishment." Some of these dealings can be conducted through oral means. Others appear more indirect: The Farrells' relationship with the drug company was purely literate, but the focus of the interaction was not the act of reading itself. The reading act was part of a wider sequence.

It is difficult to know how to understand this practical literacy. It is so embedded within other activities that it appears irrelevant to the main issues that interest us, the issues of "success" as measured by status mobility and the more principled issues of liberal "self-education" and radical "critical consciousness." The apparent ability to read the switch on a machine, a label on a tube of medicine, the newspaper, an announcement from school, an item on the family bulletin board, or the legend behind a snapshot seems such a low-level matter as to be outside what we need to understand. We think otherwise. Such literacy may not seem important given the usual means to measure importance, but it does tell us much about the family as a social world. In contrast, a focus on the abstracted level of individual skill as it might be measured in a lab through a test cannot tell us much about what reading is in fact done and for what purposes.[3] The activity of a person in a group is not determined by the person's qualities as much as by the group's identification of what that person may do under the current conditions.

Special Literacy

Let us look again at the eye ointment episode. How did the participants use literacy in this conversation? Initially, it looked as if they were involved in a search for information. This may be the way they would have talked about their reading of the label. But the commonsense statement robs the moment of its special character. At one level, all the moves in the conversation can be understood as information-gathering strategies. Whereas the overall task was curing the baby, the means were an examination of all available information in the hope of avoiding an expensive visit to the pediatrician. If we look at the impact of the various initial moves on later moves, we may recognize that the information gained through reading the label had a different force than information gained through an oral inquiry of one's peers. The label had an "interrupt" value. It stopped the conversation, it decentered the personal experience of the participants, and it redirected their search toward the expert (the pharmacist), who himself referred back to the literate text.

The simple fact that some information is printed is not what gives it a special character. It is important that the printing is not seen as being generated by the people themselves; instead, it comes from somewhere else, from a realm of experts who speak to the masses in a special voice using a special medium, a special syntax, and special words, that is, a special, symbolically marked rhetoric. The practice of literacy in this perspective is less a function of a special individual competence (which must, of course, exist) than a moment in a social exchange. The drug company "spoke" to the Farrells. The Farrells, in turn, "listened" to the company. However indirectly, they were in relationship with the company. This relationship was structured in the sense that it was differentiated from the other relationships that they had with other people and institutions.

We can go further. The special character of medical literacy is something that the Farrells, the Kinneys, and the rest of us as well personally perform. Although the Farrells could not have easily produced a text that would look like a label on a tube of medicine, such a text—if they knew that it had been produced by someone like them—would not have had the weight of a text produced by appropriately professional persons. It was imperative that the Farrells move their conversations toward the reading of the label and then redirect their investigation to the expert who could give the last word. Giving the last word to experts in specific circumstances is something that the Farrells actually and practically did. Such literacy had a sacred character. The recourse to literacy was differentiated in its communicative role from the recourse to oral confirmation. This literacy was special even when it was embedded within larger sequences. It was expert. It canceled the oral. It took the family outside of itself even though it was performed by the family.[4]

This remark carries its full weight when we begin investigating the place of school literacy in the family's conversations. Yielding to the practical power of medical literacy was not something that individual family members did singly; look, for example, at the request for a reading by the fieldworker and her subsequent reluctance to use her status as having recently obtained a doctorate. She was caught with them as they enforced on her an aspect of this status. The interpretations of the privileges and responsibilities of such statuses was not something that one could easily change locally. Medical literacy acquired its readers and doled out expertise almost regardless of the participants or their opinions. They did have opinions about it, but they had no direct handle on the "it." They had to play out the prescriptions even as they also played out their opinions. In brief, medical literacy is an issue whenever human beings are ailing within the reach of America. The same can be said for school literacy.

Homework and School Literacy

Familial, medical, and school literacies are three quite distinct social events. They are not different simply because they are produced by different collectivities of people (family members, medical personnel, or teachers). They are different because fathers, mothers, and children can themselves practically produce, within their own conversations, the special symbolic acts that mark a performance as relevant to family, medicine, or education.

As part of our data collection, we videotaped the Farrells and the Kinneys as they performed "homework." In both cases the actual event we analyzed was unique if only because we were there with our recording machinery. Although both fieldworkers felt that what had been captured was somehow representative of their respective family's usual evening round, we prefer to treat the homework performances precisely as dramatic performances. Our analysis is not based on replication. We do not ask whether these families did exactly the same thing every night. In fact, we are sure they did not. We ask instead how family members put together a school literacy event in the midst of a group involved in much else, including, that night, being videotaped. When called on by the local university to play school, to go on video record so the world could watch them display their best homework performances, what did the families have to work with? What was the script they relied upon? Who were the dramatis personae? What would allow the intended audience to recognize them? These are the questions that drove them and, in turn, drive us.

The taping was done in each case in the location where Sheila and Joe usually did their homework. The people involved (except for the fieldworkers) were the people who were usually involved; that is, they were the people who might have been involved (even though it is certain that all of them were not always actually involved).

In Sheila's case, this meant that many people came within range when she did "her" homework: mother, father, sister, aunt (with boyfriend), the performers (producers, advertisers, etc.) on television, and so on. This list could be longer; the kitchen table where homework was done and the couch where it was checked were at the center of the Farrells' social network.

Fewer people got involved in Joe Kinney's homework. This did not mean that he and his mother were by themselves: The sister, the grandmother, some friends, and neighbors all had to be dealt with (not to mention, again, the television). From all accounts (the tapes, the fieldworkers' observations, interviews, and our general knowledge of homework in American families), homework is rarely an event that is radically separated from the family's life. There must be a careful involvement of the family and its social environment even to achieve what most people think of as homework, namely, times during which children do their homework "by themselves" and "with no distractions." It can take a whole family to enforce a separation of the child.

The often assumed separation of homework from family life highlights the social complexity of the homework performance. Although the separation of the child is a social construction, it is organized to make society disappear. The appropriately dramatic representation of this separation must involve the creation of an empty physical space around the child, an absence of face-to-face interaction between the child and others during a certain time, a narrow focus by the child on a specific task, and so on. As performed, such moments are difficult to capture cinematographically in their social aspects. So we focused our analysis on the time when the parents "checked" the homework.

Checking is an optional subroutine within the general definition of homework. Teachers and schools disagree on the value of such checking, and parents do not have much specific guidance about what it should involve. Nonetheless, it is dealt with structurally as a special moment within the overall routine of the day. Separation and noninterruption are again at issue, but it is now the separation of the adult-child dyad rather than just the child.

In our families, dramatic separation was difficult to achieve. On the day we taped, Sheila did spend a half-hour "by herself" at the kitchen table. She was surrounded by much familial interaction, but she remained on its fringes. Similarly, Joe's sister was observed regularly doing her homework by herself. Joe, however, seemed rarely to have been allowed this moment of solitude. His mother told us that if she (or her own mother) did not actively participate, Joe would not concentrate. In both families, the checking sequence was difficult to arrange. The successful separation of an adult from family life is almost impossible when that adult is the center of a large household (as Mrs. Farrell was) or when she is the only adult in the household (as Mrs. Kinney was).

Although a fully appropriate dramatic separation could not be achieved, the families did hold themselves accountable for it. They performed the structural markers of separation. The many people who entered the homework scene did it as either "help" or "distraction." But the homework always remained the homework of the child in every participant's speech. The Farrells, as they said it, did not do "their" homework: Sheila did "her" homework. By another way of speaking, everyone in the family was doing homework, but Sheila was redundantly marked as the focus by being put in certain positions within the sequence.

The culturally constructed nature of homework becomes clear if we think of it as a conversation among a great number of people for a long period of time. It is because Sheila was in school that the family had to do homework. Without Sheila being in conversation with a teacher, there would have been no homework. The Farrells did not generate homework on their own. This was graphically represented to us when it happened that the day we were to videotape Joe Kinney, the teacher, "for the first time in years," as we were told, had not "given" homework. As the kind of outsiders we were, we had the authority to ask the family to do make-believe homework, which they did.[5] It was clear that no homework would have been done that night had we not been there.

The presence of School in the family kitchen was apparent in the way members spotlighted the child's performance. Even more striking was the fact that the specific talk generated as part of the homework scene was structured, as school talk is structured, to isolate individual competence displays. Such conversations followed a canonical progression that was the same as the sequences that represented the school to itself:[6] Mother asked a question, child answered, mother evaluated. This is a structure of the general classroom discourse form of /Question-Answer-Evaluation/ (Mehan 1978, 1979; Cazden 1988). The sequence can be performed in various ways. The evaluation can be delayed when the child is "right" and when a specific sequence is to be followed immediately by another. The sequence becomes more complex if the evaluation is negative. The child may question the mother's evaluation. The mother may simply reinstate the question or perhaps give hints. She may move to a full teaching mode, restating a general rule, explaining how it applies, checking for an understanding of the principle, and so on. Ultimately, the position that the mother and child occupy are asymmetrical; they cannot be exchanged. The child is the one who is accountable for the answer. The mother may check the answer in the book if she is not sure, but the child may not.[7]

The canonical progression can be thought of as a structure for a particular type of conversation in which the conversational labor is divided differentially. What is particularly interesting is the way various sequences hierarchically nest into each other. In Figure 2.1 we offer a partial model within which we can situate any moment of the homework situation.

The easy recognition and applicability of Figure 2.1 to homework scenes throughout the culture suggest that it captures many of the constraints on families when school comes home. Although family members have to perform the appropriate markers that constitute homework tasks as having been performed, the structural uniformity of the scenes indicates that the participants have little control over its organization. Whatever the families may think of the school, whatever the success of their children, whatever, indeed, the success of the families, all of them are accountable to the school for right answers, and they behave accordingly. In other words, we

FIGURE 2.1
The Structural Replication of Task-Performance Evaluation Sequences at School and Home

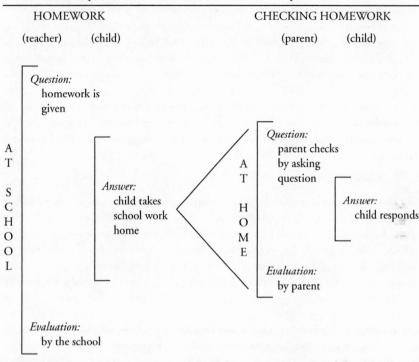

HOMEWORK   CHECKING HOMEWORK

(teacher)   (child)   (parent)   (child)

AT SCHOOL

Question: homework is given

Answer: child takes school work home

Evaluation: by the school

AT HOME

Question: parent checks by asking question

Answer: child responds

Evaluation: by parent

have no evidence to suggest that there is any major gap between the family and the school on the subject of homework and, indeed, the very structuring of education as a social interaction. These families fully participate in School.

Variations in the Doing of School at Home

The performance of the structural features that allow the family to recognize that it is performing homework never prevents the joint performance of other features that can mark other structures. The family can be "itself" at the same time that it is doing homework in a traditional manner. Families are relatively free to improvise around the imposed theme, particularly as it concerns the insertion of the school sequences within the families' own organization. We deal with these variations in the doing of school under four subheadings:

1. The sequencing of homework in the daily round (how the homework is organized in relation to other family activities).

2. Internal sequencing (how the various subroutines within homework are organized).
3. The organization of intrusions (how the entry of nonhomework tasks is managed).
4. The identifications available to the participants (what the participants imply about each other as they interact with each other both in situ and in general conversations outside of the sequence).

Taken together, these should tell us about cultural pattern and family variation, about what is controlled at the family level and what is not, and give us a look at American culture and education from the perspective of family life.

1. The Sequencing of Homework in the Daily Round

The Farrells.   It was typical for Sheila to do her homework immediately upon her return from school. It was also typical for her mother to check it immediately after. There was no need for much prompting on the parents' part. Nobody was assigned to help. Other participants were engaged in other activities. Even at the time of checking, all the participants were still engaged in a multitude of activities, but the performance of these other activities did not seem to slow down the homework process.

The Kinneys.   Homework for Joe was typically a two-stage affair. On most days, Joe first sat down to begin his homework under the supervision of his grandmother. According to all reports, this first stage was characterized by (1) a struggle between Joe and his grandmother about the necessity of doing homework before going out to play and (2) the tendency of the grandmother to do parts of the homework for him, "sometimes in her own handwriting," as Joe's mother told us. Joe generally won this struggle, which set the scene for the second stage of the homework saga. After Joe and his mother returned home, Mrs. Kinney began to check what Joe had done and what he still had to do. This could last until late in the evening. The length of the procedure was partially the product of the fact that Mrs. Kinney, at the same time that she checked Joe's homework, had also to prepare and eat her own meal, keep track of her daughter's activities, catch up with the children about their day, touch base with other members of her network, and so on. It was also a product of the way they organized homework and allowed every possible source of interruption to become a disruption.

2. Internal Sequencing of Homework

When we introduced the summary structural model of the homework conversation as a special event, we suggested that certain variations could be made on it. Like all social events, homework has a clear beginning and end and a range of things that can happen in the middle, each of which can have its own beginning and end (Hockett 1964; Scheflen 1973; Sacks 1974; Frake 1980). The variations cannot modify the basic form of the conversation, but they can, with work, accountably expand the form. At one extreme, the family can initiate the homework sequence by insisting that the child does homework-like tasks even in the absence of school-initiated homework (as the Kinneys found themselves doing when we came to videotape them). It is also possible to do more than just check the mere act of having done the work. It is possible to evaluate it, something that both families did; they were interested in the child "getting it right." This evaluation itself can be varied. In particular, it is possible to go beyond pure red-pencil-type evaluation into a full teaching sequence during which the child is made to rehearse the broken rule. Mrs. Farrell, for example, regularly went beyond identifying answers as right or wrong as she questioned Sheila to lead her to finding the right answer. This mentoring variation can be treated as a subsequence within the "parent-checking" sequence, one that is activated by any "wrong" answer. The Kinneys did not get themselves into such subsequences on our tapes. When Joe worked on a long-division problem, his mother compared his performance number by number with a completed example of the same problem. She did not teach, but if he wrote down a "wrong" number, she intervened.

3. Intrusions

Neither the Farrells nor the Kinneys could stop other family activities from proceeding while homework was happening. Even as they performed the markers that make homework special, at times the primary participants (the child and mother in both cases) were called upon to participate in other essential activities. This is a general fact of social life. Different activities co-occur. All have to be specifically performed, and they all have to maintain their borders against each other. It is not just that a social group can perform several differentiated activities concurrently. It is also that the participants must somehow handle the motion back and forth from one activity to the other. We can learn much by focusing on how they do it.

Intrusions are not random. They are concretely performed in particular ways. The structuring of intrusions differentiated the Farrells and the Kinneys.

The Farrells. In the scene we chose to demonstrate the style the Farrells used to deal with intrusions, Mr. and Mrs. Farrell, Sheila, and the baby were all checking Sheila's homework. The television, while passive, was on most of the time. Watching television was a differentiated activity, a possible source of intrusions. Mrs. Farrell followed what was happening on the television almost every time she lifted her head from the workbook. Typically, this movement occurred only when Mrs. Farrell was not "on" in the homework conversation. She did not watch the tube in place of doing what she had to do next as far as homework was concerned. The story gets more complex when one realizes that Sheila was on a related schedule. Mrs. Farrell watched television while Sheila worked on an answer to a question put to her by her mother, and Sheila in turn watched while her mother checked answers in Sheila's workbook. Even the baby could be seen following the alternating focus between homework, television, and conversation.[8] For example, after it was established that Sheila actually could do a little exercise in which she had first made a mistake, she and her mother entered into a quick sequence of moves that can be described, metaphorically, as the dance of a loving mother proudly reprimanding her daughter for a self-assurance and satisfaction both knew was well grounded. The baby followed this dance carefully, and when it ended, she turned to Sheila and laughed with her. Sheila reciprocated and sang to the baby. In the meantime, the mother returned to the homework; even self-congratulation did not break the rhythm. Homework was maintained until its school-defined end, that is, until all the assigned exercises had been checked.

When the Farrells did homework, interruptions were well timed to allow homework to continue apace. This was the opposite of the schedule of interruptions in the Kinney family.

The Kinneys.   The Kinneys also had to perform the special markers of homework, and they too had to deal with nonhomework intrusions into the special performance. Food had to be prepared and consumed. The telephone had to be answered. The Farrells taught us that such intrusions in themselves need not interrupt the flow of any special activity. Interruptions are made by the family. Watching the Kinneys do their homework, we saw Mrs. Kinney, time and again, asking Joe questions he did not answer. She did not react to this silence. It was as if she had asked the question in such a way as to tell Joe that it did not count. Often, we saw Mrs. Kinney start a sequence, get Joe involved, and then abruptly drop it so that it did not develop. Quite often, there appeared to be a clear external cause to the interruption; for example, Mrs. Kinney asked a question and then the telephone rang. She answered it. What would seem more natural than that she would have forgotten what her question was? But it was on the more subtle events that we rely in our argument that perhaps it was not quite "natural" for Mrs. Kinney not to complete sequences she started.

As Joe and his mother got ready to do homework, she leaned over, took his bag, looked in, asked, "What's your favorite subject?" Before Joe answered, she left the table to check the coffee. Sometimes she cleaned the table, sent Joe off for a pencil only after she finished with the table, and sent him off after still another false start to sharpen the pencil. In contrast to members of the Farrell family, who seemed always in tune with Sheila's homework, we saw Mrs. Kinney and Joe out of tune. To start homework was to stop homework. When she focused on his lack of attention, it was often just at the moment when we saw him already turning back to his work. They were often hung between two activities in a way that marked each as having been an interruption of the other. Together, they organized one disruption after another. In the fourteen minutes before they focused on a math problem, itself an occasion for numerous disruptions, Joe and his mother initiated homework thirteen times, and in each case they turned their attention to something new and unrelated. In an equivalent period of time, the Farrells produced six interruptions and no breaks from the homework tasks at hand.

In abstract terms, our argument is that interruptions are empty structures that gain their specific values only as a social group produces its own history. In the Farrell house, interruptions allowed homework to get done; in the Kinney house, they became disruptions that did not allow homework to get done. Even getting started was difficult. The difference between the two families was further emphasized by the presence of the teaching subroutine among the Farrells when the mother questioned Sheila about the rule that she was supposed to be applying. This did not happen in the Kinney house.

4. The Identifications Available to Participants

Another variation on homework in the two families can be found in how they talked about each other either in situ or in moments when some of them had moved to a new scene. We have noted that Mrs. Farrell and her daughter periodically took note of just how well they were doing while complaining about how they had had to struggle to get each other's attention. In the Kinney house, the same struggle was often taken by the members as an instance of how mother and son were not really good at homework. Any inattention on Joe's part could be taken not only as a source of disruption but as an occasion for noting that Joe was the kind of person who preferred not to pay attention to school—the same kind of person his mother once was while she struggled through the same school a generation before. Although Mrs. Kinney spent far more time away from the homework table than Joe and can be shown to have been the master of turning intrusions into interruptions and disruptions, she also liked to tell the story of how Joe "can't sit still." When we asked if we could videotape Joe doing homework, she warned that it would "be like videotaping an empty chair." In one embarrassing scene, Joe left the table to get a chair for a fieldworker who was crouching on the floor.

(Mother is looking into Joe's schoolbag as he is leaving the table)

Mother: Let's see what you have, Joe. A pipe. What do you say, Joe . . . (looks to the empty chair). Want to . . . (looks to fieldworker). All I have to do is bend my head and he's gone. (Laughter) Ohh, Joe. Hey Joe!
Fieldworker A: That's what I thought he was doing.
Joe: Where did you put everybody's coat?
Fieldworker B: Good guy, yeh.
Fieldworker A: He doesn't like me sitting on the floor.
Mother: Oh.
Fieldworker A: Thank you, Joe.
Mother: [Fieldworker A] went down on the floor and I didn't even notice. Thank you, Joe.

Fieldworker A: Thank you very much.
Mother: You're a good host. I'm a rotten hostess. (Pause) Which books? Where did you
get these?

The mother attended to Joe's leaving and took it to be an instance of what she had warned the fieldworker a video session of Joe doing homework would be, namely a long record of an empty chair. As the mother and the fieldworker laughed at her apparent predictive power, the child returned with a chair, and the mother then noticed that it was an appropriate move on Joe's part. From that point on, Joe was stable and the mother far less so.

Whereas in one house, homework was an occasion for noting "how well we are doing," in the other, it was an occasion for noting "how badly we are doing." What the families cannot control is that homework is an occasion for evaluation. The School will check on how the Family is doing. Nor can families control the materials on which the decisions are made. Sometimes families can manage a little control over who is included in the "doing well" and the "doing badly" categories, although never more so than is allowed by the distribution of success and failure in the wider system. In fact, in the twelve families in the Kinney and Farrell study, each had a child who was doing "well" and one who was doing "badly"; the national average played out in the average home. How the families handled the success and failure identifications was, in turn, amazingly particular and sometimes ingenious.

Culture: A First Approximation

In this chapter we have looked at two families and several sets of scenes requiring different types of organization, all open to different interpretations. Neither the Kinneys nor the Farrells were free from general cultural patterns that we qualify as American. Medical expertise and a definition of education as the getting of right answers to prescribed questions both constituted resources and constraints for the families' own dramatic reconstructions of family life and school performance in America. Visions of medical and educational expertise were available for the families to work with, and nothing they did could abolish the qualities of what was given them. But once an illness entered their homes or once a teacher assigned homework, the families were altogether free, rather than determined, to do what they could.

The Farrells and Kinneys helped us open our discussion of culture as it relates to the success/failure complex in America. The School is a cultural fact, and so are the particular ways the Farrells and Kinneys handled intrusions into the performance of homework. Culture is absolutely real as constraint. But it is also absolutely not determining of what is to happen next in local and translocal history. The freedom to do whatever one pleases with what one is given is absolute, but momentary; every new act is free until it is placed in a further sequence performed by some other person or group. To the question What time is it? one is free answer, "Go to hell!" What happens next depends on whether the addressee heard the answer; if so, it is time for a new freedom to exercise itself, and so on. A family will always do its homework in particular ways. There is a temporary freedom behind the door of one's home that cannot be totally discounted any more than it can be overinterpreted. The particularity evolved by a family is only partially controlled by that family. Soon, the homework is evaluated at school, and the results are used by others, for example, Joe's absent father, to make a new case, to forge a new context for further action in freedom and constraint.

In the following chapter, we explore further the process of interpretation, that is, of the transformation of broadly prescribed steps when performed in local groups in the real time of face-to-face interaction. We consider in part what some have talked about as "resistance," though we highlight the limits of resistance, or, as we prefer, *bricolage*, as it is resequenced within broader institutionalized performances and either radically ignored (as is the pleasure of singing together in the case we present in the next chapter) or radically overinterpreted (as is the laughter of some students in an alternative high school in the case we present in the subsequent chapter).

NOTES

The fuller report on this study is available (Varenne, McDermott, Hamid-Buglione, and Morison, 1982). Ann Morison's dissertation (1982) offers a solid account of fieldwork in Joe Kinney's family. Three other papers are also based on the study (Leichter 1985; McDermott, Goldman, and Varenne 1984; Varenne and McDermott 1986). The last one is a foundation for much of what appears in this chapter.

1. Of course, the parents are not alone in the business of evaluation. We, as researchers from a teachers college funded by a "national" institute of "education," set the parents to evaluate their children. The "criteria" for selection of the families, as these were set for us by our own context (the funding agency and a tradition of scholarship), were that some of the families to be studied had to have a child "doing well" and some others a child "not doing well." Initially we had to inquire of parents whether they had such children. Still, the parents had no difficulty entering into a conversation about the relative success of their children.

2. For a more extended discussion of these points, see Taylor (1983) and Taylor and Dorsey-Gaines (1988).

3. On the claim that the student of education should not be studying skills analytically ripped from the contexts of their occurrence and that we should instead focus on the organization of learning in ongoing social activities, see Cole, Hood, and McDermott (1978); Newman, Griffin, and Cole (1989); Lave (1988); Lave and Wenger (1991); Suchman (1987); and most of the papers in Chaiklin and Lave (1993). Cole and Griffin (1986), following Vygotsky (1986), urge us to consider that the unit of analysis in teaching and learning is not individual skill as much as the activities of which people and their skills are but a component part: "We should be trying to instantiate a basic activity when teaching reading and not get blinded by the basic *skills*. Skills are always part of activities and settings, but they only take on meaning in terms of how they are organized. So instead of basic skills, a sociohistorical approach talks about basic activities and instantiates those that are necessary and sufficient to carry out the whole process of reading, given the general conditions for learning" (127).

4. A full analysis of the incident would investigate the role of oral conversation with the pharmacist and its own interrupt function. The Farrells' recourse to the pharmacist suggests that they did not trust their collective reading of the label. In a certain way, not only were they not competent to write the label, they were not absolutely competent to read it either in its contextual relevance. In other words, all the participants in the scene, including perhaps Sheila, could "read" the label to satisfy the school. None had the power to produce a reading of the label that could be commonsensically used to cure a baby. This suggests the existence of a hierarchy of literacies and, through it, a hierarchy of readers.

5. At the time, we did not have to call specifically on the authority that came with our status as researchers in education. This authority was not under our personal control, and we could not shed it. Homework was made up almost before we realized what was happening, as if the Kinneys enforced it on us and on themselves. We could have insisted that "our research requires real homework and so we'll come back another day." This would have constructed a different history and would have led to the production of different but not necessarily "better" data. Refusal to accept what the Kinneys were doing might have been a more authoritarian gesture than just accepting their construction of what we had to be.

6. As elsewhere in the book, we are distinguishing between, on the one hand, the ensemble of the activities performed in certain settings among various people and, on the other hand, the symbols that (1) define the setting as a certain type of setting and (2) define the subactivities that can be performed with the setting. Within a family there are certain activities that are particularly "family-like," and they are used as representations of the family as a special place within possible places in the culture. "Loving" activities probably are such activities (Schneider [1968] 1980). Within family settings, scenes such as homework are themselves structurally differentiated. In school too, certain activities can be used to symbolize the School even though they are not the only activities actually performed there.

7. This does not mean that the mother is not herself on the hot seat. Particularly in front of strangers, she may demonstrate embarrassment at both her own and her child's mistakes. Displays of embarrassment are on our tapes, and the literature is replete with accounts of the way parents are made responsible for the school failure of their children. Joe's and Sheila's parents were aware of the extent to which they were on the spot. They knew they could be blamed for the failure of their children.

8. That a sixteen-month-old baby should participate in displaying the attentional structure of her family is not mysterious. It belongs with the capacity that very young children have of producing intonationally proper "sentences" and conversational routines before they begin speaking in the more usual sense (Bateson, M. C. 1975). Similarly, children position themselves relationally to reading and other complex adult activities long before they can actually decipher words (Boyd 1993; Taylor 1983).

3 The Voice of the Choir, the Voices in the Choir

Hervé Varenne
and Merry Naddeo

The first two chapters demonstrated that no understanding of educational activities can proceed in the absence of a detailed, complex account of the forces, both local and translocal, that shape what is noticed, when, by whom, and for what purposes. The stories we tell in the next three chapters could have been used to make the same demonstration. We use them instead for two related, but different, purposes.

First, particularly in this chapter and the next, we want to illustrate the complexity of action at the very moment of its unfolding. This ties in to long-standing work in Vygotskian psychology and more recent developments in ethnomethodology. Everyday behavior requires of individuals complex skills that have not been modeled to a significant degree by any cognitive theory. When individuals get together, the complexity of their concerted activity jumps to a new level, which research in interactional analysis is still sketching. The point is not to return to a more adequate psychology that would more deeply respect the personal competence of individuals. The point is to pursue a sociology of activity. At the most local levels, at the moment of historical emergence when the future of the group is still open, actors do not follow scripts imposed on them or simply repeat scripts they have become habituated to and learned. They improvise, play, resist, and they laugh. At the end, they may find themselves having reproduced their position as the product of their activity is placed on a different stage.

The second purpose of these chapters is to show how local constructions can disappear as they are placed within larger frames. A particular local performance rarely has the power of imposing its own interpretation. Adam might have been good at telling stories. People around him might even have known that about him and still forgotten, discounted, or otherwise ignored this as they identified him under other circumstances for particular purposes framed by other constraints. Translocal evaluation of local constructions is not under local control; neither are the materials offered to the locality or the original patterning of these materials before actors move into the room. All this is given prefabricated to local participants. As we showed in Chapter 2, the shape of these "gifts," their interpretation by those who made them as well as what they will do with the local performances does not absolutely determine what the participants will do. When Merry Naddeo entered the "Inn of the Good Shepherd" and offered to start a choir, she was improvising. When new residents moved in and when some responded to Naddeo's offer to join her choir, they were improvising too on a theme they may never have before practiced. The inn itself had a long history. It arose and was fitted within a religious, ideological, and institutional world that was even older. The music they all sang had another long history. Still, they made something that we present as essentially successful: A good time was had by all. What that good time produced, individually, we do not know. We know, however, that the good time did not prove consequential. The good time did not change anything in the identification of the young adults by those around them. It is as if they had done nothing, and they themselves helped in this reconstruction. Good times in a group does not demonstrate "talent" in any of the participants and thus cannot be used for individual advancement. Let us now see how this works.

Religion, Therapy, a Lutheran Italian Choir Director, and Some Street Kids

The issue at the Inn of the Good Shepherd, a pseudonym for a charitable institution, is not education but "saving street kids." The inn was started a few decades ago by a person who dedicated his life to taking runaway children who had drifted into the seamiest areas of New York City and bringing them back to an institutional version of normal life. In his various writings about the "kids" (his word) who came to him, the founder insisted on their loneliness, on their inability to trust and form proper human relationships. The imagery was one of fallen angels, though not because of any moral fault of their own. The causes were in the parents or society, and salvation was always possible through the right word or silence said or performed at the right time. Given the allures of the streets outside the inn's building, talking or listening might not always work. But the possibility of redemption remained—one kid at a time.

In the everyday life of the inn, the religious vocabulary the founder used in fundraising newsletters was in fact downplayed. The dominant language was therapeutic. The kids did not fall from grace, but they had developed low self-esteem. They were not in need of salvation, but they were in need of therapeutic interventions that would make them feel good about themselves and thereby allow them to enter the unconflicted middle class. The religious and therapeutic languages were in fact quite consistent in their underlying ideologies of what it means to be human: Human beings are fundamentally good (balanced); through various experiences they may develop personality problems that may in turn be reinforced if they remain in the same environment that originally produced the problem; through a change in the environment and specific help they can build on their fundamental goodness and free themselves from these problems. This ideology, as many have noted, is deeply individualistic in the American mode. The ideology allows for a commonsensical expression of a view of the world where many people end up confused. It allows and, in its liberal variation, even encourages an understanding that emphasizes the environment or social context as the cause of confusion. But the unit of concern, and the unit of solution, remains the individual. Society (family, the streets, etc.) enter only as powers that put pressure on a well-bounded object, the person. Improvement is best achieved through measures to limit social pressures (by, it is hoped, transforming them). Working for this kind of change is good but may not help those currently suffering. One may thus help most immediately by taking the individual person away from the place where the negative pressures are strongest and/or by helping the person to build stronger defenses.

We are not directly challenging the ideological formulations underlying this individualism. When one has been caught within the symbolic landscape constructed over 2,500 years as the people of Europe confronted their neighbors and each other, one cannot fail to work with it and through it. No one can escape such an ideology even after one has come to see the limitations imposed by the American pronoun 'I,' along with its semiotic connotations. The Chinese 我 is not available except as proof that the American pronoun is indeed a cultural construction. American individualism feeds our assumptions, but it remains our argument that, like all ideologies, it hides as much as it reveals, particularly when used commonsensically to deal with pressing problems that excite one's sympathies. What else can one do with a sixteen-year-old prostitute but try to get her, as a unique person, away from the street corner where she has been placed by a pimp? We do not want to blame the inn for trying to do something. Our task, as in the case of the teachers and administrators of West Side High School, Mrs. Kinney, or Adam's entourage, is not evaluative in the traditional sense. Our task is to give examples of things that the kids can do that nonetheless disappear in the normal telling of their lives. In the long run, we hope that our analyses lead to a rethinking of the design of helping or teaching activities. If persons are multiple, if they are best thought of not in terms of an "identity" but in terms of a radical presence resisting identifications and continually making new ones, then perhaps policy should be less designed with the goal of "changing" the person than with the goal of opening new possibilities.

At this point, we want only to highlight how much people can do together with and in spite of various identifications that none of them can escape but that are not fully determinative either. We talked, for example, of street kids, pimps, and prostitutes. We reported the accepted diagnosis that the inn's psychologists used: The kids had "low self-esteem"—it took them to the streets and then prevented them from acting in trusting concert with others around them. The "kids" can also be described as being in their late teens, as African American and Hispanic men and women, as small-scale hustlers who used the inn for what it could offer while generally maintaining ties with their networks on the street. They came together with a forty-something Italian Lutheran woman who had never worked with such a population. Merry Naddeo was on a leave of absence from her position as a music teacher in a working-class suburban middle school. She had a lot of experience directing choirs and had also worked as an organist and music director in various churches. The heterogeneous group she assembled made music for several months. This accomplishment, however, did not seem to count for much, as the kids themselves built upon the individualism that separated them from each other and thus were replaced in positions where their failure could be displayed for the whole world to enforce.

Coming Together

When Merry Naddeo first arrived at the inn, there had never been a choir there. While she was there, a choir met once a week. After she left, there "had been one," though perhaps only as long as the memory of it remained. Part of the story to be told centers on the construction of the choir and the many people who participated in giving it a place in their lives. Another part of the story centers on the construction, every week for several months, of a rehearsal. At the beginning of the day, there had not been a rehearsal. At the end, the rehearsal was a fact in the history of one to two dozen persons. The rehearsal itself was made of many smaller parts. Each part had to be constructed separately, sequentially, and contingently to fit each within the broader whole without calling attention to itself. For a rehearsal to have been built, songs had to be chosen from a repertoire; the order for the singing had to be decided; the singing of each song had to begin, proceed, and end; the transitions between the songs had themselves to be constructed, and such transitions were themselves complex interactional events requiring cooperation by all involved. Each step in these sequences of sequences was sensitive to what came before and would come after and to the whole sets of scenes within which it was placed. Out of these stones, a wall was made in the history of the participants, a cultural fact with particular properties: A song ended and another song started, a rehearsal was accomplished, and the choir became a topic of conversation in the management of the inn, in a dissertation, and now in this chapter.

We focus on a particular rehearsal someplace toward the end of the series of rehearsals that constituted the choir at the inn. The choir had already established itself. It was a fact both for the administration and the residents (as the "kids" were called after they had moved from the streets to the inn).[1] We focus particularly on a moment within the rehearsal after it had established itself. Beginnings had been completed ten minutes earlier, three songs had been rehearsed, another song had been started. Naddeo was at the piano, some singers were standing in a C formation around the piano, a small audience was seated, and the camera neatly framed the scene. Then something happened. Before we look at what happened, we must outline the complexity of the activities that led to it.

Cultural facts, like the choir and its rehearsal, arise out of and require a change in the everyday life of the people touched by these facts. The set of the people touched by the choir thus constituted it. These people included not only Merry Naddeo and the singers but the administrators who had given permission, those who had been assigned the task of setting things up for her, the man behind the video camera taping the scene for research purposes, and indeed Hervé Varenne as the sponsor of Naddeo's dissertation. All of them, in one way or another, made a space in their lives for the choir. This involved a rearrangement of other aspects of their lives. The rearrangement can be thought in terms of a resequencing of all other activities as the interactional requirements of the choir became evident. Doing choir, like doing homework, is a set of differentiated activities sequenced in any person's life with other activities. Obviously, the choir was something one did while it was "on." Less obvious but perhaps more important, it was something the persons involved did when it appeared to be "off" (for example, earlier in the day when one had to plan to be at the right place at the right time for the rehearsal). Conversely, when the choir was "on" other activities may still have had to be performed concurrently. Merry Naddeo, for example, was indeed doing "dissertation" as well as doing "choir." Some administrators were doing "helping street kids," others were doing "their job," others (or the same ones) were doing "internal institutional politics." Some singers were doing "courting" and others were doing "trying to make it in the music business." Everyone was doing "getting through the day."

For everyone, then, the choir required specific kinds of activities. The basic one was presence in a designated room organized for the choir to assemble. Designating and organizing the room required activities by Naddeo and the inn's administration. Being there, singing, and directing required activities by Naddeo and the singers. For anyone of these participants the requirements were absolute. Either people performed the prescribed activities or they were not members of the choir or rehearsal. It is in this sense that the choir was a fact of social import. All potential members were accountable to the choir in their particular position. For some (the administrators, for example), the accountable activities consisted of such acts as giving permission, making the existence of the choir known to the residents, perhaps encouraging them to join, booking the room, and making sure that a tuned piano was available. For each singer, the accountable activities consisted mostly of arranging for one's presence (which must have meant arranging for one's absence from somewhere else) and then arranging oneself to do the actual singing. This actual singing, as we already suggested, was a complex task with a set of subrequirements. Singing involved not only singing but doing the social beginnings and endings of songs, doing the various transitions from one song to the next, and so on.

These activities were defined by the choir itself. They were performed by individuals, but we do not have to assume the participants had any clear idea or articulated understanding of the connections made by their activities. There is every evidence that to the extent that they had any understanding of what they were doing, this understanding—as it might have been elicited by questions such as What did you do last night? Why did you do it? and so on— was quite idiosyncratic. Through informal conversations, Naddeo found that the participants pursued a multitude of agendas: Some came to the choir because they were courting a member, some hoped that the choir would be a first step toward a professional music career, some hoped that the choir would help the kids complete their return to a normal career toward adulthood, and some thought it was a requirement of their job. One did it, among other reasons, because it was part of data collection for her dissertation. That person, Naddeo, had a lot of musical training. She was a professional musician, music teacher, and church choir director. Others had no training at all and altogether didn't care (or didn't have to care). Some of the singers had sung some of the songs in earlier church services but not in the musical style adopted by Naddeo. Others had never sung.

There are severe limitations to understanding the choir as a group of individuals with motivations and understandings (Schutz 1951). Indeed, it would be inappropriate to think of the choir as the product of its members. There was no membership list, and there was quite a turnover in the people who sang. It is more helpful to understand the choir as existing before and apart from any one of the persons who, at times, were captured by it, and only to this limited extent can they be said to have thereby become members. The choir carried each individual along. If none of the participants had shown up, then of course the choir would not have come to life. But when it had, anyone who came into its orbit had to handle its interactional requirements. A person could refuse participation (as most of the residents who were invited did). Another could accept and then resist (as none of the singers did—the only case of resistance came from one of the administrators), or one could accept and be carried along to perform whatever was being done. One could even actively pursue an alternate agenda—as long as it was done in such a way as not to disrupt the flow of the choir. The choir was condition and resource for the participants. It was not something that they constructed in the shape that it actually had. Neither was it something that determined them. Nor was it directly dependent on the constitution (knowledge, sense, *habitus*) of those who came. It was a cultural fact for all those it touched.

The Rehearsal

On the day we are concerned with, the choir was an established fact for all participants. Naddeo and some residents only had to organize their personal lives to be together in the same room at the same time. Enough of them did for the rehearsal to be actually constructed. The residents who did show up were not exactly the same ones who had always come. Given the institutional setting of the choir, there was no way to make attendance an accountable event as absence may be in a school. One cannot be absent from a group that has no membership list. One can only be present. About twelve residents showed up regularly. Each rehearsal also included two or three first-timers who had to be introduced to the evolving history of the choir. This was the case on the day in question. Besides Naddeo and the singers, the rehearsal also included two administrative visitors from the inn. They were on an inspection and evaluation mission. It also included the cameraman and the toddler-aged child of one of the singers. At the boundary of the rehearsal, there was also another small group of people. They were setting things up for a talent show at the other end of the auditorium. They were certainly not part of the rehearsal, but they had to deal with it just as it had to deal with them—particularly since some of the singers were being recruited to set up the talent show, which also involved making music.

The tension between the groups illustrates that the rehearsal required continual and sometimes onerous work from those it had captured. The catching itself was not settled at the beginning. There were latecomers. Some residents drifted in and out of the singing. At some points, only a few could be seen around the piano. At other times, the gathering looked like a crowd. Something particular that we call the rehearsal did, however, arise, and it never broke down. It proceeded apace through the work that everyone in the room, those who sang and those who didn't and those who came and those who went away, performed collectively. The rehearsal remained something that all took into account, whatever it was that they were in fact proceeding to do, whether coming or going, whether taking care of her baby or of his camera. The sequencing of these multiple activities was accomplished in such a way that even when they threatened to interrupt the rehearsal (as the setting up of the talent show did), they were handled in such a manner that they did not in fact become interruptions.[2]

The rehearsal essentially consisted in an alternation between singing and two main types of transition between and within songs. Naddeo would give brief directions about the next song and the way the singers should do their parts. She would give a signal (musical and gestural), and the singing would start. After a while, the singing stopped, a new transition was performed, and singing started again. In Figure 3.1 one can see the contrast between the "transition" and "singing" positionings.[3] In the former, members were still organized around the piano, but their attention was allowed to wander over the room without their being called to account for "inattention." In the latter, all attention was focused on the multiple tasks involved in singing. As one can see by looking at Figure 3.2 the transitions were always brief events (less than a minute) by comparison to the singing (two to four minutes). Over the first thirteen and a half minutes, four songs were performed (two of these were repeated once). The choir sang for about twelve of these minutes. The first three songs were sung straight through with brief time-outs to explain details to newcomers.[4] The last was still in the process of being learned, so its performance replicated the organization of the whole rehearsal with singing segments interspaced with explanatory or transitional moments as Naddeo led the rehearsal through one section and then another.

For those who remained main participants during the whole half-hour, the main work consisted of arranging their bodies and activities in terms of the task at hand. This required continual monitoring of the other participants, and it was particularly striking during transition times. At such times, the interactional thread provided by the musical score itself was absent. The participants were back to improvising on "the rehearsal" theme, requiring that the group open up to a multitude of diverse activities (involving, minimally, shuffling sheet music and, maximally, dealing with behavior from outside that was put on hold during the singing, e.g., taking care of one's child). The rehearsal theme also required that the group eventually come back together in such a way that all could start singing, accompanying, and directing at the same time.

FIGURE 3.1
Major Positionings

Transition

attention of members is directed in various directions; some move into, others away from the group; the baby cries out

(image taken from transition #2)

Singing

all members are now focused on their part within the singing; nonmembers have receded into an audience position

(image taken from sec. 560)

The group did this consistently and concertedly with no particular prompting. Although the activities were differentiated enough that Naddeo had to perform a directorial gesture to complete the new beginning, it is clear from the video record that by the time she performed it, the singers had already organized themselves into the recipient posture. There was no need for calls to "get ready to start."

Most of the people caught by the choir were not main participants during the half-hour. Many came and went. Their activity may thus be even more interesting, since common sense would suggest that they were the persons most likely to disrupt the flow of the rehearsal. In fact, their comings and goings were so sequenced that they didn't. Singers sometimes, just moved away. Others simply came to the piano, glanced at the sheet music held by a neighbor, and then proceeded to sing. Their

FIGURE 3.2
First Half of Group Rehearsal

sec.	Major Positions	Song Performed	Some Minor Positions & Intrusions
20	SINGING	"My Lord What a Morning"	
40	SEGMENT		[[minor transition]]
60	#1	"Swing Low, Sweet Chariot"	
80			[[minor transition]]
100	(4 mn 26 sec.)	Partner Song	
120			[[minor transition]]
140			
160			
180			
200			
220			
240			
260			
280	TRANSITION #1		
300	(42 sec.)		
320	SINGING	"My Lord What a Morning"	
340	SEGMENT		
360	#2	"Swing Low, Sweet Chariot"	
380			
400	(2 mn 32 sec.)		
420			
440			
480	TRANSITION 2		
500	(62 sec.)		
520			
540	SINGING	"The Clouds"	
560	SEGMENT		
580	#3		
600			
620	(6 mn 24 sec.)		<where? here!>
640			<where? here!>
660			<here! O.K.!>
680			<here! O.K.>
700			[[minor transition]]
720			
740			
760			
780			
800			
820			
840			
860			

(Continued)

FIGURE 3.2
(Continued)

sec.	Major Positions	Song Performed	Some Minor Positions & Intrusions
880	TRANSITION 3		
900	(1 mn 2 sec.)		
920			
940	SINGING	"Rocking Jerusalem"	
960	SEGMENT		
980	#4		
1000			
1020	(2 mn 31 sec.)		
1040			
1060			
1080			

presence or absence did not transform the choir. They were the ones who changed as they paid attention to the signals given by the rehearsal for participation. For a while, they put their other activities on hold as they sequenced the rehearsal in their own flow. There is evidence that this flow itself was not disrupted. We saw people waving to others off camera, we saw people exchanging jokes, and we saw them coming back to the rehearsal at the moment they were needed.

The activities of two other people are also interesting for what they suggest about the power of the rehearsal as fact. As mentioned, the cameraman himself was a participant in the making of the record. His activity was mostly remarkable in various shifts in focus and framing. Significantly, all these shifts took place during transitions. During the singing, the focus remained stable and was organized to segregate the choir from the rest of the room. In this way the separation of the rehearsal as a distinct activity was reconstructed, as it was by the singers themselves. Another borderline participant was the toddler. He was mostly off-camera and only noticeable through his crying or through the activities of his mother as she took care of him. But the crying, much like the baby's involvement in the Farrell's homework, took place only at transition times, thereby reconstructing again the rehearsal and its interactional boundaries. The baby's activity never transformed into an interruption of the choir.

Naddeo's own movements in and out of the rehearsal are also quite interesting. She did not get up from the piano bench for the whole period. She did not stop playing for more than a few seconds (she continued playing variations of the song just finished in a "background music" style during many of the transitions mentioned previously). We could see her continually monitoring both the activities of the singers and the activities of the nonsingers. In general, Naddeo just proceeded as if nothing but the rehearsal was happening. At other times, she acknowledged the arrival of a newcomer through a brief comment while continuing to accompany the other singers. At all times, these asides were performed in ways that minimized the attention of those not directly involved, and she would soon turn back toward the other singers and continue to direct them. In fact, these asides may have been an aspect of the directing activity itself. Given that the choir was sometimes divided into sections that sang different parts, each of which had to be monitored, it was in the nature of the rehearsal that the attention of the director should move from section to section and from one soloist to the next.

The same could be said of all the times when she had to deal with the activities of the other people in the room, particularly those who were setting up for the talent show and threatening to drown the rehearsal in their own noise-making. We could see her turning away, we could see the singers move their gaze in concert with hers, and we could see them all coming back together, all the while proceeding with the singing.

And Then, Something Happened

Strictly speaking, nothing else happened than the rehearsal itself in the frame we have chosen. Nothing that was directly related to the rehearsal disrupted it, and nothing interrupted it. It ended in an appointed way, though not quite on the appointed time for reasons discussed later, reasons that had nothing to do with the choir per se. Nothing in the choir was marked as being in any way extraordinary.[5] We do want to focus on one of the many events that, through their happening, ensured that nothing in fact happened.[6]

Until now, we have treated the singing itself as somehow less problematic than the transition times and the sequencing of the rehearsal with all the other events that required activity by the participants. The singing itself was not so simple a task. Musically, this was indeed a choir, not just a group of people singing. The singers were organized in sections, each of which sang slightly different parts of the same song. To do this, all singers had to pay attention not only to the words but to the director and to each other. Their "singing" was an alternation of times of silence and times of actual singing. The issue of sequencing that we encountered at broader levels is found here also. Newcomers had the task not only of orienting their other activities and then their bodies to the singing; they also had to find their particular place around the piano and within the singing. It is clear, when looking at the record, that many did not quite know how to do the detail of these things: Where does a soprano stand in relation to a tenor? Where does one enter in a multivoiced piece? or even simply, Where am I on the sheet music?

Some of the newcomers did not have a clue, but there were clues all around them. They picked them up, sometimes with the help of others, and everything proceeded apace. Let us now focus on four brief moments when a clue was searched for, presented, found, and used, first by the person to whom it was presented and then by the group as it became an occasion for a correction routine.

At the initial moment (at about second 560—see Figure 3.1, bottom image), the group was in its full singing mode. It remained in this mode throughout the event (see Figure 3.3 for detail). The camera stayed stable around a scene at the center of

74

FIGURE 3.3
Detail of Singing Segment #3

sec.	"The Clouds"	Naddeo	Angie	Nan
540		PLAYING,	[SINGING	[singing ...
2		SINGING &	THROUGHOUT	
5		SCANNING#		
7		THROUGHOUT		
550		←		
2				
5				
7	[turn to p.4]	↑		[turns page]
560				
2		←		
5				...]
7		↗		[searching
570				?
2				?
5		←↲		?
7				?
580				?
2	[turn to p.5]	↑		?
5				?
7		↖		?
590				?
2		↗		<---¿*where are we?
5				
7				<---¿*where are we?
600			¡*here we are!	*thank you
2				?
5	[turn to p.6]			?
7		↗		?
610				?
2				?
5		←↲		<---¿*where are we?
7		↖	¡*here we are!	...
620				*thank you
2				?
5		↗		?
7				?
630	[turn to p.7]	↪		?
2		←↲		?
5				?
7			--->¡*this is where we are	*thank you
640		↖		?
2				?
5				?
7				?

(Continued)

FIGURE 3.3
(Continued)

sec.	"The Clouds"	Naddeo	Angie	Nan
650	[turn to p.8]	↗		?
2				?
5				?
7				?
660		←↲	--->¡*this is where we are	*thank you
2		↖		
5			[waves to someone	
7			behind the camera]	
670		←↲		
2	[end song]	↖	ENDS SINGING]	
5				
7		↗		
680				

#Arrows suggest Naddeo's movements during the song:

←↲ —forward toward the piano:

↑ or ↗ —up or up and to the right

↪ —behind her:

*interpretation of the speech act jointly performed by Angie and Nan

which was the upright piano with Naddeo playing and directing. She was surrounded by seven and eventually eight men and women (the "residents") arranged in a double C formation around the piano. Four women formed an inner C. The men stood at the periphery. Directly facing the camera at the farther end of the piano, two women, Angie and Nan, were organized for singing. They stood in a parallel position, holding a six-page stapled sheaf of music that contained the score for all the voices and accompaniment in this arrangement of "The Clouds." They were finishing the opening statement, or theme, of the song, and all the singers had turned the first page of the music.

To understand the complexity of what happened next between Angie and Nan, we must back up briefly to give more details about them and the song. Angie was one of the singers who had been most faithful to the choir. She had rehearsed the song several times. Nan was a newcomer. She had never before performed with this or any other choir. She appeared not to have had experience with reading complex musical scores. In the transition before the singing, a new set of sheet music had been distributed with no explanation. Everyone had taken a copy, and the group had arranged itself for singing. "The Clouds" was part of the routine and so was the particular arrangement performed. Upon completion of the initial statement by the entire group, the piece went into a canonic statement using the same theme with different lyrics. It was at this point that the singers split the two parts between the males and females, each group having to follow separate lines (staves) of music. The separate staves made it necessary for the singers to skip over the music of the other part instead of following straight through, as they could in the initial unison statement. The second section created its own harmony simply by restating the initial theme in canon form.

The result of this complexity was that one could not simply use commonsense musical knowledge to stay with the choir, particularly if one had never before sung the piece. The whole song was spread over six pages. Singing thus involved turning pages and staying on one's line until the song's completion. The situation was somewhat analogous to Adam's in Chapter 1 when he was confronted with a recipe that listed separately the ingredients and the instructions about the order in which to mix them. Nan, like Adam, had to look around for clues.

Another solution was to ignore the music, sing the lyrics from memory, and follow Naddeo's direction as she indicated to each voice when to join in. After following the music on the first page and having turned to page 2, Angie did just this. She stopped reading and looked out toward Naddeo (and sometimes beyond). At about the same time, Nan stopped singing. We saw her hesitate, start again, stop, look intently at the music, and, eventually, lean over Angie's shoulder. As she did this, Angie organized her body in a complementary relationship to Nan's. Without breaking her singing, she turned to page 3 and pointed to a place there. Nan turned her own music to page 3 as Angie went back to her initial position. Figure 3.4 shows three frames from this sequence.

Ten seconds later, the scene repeated itself (Figure 3.5). Nan had not been able to stay with the singing. Again she leaned toward Angie, and both of them performed a complementary "where are we?–here we are!" scene. At the end, both Angie and Nan were singing and following the music. The next page turning was done in unison. At this point, a variation on the scene was performed as Angie leaned toward Nan and pointed at a location on Nan's music (Figure 3.6). Angie had stopped singing, appeared to give oral directions, and then returned to singing. Nan nodded her head affirmatively, but she did not start singing. At the next page-turning moment, Angie leaned again toward Nan, and both performed again what we might identify as "this is where we are–I understand" scene. For the fourth time in less than a minute, they moved in and out of a complementary relationship (Figure 3.7). In the meantime, the singing, which had never deviated from course, came to the conclusion of the song. Everyone, including Angie and Nan, held on the finishing long harmony; Naddeo played the final chord and proceeded with her next task.

Laid down in this linear fashion, the multiple pairings between Angie and Nan look more momentous than they appeared on first viewing. The overwhelming reality of the rehearsal and its singing may even have prevented one from noticing that something else was happening, but the pairings did happen, just as the singing did. The relevance of the pairings is what is at issue: their "meaning," if one takes this term in the structuralist sense, and their consequentiality within the rehearsal, if any. A conventional telling of the scene might proceed in the following fashion: Nan

FIGURE 3.4
Asking for Information (first occurrence)

Nan has been searching through her papers for 25 seconds. She suddenly leans towards Angie and looks at her paper. Angie moves herself to allow Nan to complete her movement.

(image taken at the peak of Nan's movement towards Angie)

Angie turns towards Nan, moves back a page on her handout, and points on it at the place where Nan should be reading. Angie does not stop singing.

(image taken 2 seconds after earlier one)

Nan looks at her paper, along with Angie and appears to begin singing

(image taken 2 seconds after earlier one)

FIGURE 3.5
Asking for Information (second occurrence)

Nan has continued searching through her papers. She appears to have missed the turn to page 6. She turns her head to look at Angie's papers

(image taken near the onset of Nan's movement towards Angie)

Angie turns her upper body towards Nan. She does not stop singing.

(image taken 2 seconds after earlier one)

Angie turns pages in Nan's packet until she finds the place where Nan should be.

(image taken 2 seconds after earlier one)

FIGURE 3.6
Giving Information (first occurrence)

Nan has continued searching through her papers. After the next turn-paging moment, and half-way down the page, Angie turns herself towards Nan who is staring at her page.

(image taken near the end of Angie's initial movement towards Nan)

Angie points to the place on her paper where Nan should be.

(image taken 2 seconds after earlier one)

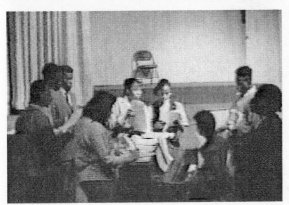

Angie, who has not stopped singing, moves away from Nan and makes eye contact with Merry Naddeo. Nan continues her search

(image taken 2 seconds after earlier one)

80

FIGURE 3.7
Giving Information (second occurrence)

Nan has continued searching through her papers. At the next turn-paging moment, and half-way down the page, Angie turns herself towards Nan who shuffled through her papers.

(image taken Nan comes toward Angie)

Angie points to the place on her paper where Nan should be. Angie looks on.

(image taken 2 seconds after earlier one)

Nan shuffles her papers to the correct place.

(image taken 2 seconds after earlier one)

loses her place, Nan may not know how to read music, Angie does, Angie helps, Nan appears to learn. As scripted, this little scene could be expanded into a story of personal trouble that becomes a story of small-group trouble (as Angie becomes involved in Nan's problem) that does not become a story of larger-group trouble (as the director and the rest of the singers ignore the problem) and develops into a story of getting out of trouble. Many movies have been written on the basis of such a script but treat this trouble in a particular way. It is the particularity that, here again, we want to emphasize.

Initially the trouble was dealt with as an information problem: Where are we? It was then dealt with as a brief learning problem: This is where we are; are you at the same place? Eventually, it became the occasion for a full-blown learning session as it was reintegrated into the rehearsal: As Naddeo lifted her hands from playing the last chord, she moved in one unbroken swing toward Nan and another resident who stood by her and had had Nan's problems also (but had not sought or received any help). The three of them organized themselves in complementary positions for a more complex version of what Angie had last done with Nan. Naddeo pointed on the various pages where Nan should be ("top line . . . , top line . . . , top line"). Nan followed and nodded her head. Meanwhile, the rest of the group had opened into the "transition" positioning. The members chatted, addressed people outside of their group, and so on. They did not drift away but stayed around the piano. Less than thirty seconds later, everyone started again from the beginning of "The Clouds," and the singing part of the rehearsal proceeded.

By sequencing her dealing with Nan's trouble within a transition, Naddeo placed them back within the rehearsal structure, a structure that not only allowed for the correction of errors but required that certain types of errors be discovered and handled. If Naddeo had not corrected Nan, she would have corrected somebody else.[7] By contrast, in a formal performance, the teaching routines would have been suppressed and errors, masked. Once again, the interactional and social consequences of "trouble" revealed themselves to be relative to their interactional sequencing.[8] Ignorance does not necessarily "mean" problem. During the singing, the trouble was something that happened in such a way as not to be noticed as happening. Something happened in one social scene (the one involving Angie, Nan, and perhaps Naddeo) that did not become an event in the social scene that encompassed Angie and Nan (the rehearsal, as a scene within the choir, as a scene within the inn, as a scene within New York City, etc.). It disappeared as, at most, a kind of background noise within the rehearsal. During the transition it was noticed as an occasion for teaching-in-a-rehearsal. In neither case was what looked like trouble (and may have been so for Nan) handled as trouble.

Pulling Apart

Eventually, the rehearsal ended and the choir was disbanded. By all accounts, while the choir lasted, a "great time was had by all" who participated. Residents continued to come and to bring friends until the last. The administration of the inn itself came to see the choir as a good thing and tried to get Naddeo to continue. Our own fascination with the choir has to do with the evidence it offers for the possibility of scenes where people like the "kids" of Forty-second Street reveal themselves as experienced and active participants in the construction and reconstruction of the social world around them.[9] The choir, as an event in the history of the inn, was a success.

It was also an inconsequential success, and our task at this point is to trace various properties of the broader cultural structures within which the choir was sequenced that made it impossible for the success to be noticed as transforming the life of the people in it. They remained in the position of "kids," "residents with psychological problems." There is no way, of course, that we can trace all these properties. They are related, although different, from those we trace in the other chapters. At this point, we want only to follow briefly the participants as they engaged in related activities.

The end of the choir was precipitated by the end of Naddeo's sabbatical from her regular job as music teacher in a New Jersey middle school. Our discussion of sequencing and the changes that occur in the life of participants when a cultural fact like the choir catches them was intended to highlight the practical and temporal aspect of such constructions. Although we can say of cultural facts that they embody ideological structures, we must also realize that they are not purely ideational. They take time and energy (physical, emotional, and economic). Eventually, Naddeo had to resequence her own life with the institution that allowed her to survive economically in the United States.

Biographical details are so commonsensical that they are easy to ignore when writing about the development of programs such as Naddeo's (or Rizzo-Tolk's, discussed in the next chapter). The choir was a charitable and research activity in Naddeo's life. It was a special event that could not have become the organizing center of her life without major changes in other institutions. Minimally, the inn would have had to find ways to fund her participation. The funding activity itself has special requirements, one of them in this case being a justification of the usefulness of the choir in helping the kids. This usefulness could have been legitimately shown only through an experimental design with controls that would establish that the choir experience had, for example, significantly increased each resident's (or at least some of the residents') self-esteem. The residents' participation and pleasure would not have been evidence enough of success; nor would they evidence that, whatever these kids were suffering from, it was not "low self-esteem," "alienation," or any other euphemism as currently understood in the psychological literature.

The choir as organized by Naddeo could thus not have been justified in the same manner as the regular therapeutic programs on which the inn depended for the demonstration of its own success. In the imagination of institutions such as schools and welfare agencies, choirs do, however, have another interesting feature that brings us back to the overall constraints that the most general level of American ideology places on people in the United States: Choirs are good, good choirs are better, and the institution that can display itself through a good choir has a new resource in its competition with other institutions for recognition and funding. Choirs are both frills and decorations. They may thus be judged under certain circumstances on different criteria.

In her New Jersey school, Naddeo discovered that she was all the more popular with her principal to the extent that he heard good things about the choir. In the inn too, the support that the administration gave to the choir grew to the extent that it started to hear good things said about the choir. There is no clear evidence for the exact nature of the "good things." Still, the school, and to a certain extent the inn, responded in the same manner: They identified Naddeo as someone with "talent" in organizing and directing choirs, and they suggested to her that she make of her choir a "good" choir by recruiting and focusing on students or kids with "talent" themselves. And so the school required that she have auditions to determine this talent—something that she resisted in various ways but not quite successfully. Interactionally, auditions focus attention on the individual person, this or that person in particular, and by definition produce a number of "failures" as various kids are determined to (not) have talent. An audition that would result in all people heard being accepted would be a sham.

The choir never became so institutionalized at the inn that Naddeo was under administrative pressure to have auditions and so to "raise" the quality of the choir. The pressure came from the residents themselves.

The Performance of Talent

In our discussion of the rehearsal, we mentioned briefly the setting up of a "talent show" in another corner of the auditorium. This talent show competed with the rehearsal in several ways. Most noticeable was the competitive playing of other music. Another issue centered around the fact that some of the singers were being recruited to perform in the talent show. Those who did move between the two groups did it in such a way as not to disrupt the rehearsal. Still there was pressure, and Naddeo brought the rehearsal to an end sooner than she might otherwise have done. More important on a broader scale is what happened before this rehearsal and a few others: Several residents requested times for solo performances, and they requested that they be taped. Others requested private music lessons. Some asked for contacts in the music business in the hope of getting auditions , for example, to perform at the Harlem Apollo's amateur night or to secure a recording contract. Naddeo could not accede to the latter type of requests. Her contacts were in the classical music networks, and the residents were more interested in rap and other popular genres. She tried to accommodate the other requests, and she did tape several solos and duos. She bought special music. She offered to teach one of the women how to play the piano.

None of these efforts amounted to much. As a professional musician, Naddeo could differentiate between "good" and "bad" voices on several evaluative scales. She was skeptical that any of the individual voices she was presented would be heard as "good" at the professional classical level that she knew best, though she hoped that

some would be found "good" in the musical tradition the singers hoped to join. Behind this was the problem that a request for an audition and a determination of the
quality of one's voice was also a request for something that could be quite painful for
the recipient. Even the request for piano lessons became a dilemma for Naddeo. She
knew that the girl who asked did not have a stable residential life, and there was little
likelihood that she could spend much time practicing. Naddeo feared that she would
become discouraged and experience herself again as a "kid who failed."

Talent, by the American definition that the residents of the inn reconstructed, is
an individual property dependent only on individual resources. This was strikingly
displayed in the recording of the solos, one of which took place just before the rehearsal examined. A solo—by name and in performance—is something that ONE
person does. But words, like performances, are embedded in cultural history, and
they gain their meaning through the activities of those who arrange them. The request for a taped solo was a social scene between the requester and Naddeo. The organization of the taping required many more participants arranging themselves in
particular ways. Naddeo became the accompanist, arranging her playing to fit the
singer's voice. The cameraman had the task of focusing on the singer and hiding
himself and any other signs that this was not in fact a solo performance. Everyone in
the room was transformed into an audience. All this flowed without a hitch to its
scripted conclusion; the crowd actively cooperated and disappeared, and the soloist
revealed herself for evaluation as someone who might (not) become an individual
success.

In all these ways, a solo designed to display talent reveals itself as another version
of a child's homework, as a display of that child's intellectual aptitude. A crowd has
to arrange itself so as not to be seen, and then some members of this crowd, particularly people who were not physically present at the time of the performance, make
an overwhelming consequential interpretation that is also an evaluation when it is
made in psychological or educational contexts: At the time they might say this person is a person with low self-esteem, no talent, and little aptitude for advanced education, in consequence of which she should receive psychological help in a specialized institution. In this evaluation, all the work that the crowd performed and all the
work that she may perform at other times is radically discounted.

NOTES

This chapter is based on Merry Naddeo's work (1991, 1993).

1. In the fund-raising literature distributed by the inn, the "kids" were typically fourteen-
to sixteen-year-old runaways. The "residents" were typically three years older. The age limit for
residence was twenty-one.

2. The very fact that some came, went, and conducted other business in parallel to the
choir means that we were able to document on tape how this sequencing can be accomplished.

3. See Appendix A for details about the conventions used to make the figures used in this chapter. For an introduction of the concept of "positioning" in interactional analysis and a further discussion, see Chapter 8.

4. These were the "minor transitions" mentioned in Figure 3.2. They did not involve a major shift in the gestural stance of the members who relaxed and possibly started scanning the room but who did not actually move out of the major "singing" positioning.

5. See Robin Miller's work (1993) on the catastrophic disruption of concerted activities.

6. The classical text on "nothing happening" is Sacks (1984). See Varenne (1992: 95–96) for a further discussion.

7. However "good" a choir, such errors will always be made if only because the choir will always be pushed beyond its limits by being asked to perform more and more complex pieces. Within this structure, the only trouble Nan's inexperience may have caused consisted in preventing Naddeo from correcting more complex errors in the choir's performance. This "trouble" was not consequential for the rehearsal. In fact, it maintained the choir at its broader place as a choir made up of inexperienced singers, a choir of amateurs, residents in a charitable institution.

8. We have been talking about sequencing rather than context in order to escape some of the problems discussed in Chapter 1. We are not talking about a container that actively shapes its contents. We are talking about the way single moves, smaller and larger scenes, and so on place themselves and are placed within larger scenes. Moves, scenes, settings, do not change meaning as they are placed within various other scenes. As a long tradition of work in communication and interactional analysis has shown (Bateson, G. 1972; Kendon 1990; McDermott, Gospodinoff, and Aron 1978; Schegloff 1984), single behavioral sequences (phonemes, morphemes, utterances, scenes, etc.) have no meaning except as constitutive of particular sequences at the next higher level.

9. That demonstration can be done by looking at the complexity of surviving in the street (Hannerz 1969; Liebow 1967; Valentine 1978). Our common sense refuses to see in such "asocial" activities as prostitution and retail drug selling the proof of a general kind of social competence applied in the particular settings available to the actor.

4 Joint Action on the Wild Side of Manhattan

Hervé Varenne and Rosemarie Rizzo-Tolk

Chapter 3 told the tale of an instance of under-interpretation. Something happened and disappeared. It had no social consequences either locally or in broader circles. Our first temptation was simply to stress that something good did happen and to chastise many for not recognizing it. But this is not enough. The recognition of the erasure must move us to figure out the practical processes through which such erasures are achieved. To do this, we now look at an incident in which a performance was overinterpreted as it was placed within a broader frame. The story could have been told to emphasize the points that we have already made. Again, we meet a person who, like Adam or Joe, is identified as a failure in spite of documentable skills in handling the world. Again we see a group at work, like the choir, making something specific and complex, something that worked and may even be said to have been truly educational in the grand tradition of Rousseau and Dewey. In addition, we will see the relative success of each individual within the group and the success of the whole group get erased through the active overinterpretation of a single communicational sign made ambiguous when taken from context by institutionalized interpretations. The scenario shows a group of students discussing a school project and, at a crucial point, laughing together. The laugh offers observers the handle with which they can identify the students as just what they have always been: students who have failed in the New York City Public Schools and who will probably keep on failing.

West Side High School: Center and Periphery

West Side High School is a noble experiment. It flourishes at the periphery of the huge bureaucracies that appear to be necessary correlates of efficient industrialism and the contemporary nation-state. At West Side, a few hundred students who have dropped out, been kicked out, and otherwise have found themselves estranged from the mainstream high schools of New York City can drop in and complete a regular high school program in two years. There, eighteen- to twenty-year-olds, some already fathers and mothers with their babies, can try to complete an interrupted schooling. There, African Americans and the children of recent immigrants from the Caribbean can, perhaps for the last time in their life, spend extended periods of time with each other and with representatives of the white middle classes with whom they are likely otherwise to have but minimal and extremely ritualized contact. There, two dozen older adults of mixed origins and creeds—European and African Americans, liberal Jews, Catholics lapsed and conservative, Muslims, Baptists, and agnostics of various stripes—people who were born and raised in the least-melted neighborhoods of New York City and in places like Michigan, make their lives in a place that is as exciting as it is difficult.

West Side High School *is* a difficult cultural dwelling in a run-down building that is Gothic in more than its turn-of-the-century architecture. It is not quite hell, since both students and teachers are told upon entrance never to abandon hope. There is always tomorrow, when new beginnings can be made, and help is always available to those who ask. In the local lore of the public schools, this is a "good" school when compared to other "typical" high schools. It is small and run by a dedicated principal who encourages teachers to think for themselves and take initiative. There is much interaction among the teachers, and most of them know most students by name and life history. There are no metal detectors at the entrance, and there have not been any serious fights in a long time. It is a place where human beings do flourish, a place where things get done. Success stories get told as a good number of students graduate and enter the more satisfying sectors of the working class, and teachers—as we document here—do find work by their students that they can display proudly.

The students are quite aware that all this is available and that in many ways this is, positively and negatively, "the end of the line." As one student put it, "If you don't make it here, you won't make it anywhere." Still, most of them are in the school because they have not "made it" in other high schools, sometimes for academic reasons and often because they have been caught doing something that goes beyond what is usually ignored: being continually truant, carrying guns or knives, getting into fights for which they have been arrested, dealing drugs, and so on. Above all, many of them are older; they are "kids" in a structural sense only. In all other senses, they are adults. They are probably more properly adults than their contemporaries who attend Columbia and Barnard a few blocks north. They come from the most difficult places in which to make one's life. They are not all poor, at least in the sense that some have access to large sums of cash, but they all know the street and what it takes to survive there.

Inevitably, they bring the street into the school, and for all that can be said positively about West Side High School, it is still a place that is constantly simmering from an unlikely mix of people being thrown together into a pot that may not be melting them into each other as much as it stays close to the boiling point. It is a place that continuously generates stories that tempt an observer to wax lyrically along romantic liberal lines or to thunder apocalyptically along realist conservative ones. It is also a place of routine practical accomplishments where people daily improvise a life in common with some of the worst circumstances modern urban society can mete out to the people it organizes. These people—students, teachers, administrators—often suffer. They are rarely "successful" in the sense that is usually meant when one says that a school is a success. Still, through the direct activities of these several hundred people, the school does reproduce itself. It recruits teachers, some of whom stay with the school for years. It attracts students and places them in settings that are common-sensically identifiable as "educational": classrooms, counseling sessions, "family groups" (as homerooms are called to emphasize the added moral responsibility teachers are expected to take for their students). The students graduate; a few move on to college, complete it, and become teachers, social workers, or even successful entrepreneurs. They do so at a rate comparable to that of the other "normal" high schools of the NYC public school system. It is quite possible that without this school and its program, most of those who attend would not have graduated. And all this has been going on with little change for more than twenty years.

How any of this is possible cannot be fathomed unless one abandons models of social action that center on the separate ability, knowledge, or even "culture" (in the usual ethnic-racial sense) of the participants. More useful would be various theories of resistance that emphasize the extent to which people who differ in culture, class, or gender background can still penetrate practically, if not analytically, the conditions set for them. At West Side, displays of resistance are common indeed. "Fuck you, you white bitch" is always available as a rejoinder to a teacher's attempt at discipline. But students rarely resist to the point of destroying the institution. Given everything else, this must be precisely at issue. The students refrain from ultimate, destructive resistance, and the teachers persist in trying to find new ways to save them from the ghettoization to which many would confine them. To understand how they achieve this balance we must look at what is *done* by the people in local scenes they construct *together*. This, in our sense of the word, is West Side's culture. It is the historical pattern to which all participants are accountable—whatever their position and type of understanding.

The Study: One Moment in American Time

A culture is best analyzed in the detail of the dramas it organizes. In this spirit, we report on a half-hour of classroom time in West Side High School. This half-hour was videotaped, and a five-minute segment was examined closely. The locally accountable task (what the participants would have said they were doing) was a discussion of a larger project conducted by the students and Rizzo-Tolk on being homeless in New York City. This task was accomplished effortlessly by a very diverse group, and to this minimal extent, it was a success.

Because of its anchoring in the pragmatics of everyday life, the study fits within a tradition of classroom analyses criticized for making much about little. This particular study is grounded by the several years Rizzo-Tolk spent as a teacher in West Side High School, the perception of her successes and of the limited value of such successes on a broader stage. A sweeping description of the school and its classroom—a description that would enrich the sketch we have been providing—would not tell us much more than we already know, ethnographically and theoretically, about the situated erasure of what appeared to be interactional achievements.

We do have general accounts of the kinds of classrooms found at West Side, particularly in the excellent work of Reba Page (1991). In many ways, the "normal" pattern of West Side classrooms is the pattern she identifies as "the caricature" of the best in liberal academic high school instruction. In this pattern, the attempt to have the students think for themselves in a self-directed manner with the teacher as moderator becomes a continual exchange of half-joking challenges, games, life-history details, and so on that justify the teachers' overall interpretation of the students as "your basic bottom." Page talks about this process as "chaos," whereas we see an overwhelming order. She does describe it as something that reproduces itself from day to day and from year to year. She wonders why the students' resistance remains within limits and does not threaten the organization of tracking in the schools she describes: The students do not challenge the wisdom of having a "lower track." They do not resist to the point of dropping out altogether or directly revolting against the school.

Reproduction in large groups and over long periods of time has been well documented. It is the stuff of general sociology. Much theoretical speculation has been built upon it by those who have not always understood that to demonstrate the structural functionality of an institutional organization is not necessarily to have said anything as to how actual human beings do reproduction in face-to-face interaction. This is the challenge we are picking up in a dual movement. On the one hand, we anchor teachers and students within New York City, its board of education, and the American definition of schooling. On the other hand, we pay close attention to the second-to-second and hand-to-hand construction of a moment in time to marvel once again at the sensitivity of students and teachers to the organization of their setting.

We do this in several steps. First, we highlight the rhetorical ways through which the classroom project is constructed as something controlled by the teacher in charge. Second, we highlight how students can deconstruct such projects by playing on the properties of the rhetorical pattern. Third, we focus on the exact process of such construction and deconstruction during the taped half-hour. In a fourth and final step, we show how such local performances get replaced within less local ones in the context of West Side High as an alternative school of the New York City board of (American) education.

Classroom Construction—A Teacher's Task

The rhetoric[1] of what we gloss in this book as "the School" does not easily allow for accounts of schooling that emphasize the joint activity of teachers and students. It allows for fragmented accounts "from the point of view" of each of the formal roles. Nothing seems more commonsensical, for example, than the following account:

> I was hired at West Side High School at the beginning of 1985. Approximately one month later, 20 newly enrolled students were about to enter the school. I convinced the principal and others who were present to assign the new students to me so I could try out the idea I had for a class, a course called Social Issues.
>
> Towards the end of the course and during the first discussion we had about homelessness, I asked the class what they knew about homeless people. One of the boys honestly and

solemnly confessed that he knew little except that he and his friends had "lit one on fire" several years before. The class roared with laughter. I was shocked by both the story he had told and the class's response. Further class discussions revealed strong and biased opinions about the homeless. They were considered common street people. Bums were useless, either lazy or crazy. Students discussed homeless people much in keeping with society's view of the homeless and less sympathetically than one might expect. For the most part students came from poor or disadvantaged homes, and it would be logical for them to believe that the poor would become poorer because of conditions set by the society which were beyond individual control. However, downward mobility was believed to be earned and, within each person's purview, by design and will, a result of active, individual choosing.

A part of me honestly believed that the students were used as an arm of conservative social thinking when they harmed the homeless. Encouraged to do violence by covert messages in the society, teenagers like the boy who set fire to a sleeping man are in a sense victims. I was fearful that without further discussions, they and the homeless would be further victimized. In an attempt to reduce violence, to protect the students and the homeless, and to evoke a more moral response regarding the homeless, I asked the students if they would be interested in participating in a documentary-making class exploring homelessness in New York City. Approximately twelve students registered.

The students in the documentary class were taught to use portable video equipment. Soon they began video taping street scenes, surveying everyday moments, capturing interesting settings related to homelessness. Film crews attended conferences and public hearings and held interviews with knowledgeable people on the subject of homelessness. The class talked with homeless people, homeless advocates, professional homeless representatives, and spent considerable time in a squatter settlement on the lower east side of Manhattan.

Students began to talk about feeling differently toward the homeless. In the middle of the documentary-making cycle, the students began telling unsolicited stories of how they helped a homeless person get a cup of coffee or some food, how they helped protect a person or his property, how they gave someone some money or helped find a place for a homeless person to live. Each time the students returned to the squatter settlement, they brought something to the residents. At first the students easily collected uneaten school breakfasts. Later, they brought clothes, blankets, and cooked meals from home. It was clear to me that the students were becoming more sympathetic toward the homeless and more keenly aware of the problems the homeless had to face everyday.

A private funding source granted the school $2,000 to turn the students' tapes into multiple copies of a finished documentary. In consultation with a professional editor, I helped recount the students' research journey. We assembled the film pieces to reflect the students' experiences. The result allows an audience to participate in the students' odyssey and to allow the same conclusions to be drawn. At the end of the film Yasmin summarizes: "You have to watch out, 'cause it could happen to anybody."

The tapes were delivered to the school early in October. An after-school workshop was held to give the students an opportunity to see the finished documentary for the first time. (Rizzo-Tolk 1990, ch. 1)

To underline the cultural construction of such a story, its artfulness if not its artificiality, is not to denigrate those who may see nothing strange about it. They are accountable members of a world that is consistent in the image it proposes. It is a complex world with schools of education where people are transformed into legitimate teachers, with bureaucracies that require proof of individual professional competence and, when evaluators are most sensitive to educational theory, proof of *individual* creativity. All this ties not only with what is most powerful in the United States but to what is best in America, to the fundamental striving to construct institutions that "foster the ability of individuals and communities to elevate their levels of competence, increase their number of life options, and disseminate human and ethical values that will help insure all citizens equal access to a democratic society in a world at peace." So the goal is put forth in the "vision statement" of a major school. Such strivings should not be abandoned. But waving flags will not get us where we want to go if we do not also severely criticize the ways we have chosen in our earlier strivings.

Classroom (De)Construction—A Student's Task

The rhetoric of the School allows for a "student's point of view," but its expression is not equally consequential to the teacher's. In School ordinary times, there is no setting where a student can justifiably say, "This is the classroom that I designed for fifth period." A teacher or researcher can ask a student to produce a text, and this text can be edited and made to look like an adult text and thus become the proof that students can understand what is happening to them. But these are extraordinary texts. A student's articulation must proceed along different performative ways. Mostly, in the world of the School, Student responds with what Teacher suggests.

We capitalize words such as Student, Teacher, Class, Time, and Test to make the same point our capitalization of the word School has made: All participants are caught in a world of complex categories and prescribed sequences. They must take these categories into account as facts: Anything they do can be evaluated as parts of the prescribed sequences. This is certainly what happens in West Side. There, as anywhere else, students can always be seen taking the School frame into account. They never fail to acknowledge that they *are* "in school." If they didn't, West Side would cease to be a school that is an identifiable instance of "the School." If they stopped acknowledging the relevance of the various frames, the students would cease to be students, and the broader social forces, in the guise of a central board of education, would enforce what could then truly be called a collapse of the social order. But the social order does not collapse in West Side. The students participate. Later, we examine in more detail how they do so. Let us now look at a moment when a few students constructed the main formal features of a classroom and, at the same time, all but deconstructed it in an altogether postmodern fashion:

The Setting

A poetry class.

The Time

Before lunch (some minutes before official ending time).

The Protagonists

The teacher,: a white, middle-aged, middle-class, midwestern woman.
The students,: five young men and women, some black, some Hispanic.

The Action

A student begins, the teacher responds, and they proceed with the following exchange.

S: What time you got?
T: Ten to twelve.
S: Man, you got the wrong time. Where did you get your time?
T: I listened to the radio this morning.
S: You got the wrong time, it's time to go to lunch.
T: It's not and you cannot leave until the end of the period.

(The students stay in the room until the end of the period.)

In the introduction we distinguished a few types of "What time is it?" conversations, particularly the "information-seeking" and "knowledge display" conversations. Canonically, the former ends with an acknowledgment that information was given ("Thank you!"). The later ends with an evaluation ("Very good, John!"). In the quoted exchange, we get a "What time you got?" conversation governed by the existence of an accountable boundary for a scene that, like most social scenes, is legitimate only for a Time. It is a conversation in which the accountable answer is "It's (not) time (yet/now) to end a time-bounded activity." As such it is an extremely appropriate conversation in what some are describing as "the cultures of the clock," which human beings began constructing in the nineteenth century (Frykman and Löfgren [1979] 1987).

The students in this West Side example take the boundary-making process seriously. They do not ignore the social fact that classrooms are timed constructs and that, during Time, only Teacher can free Student from Classroom.[2] In this instance, as in most instances, the students stayed and played with one significant feature of the frame, namely that in a school without bells, the teacher is the keeper of the clock that will eventually free the students (and teacher) from Classroom. Thus the accuracy of the teacher's clock can accountably become an issue without challenging the place of the teacher. Teacher is paradoxically constructed by the very fact that a question about the teacher's watch is asked. Eventually the students yielded, thus revealing that Classroom is indeed Teacher's to construct.[3] And yet through the very fact that they for an instant revealed the structural framework of Classroom, they literally "took apart" the actual classroom with the effect that, as with any other human object that is taken apart and lying deconstructed, such as an engine in a mechanic's shop, this classroom stopped working. Such sensitive deconstructions may delight those of a nihilistic bent. Teachers and students do not have this luxury, and often they despair. Like most of us, they prefer that their machines and other cultural artifacts get put back together and purr smoothly as they perform the tasks of life.[4]

A Teacher's Task for Her Students

Let us now look in detail at a moment when the machine was together, smoothly performing a task. Let us look at it as something that was jointly produced by equally active participants. The task was given by Rizzo-Tolk in a kind of epilogue to the much broader task of making a documentary on the homeless.

Before the video was to be shown to the whole school, the students who had been involved in the project were invited to a discussion and showing. There was a lunch in their honor. They received a certificate. They were a major success story. Then, they proceeded to a classroom where they were first asked to discuss homelessness as it affected them. Besides the six students and one student's two-year-old son, Rizzo-Tolk, an assistant teacher (Chuck) and another guest were present. The discussion lasted about half an hour and was videotaped. The students were assembled in a circular fashion. They were asked to present themselves to the camera, and then Rizzo-Tolk started the conversation with a question. The students responded. Rizzo-Tolk asked other questions, and this went on for about twenty minutes. Figure 4.1 summarizes the main "tasks"[5] that the students let the teacher give them: They remained physically stable, in focus, and never resisted.

At the end of this long sequence, the students were asked to rank order a list of options they might have if they became homeless. In many ways, and certainly in contrast to the fieldwork the students had done to make the documentary, this task was fully under the control of the School at its most traditional. It was a final exam of sorts designed to capture a display of the new knowledge that the students had gained through their work. We now focus on this final task for a more detailed analysis. The students did it as a matter of course, neither requesting nor requiring help. They were done in less than five minutes.

We focus first on rather gross behavioral units to illustrate what happens when human beings hold each other accountable and can be held accountable by principals and boards of education to the positions of Teacher and Student as asymmetrical though jointly performed. At such times, it is not enough for each person to be aware of a role or status within the structure of the School. She must also bring into accord her actual performance with the performance of the people in the complementary positions. That this is what indeed happens is abundantly clear when looking at the tape, and it is easy to segment the total performance into units related to what has been called "positionings" (Kendon 1990; McDermott, Gospodinoff, and Aron 1978; Scheflen 1973). A first analysis reveals units that have a specific label in the participants' vocabulary. They may be explicit dramaturgical answers to a command, or they could gloss what the participants would offer when asked, "What is happening here?" For example, Rizzo-Tolk declared, "We have a task for you to do," and the students later performed something that she took as evidence that they had done the task. Eventually, a student asked, "What do we do now?" as the whole group that had shaped itself into a huddle of sorts opened up again and faced the teachers as it had at the beginning when "given" the task. From this point of view, we can summarize the whole sequence into a series of subsequences:

FIGURE 4.1

Major Segments during first 20 minutes

Segment	Length of Segment (in mins.)	Introductory Statement	Summary of Movements During Each Segment
1	2.5	"Could we start by having you introduce yourself first? Say your name to the camera so that when we look at it, when we look at it we can identify who you are in the discussion. So one at a time . . ."	After further explanations by R-T, each student stands up and speaks directly into the camera for less than 10 seconds.
2	1.25	"There are going to be two people here that you don't normally see. Natalie, who's just walked in, and Chuck is here to tape us also. And the reason that we're doing this is because we think it's an important project . . ."	Further explanations by R-T; students listen.
3	3.0	"Under what circumstances would you choose to be homeless? What would happen in your life that would make you choose to be homeless?"	Under prodding by R-T, who controls the turn taking, one student and then another answers the question until all have.
4	6.0	"If you ended up having problems with your parents or if your parents were no longer living and you found yourself faced with a bad situation and you ended up being homeless, who might you go to as the first person that you would feel comfortable living with? Let's say something happened tonight. I'm talking about immediately, who would you go to?"	Same as 3.
5	1.75	"Are homeless children, kids, adolescents different from homeless women, homeless men?"	Starts like 3 and 4 but only one student speaks for the whole time; others stay silent.
6	3.5	"Do you feel different about a homeless women than you do about a homeless man?"	Same as 3 and 4 but not all take a turn; there is elaboration by some whose turn it is not.

Note: During the 20 minutes, the students hold the same position: they sit in a circle, bodies facing each other. When they speak, they turn their head (but not their bodies, which remain almost motionless throughout) toward R-T, who stays invisible on the side of the camera.

1. Teacher and assistant define a task for the students to perform.
   1.1 Teacher makes general statement about the fact of task to be performed.
   1.2 Assistant teacher gives the detail about the task.
2. Students perform task.
   2.1 Students settle themselves to perform task.
   2.2 Students perform the task.
   2.3 Students complete task.
   2.4 Students engage in a conversation tangentially related to the task.
   2.5 Students call on the teacher to announce their completion and to ask for a further task.

Things are in fact somewhat more complex, as can be seen by looking at a transcript of the first minute and a half of the sequence in Appendix B. Notice the group laughter at the end of Charmaine's reading of the choices to rank. This laughter stands out because, in contrast to the other recorded speech, it does not seem to answer a specific question. Thus it reveals the need for a finer-grained analysis of the sequence, an analysis in terms of positionings that are jointly performed units of behavior that have no verbal gloss but have clearly served to organize the group for a while. The need for such an analysis is particularly clear when examining the visual record, where we see major alternations between various organizations of the bodies in evidence. We can then summarize the sequence into four basic positionings:

Gg Getting/giving instructions.
Rg Reading cards/listening to the reading/attending to the reading.
Lg Laughing/attending to the laughter.
Dg Discussing the choices/attending to the discussion.

Each positioning is typified by the relative physical positions of all the participants (teachers and students). During getting/giving, laughing, and discussing, the basic distinction is between students and teachers. During reading, we have a further subdivision among the students as one reads and the others listen. See Figure 4.2 for a summary of the temporal progression of the segment in terms of these positionings.

This analysis helps us realize, first, that what the students and teachers did is somewhat more complex than our common sense would have led us to expect. The analysis emphasizes the common achievement of all the participants. Things proceeded smoothly, as the structural mechanisms that we are now exposing were never brought to the attention of the group in a metaconversation that would have stopped the flow of the task; there was nothing equivalent to the displays that deconstruct classrooms. None of the teachers in the room saw anything extraordinary, and the concerns they later expressed about what the students had learned had nothing to do with the coherence of what was done. The students' accomplishment

FIGURE 4.2
Sequencing of the Positionings During Student Discussion

sec.	Positioning	Students	Teachers
0 10 (13) 20 30 40 (47)	Gg^1 Gg^2	getting instruction getting instruction (see Fig. 4.3 #1)	R-T giving instruction Ch giving instruction
50 60 (65)		[TRANSITION]	
70 80 90 (92)	Rg	one student reads other listen	attend
100	Lg^1	full group laughter (see Fig. 4.3 #2)	attend
110 120 130 140 150 160 170 180 190 200 (209) 210 220 (223) 230 240 250 260 270 280 290 (298)	Dg Lg^2 Dg	discuss choices (see Fig. 4.3 #3) part group laughter discuss choices	attend attend attend
300 (308)	Lg^1	full group laughter	attend
310	Gg	return cards (see Fig. 4.4 #1 & #2)	

was not a trivial feat. Consider, for example, how the assistant teacher presented the task: "We want you to rank options that you would have if you were, uh, faced with being homeless; what type of choices you would make, I mean where would you go from there: Where would you sleep? What would you do? That kind of thing so, uh, on the index cards there's nine options and we just want you to rank them as a group, decide in what order you would do these things if you were homeless." What, in particular, could ranking options "as a group" possibly mean, literally and performatively? What should get done for the teachers to recognize that the students had indeed done what they were asked to do? Most of the details were left to the commonsense understandings of the students who accepted the task matter- of-factly.

These descendants of African slaves, Amerindians, Spaniards, and other Europeans—people at the far periphery of the official middle class, who had "failed" all schools of the hegemonic center, who did not speak standard English easily, who were children of parents (who may not have spoken English at all and who had probably failed in school themselves), and who were usually presented as the prototype of those outside the mainstream—expertly organized themselves in a huddle and proceeded to rank options as a group.(Figure 4.3). One person, Charmaine, acted as a secretary of the group's process. She held the cards, read from them, informally ensured that everyone spoke, and recorded the emerging decisions. Four minutes later, they were accountably done, the nine choices had been ranked, and the cards were turned back to the teacher, who in the Classroom frame was the only one who could actually close the sequence.

Then there was hesitation. The cards had been taken away, and the students had returned to their huddle and to a conversation heavily marked by behaviors that were not performed earlier: laughing, covering the microphone, whispering, jostling, and such. Eventually one student asked, "What do we do now?" as the whole group reoriented itself toward the teacher. There was no place for them to generate School tasks. What they had been doing since the cards had been handed in was "nothing," no-School-thing, a negative of the accountable positive. All they could do was keep themselves in School. By asking the teacher what they should now do, the students practically disciplined her. They enforced Teacher on her in a way symmetrical to the way she enforced Student on them when she gave them the task.

In the process, and against the common sense with which the students likely operated, a teacher's task for the students was revealed to be what it always also is, that is, a student's task for the teacher. As the teacher responded coherently to the students' call, she was enforcing Teacher on herself in the same manner the students enforced Student on themselves. It is only in the formal educational rhetoric that what a teacher does and what a student does is distinguished. Analytically, we must step out of the rhetoric and consider that teacher and students are always together, that they are a unit predefined and actually constructed through the feedback mechanisms that keep everyone on track.

FIGURE 4.3
Start of Ranking Sequence

#1

Chris gives instruction:

on the index cards there's nine options and we just want you to rank them as a group, decide in what order you would do these things if you were homeless (sec. 37–47)

the students listen.

#2

FIRST LAUGHTER SEQUENCE

#3

The students discuss

The Voice of the Group:
Laughter, Resistance, and Reconstruction

We can now proceed to a finer-grained description of certain exchanges among the students while they were "ranking the options." Not only did the five-minute conversation move smoothly to an accountable ending but in the details of specific exchanges the students' various contributions to the discussion meshed smoothly.[6] They were not simply "conversing" but producing something that was more akin to a multivoiced, improvised conversational choir: They terminated each other's utterances, expanded on them in other directions, agreed on the relative position of the choice, and moved on. They were a single voice speaking through various mouths.[7]

How are we to understand the students' accomplishment? They did exactly what was asked of them. They came to an agreement as a group, and did so in a manner that demonstrated that they were a group controlled by a set of cultural conventions that they had incorporated into their speech and their bodies. For example, we could celebrate how most of the participants did talk, made comments that sometimes were at odds with what had just been said, and yielded politely to the expression of the majority—e pluribus unum in the best and great tradition of American democracy. Indeed, when Varenne first saw the tape and before it had been contextualized for him, he saw—as probably many would have if they did not play close attention—a group of middle-class teenagers from a middle-class suburb having a discussion in a school or a church group. The fact that one of the teenagers was holding a baby that was taken away from the group as it started its task, the fact that some of the participants were phenotypically black and others probably Hispanic, these commonsense signs that this was a conversation from the bottom of the social hierarchy were made to disappear.

And yet the educational tale we used earlier to summarize the historical organization of the project underlines that the students' task was framed by the School's identification of these students as being in trouble. Rizzo-Tolk herself was moved to design the project by her experiences in a class in which students laughed at putting a homeless man on fire. At that moment, her students revealed themselves to be what they were known as being: the "worst" and "just the kind that comes to West Side." She was moved to conduct the research when, on first watching the tape and talking about it with others, a doubt crept into her mind about the extent of what she had thought until then was a success. The experience had been quite satisfying for her. She was quite sure that it had also been satisfying and useful to the students. They had revealed what they could do if given the chance. Other teachers were not so convinced.

One moment particularly stood out. Let us look at it briefly. One of the choices to rank was "living in Shantytown." This referred to a settlement of people in a vacant lot on the Lower East Side of Manhattan. The group had visited it several times during the filming of the documentary, and because of the political awareness of the settlers and the fact that they had organized themselves into an active and caring community, they had served as the model of what to seek if one was forced by circumstances onto the streets. The educational message had been strong and consistent: Shantytown was the kind of place that should not have had to exist in a proper America, and one should change conditions in order to make it unnecessary for people to live in such places. In the meantime, those who found themselves homeless would find the most help in such a community. Not only would living in Shantytown help those who lived there but participation in an organized alternative community would ideally help the political movement that would change the conditions.

In the final ranking, Shantytown came last. And to make things apparently worse, the students laughed when they established this ranking. There was an episode of group laughter after Charmaine finished reading the list of the choices and as the students settled into the discussion. The laughter that interests us now came at the end of the task and, in formal terms, can be seen as the symmetrical marker to the first one. As the laughter subsided, the students moved out of the "task" positioning, shifted their bodies, shifted their voices, and moved into a "waiting for the teacher to give us a new task" positioning (Figure 4.4).

An identification of the laughter as an interactional marker is the only proper one to make within the strict framework of conversation analysis. General audiences and official evaluators (other teachers, inspectors, accreditation boards, curriculum designers, etc.) unfortunately are not constrained by the same intellectual concerns, and eventually, it is through them that the power of the center exercises itself. To them, there is something powerfully evocative in an act that seems to reverse the priorities suggested by the educational effort (placing Shantytown last rather than first or even second or third). Possibly it ridicules the whole effort.

While laughing, the students talked briefly about the visit that some of them had made to Shantytown after the project was officially finished (and thus at a time when the School had relinquished control over them). Mention was made of being afraid of the roaches and the smell. For the first time, one person attempted to put a hand on the microphone, apparently to block the recording. Toward the end of the sequence, one student appeared to resist what her peers were constructing and affirmed that things hadn't really "been so bad." We cannot imagine what evidence could help us produce a definitive statement of what any student had learned. An act like covering the microphone could be seen as an indication that one student at least had learned what she was supposed to have learned but that she was not going to use it. Could this be proof of independent, possibly "critical," thinking ("Yes, I know what want you want me to learn, but I do not think this is the way the world works, though I am going to try to prevent you from finding that out")? Could it be proof that she had fallen prey to peer pressure? Could it be an instance of the displays of distanciation that true believers perform when they make fun of their deepest beliefs by emphasizing what they know those who do not share their beliefs would consider most absurd? The laughter could thus be considered a negation of the negation, and the overall effect may be that the moment must remain ambiguous. Covering the microphone, like any other act considered in isolation, could be a display of confor-

FIGURE 4.4
End of Ranking Sequence

#1

SECOND LAUGHTER
SEQUENCE

(notice the teacher standing
with arms crossed at the
back, attending to the students' discussion)

#2

The girl who recorded the
rankings attempts to return
the card to the teacher.

#3

About a minute later, the
students are now in an informal, non-teacher sponsored
conversation. The girl at the
back tells a funny anecdote
about going back to Shantytown; all laugh; she playfully
covers the microphone with
her hand.

mity, resistance, or resistance to resistance. What we do have is a display that was wide open to co-optation by any of the parties to whom the local group may have found itself accountable.

The Voice of the Center

Many parties might have made this local group accountable to their own organization. We can only wonder what might have happened if this tape had been shown to Charmaine, Rob, or Yasmin during a party of peers far away from school. When would they have laughed? Would they have started talking about homelessness? Would they have worried whether they had failed? We do have some information about what happened when the tape was first looked at by people in the Teacher mode: They focused on the laughter, bracketed away everything that happened earlier, and engaged in a conversation structured around the issue of failure. In so doing, they performed locally a version of what we are doing on a broader stage in this chapter. Like the teachers, we, the authors and anthropologists of education, watch the tape for an answer to the question that has organized the scholarly and professional conversations that America has conducted for many decades: Why can't Johnny read? Why do students who have spent many months or years attending West Side continue to score so low on national tests?

This conversation defines what the School is all about. It is particularly intense at West Side High, perhaps because everyday practice there has the potential to challenge its grounds. Probably not one day passes without passionate, soul-searching exchanges centering, sometimes optimistically, sometimes pessimistically, on the relative success of the school, of its programs, or of the teachers' teaching. This soul-searching is particularly difficult for the teachers, since the students rarely succeed according to the canons of academic success. They come with universally acknowledged "low skills," and their attendance is spotty; their skills improve, but rarely to the point where they can compete meaningfully with students from any but a few other urban high schools. The simple version of the teachers' question to themselves may be: What are we doing here?

One answer is that the teachers are trying to get students to read at an advanced level. Sometimes, other answers are given: West Side does go to great efforts to provide an institutional environment where students are helped, understood, and always given another chance, as they would be in a "family" (the model the principal uses in order to counter the indifference of the streets and other institutions to the fate of the students). The hope is that through a modeling of caring, the students will care for their own and for each other. The goal is changes in behavior, not increases in stored amounts of information. This was the goal Rizzo-Tolk gave herself, and she has much evidence that such changes occurred among her students. They might still have had to laugh about the homeless in certain contexts, but they told stories about how they had started to help homeless persons in direct and practical ways. It was hoped that they would continue doing so. The principal likes to say that the school is not working necessarily for the immediate success of the current generation. It is working to provide a basis on which to build in the hope that, twenty years from now, a student who is now abusive and rebellious can be heard attributing eventual survival to the "the great teacher who disregarded my adolescent nastiness and gave me the under-standing I needed so that now my own children can go on to college."

Such alternative answers to questions about the finality of a high school education are made necessary because no matter what is tried, Charmaine, along with most of her peers at West Side, did not demonstrate that she had learned in such a way that teachers, locally or on broader stages, could say unambiguously that she was an acad-emically successful high school student. In fact, Charmaine displayed redundantly, like Adam did in the relevant settings, that she had not learned, that she was not suc-cessful, and that her identification as a failure was well established. The identification of West Side High as one of the "worst" schools in New York City was also well es-tablished according to the legitimate criteria to be used for such rankings, and it re-dundantly presented to the world the face that justified this ranking. The same could also be said of New York City public high schools in general, at least in contrast to suburban or private schools.

Traditionally, the behavioral sciences, when applied to education, have fully par-ticipated in the conversation and, eventually, in the rhetorical identification (or la-beling) of students, teachers, and school systems. This is true even of those research traditions that have criticized this or that identification. To the extent that re-searchers have tried to give a better answer to the question Why can't Johnny (or Adam) read? they have fallen victim to the cultural constitution of the question. Demonstrating that Adam, and the participants in the choir and the homeless pro-ject, could under many conditions be seen as interactionally successful and indeed knowledgeable must lead to an analysis of the conditions that deliver the failing la-bel. Practically, we must understand the fascination with the questions about success and failure that the School imposes on those who wonder about its operation.

As anthropologists, we are led to the broader question by the logic of the ethno-graphic research that reveals the central character of the success-and-failure system. Descriptively, we could stop as soon as we completed the analysis and highlighted its sources. As Americans, we must question the "native" question about success and fail-ure because there is evidence that real personal damage is done to those who make their life in such places as West Side High School, particularly when their experience is framed by the failure made apparent by the institutionalized "success" conversation. We talked earlier about our desire to celebrate the effort of all the people at West Side. We were tempted to couch our celebration in language well stated by Perry Gilmore in the conclusions to her work on "sub-rosa" skills: "Teacher expectations should be raised through an awareness that students are capable of doing more with language when they are given the room and respect to do so" (1984: 390; 1986). This approach indeed guided Rizzo-Tolk when she designed the homeless project.

Eventually, we came to doubt whether a scholarly celebration of student perfor-mance, although hard won and essential, was quite enough. We were alerted to the problem by the careless identification by some West Side teachers that the students' laughter demonstrated that they had indeed "not learned." We could have tried to argue that the teachers were mistaken, that it was they who "had not learned." But by doing so we would have shifted the blame and stopped our investigation where it really should have begun: How is the world so constructed that School success cannot be demonstrated? Gilmore showed the way in her comments about children's folklore: "Once [this folklore] is neutered, colonized, and socially controlled by the school, it is, in fact, no longer children's folklore" (1984: 390).[8]

A celebration that proceeds by shifting the blame is certainly not what we need. What is marvelous about the people of West Side is that they persist in building an everyday life in spite of the persistent negative reinforcements they give each other along lines enforced by the less local stages on which the teachers, at least, continue to perform. All the teachers have "succeeded" in schools. Many of them have advanced degrees from major Schools of Education. All of them read the papers, watch television, and listen to Superintendents and union Presidents talk about "improving education in our failing schools." Still, they persist, and at times as they wonder, "What are we doing here?" they show us, perhaps more than most scholarly analysts of education, that they are aware of the artificiality of the task they have been given.

Where does the School (in all its performative and dramatistic aspects) come from? Why is it that for the past 200 years, all the cultural productivity of Euro-American civilization has strained to make schooling available universally and even to make it compulsory? Why did the United States and France risk civil war to separate Church from State while trying always more fully to integrate School with State? There are philosophical and political reasons for this, and we are not necessarily criticizing them by calling our attention to their overwhelming presence in the conduct of our everyday life in schools. Still, the practical reasoning that makes of "success," as measured in School, a central category in American culture cannot remain the frame of our inquiries. It must become an aspect of our field.

NOTES

In the title to the chapter, the qualifier "wild" is a homage to Lévi-Strauss ([1962] 1966), who dared say—in French—that wildness, *sauvagerie*, is a property of humanity in cultural action: *La pensée est toujours sauvage*. Because one must challenge even our recent common sense about anonymity, we decided not to disguise the school after discussion with the principal, Ed Reynolds, to whom we showed a late version of the paper of which this chapter is an expansion. He lives the constraints we are trying to describe and wants to be part of the conversation. All other names have been changed. This chapter is based on a dissertation by Rosemarie Rizzo-Tolk (1990). It is a rewrite of one of her papers (Rizzo-Tolk and Varenne 1992). See Appendix B for more details on the fieldwork.

1. See Varenne (1978, 1983) for a further elucidation of this tack in analyzing schooling.

2. This does not always prevent actual students from leaving with or without speeches explaining their departure in Classroom terms. We are talking about rules for accountability

(defining the kind of explanation one can give for behavior or meting out consequences), not deterministic mechanisms.

3. This is an altogether mild example of student resistance. Most teachers at West Side appear to have more ominous stories in which the resistance leads to a radical break of the classroom frame as students organize themselves into a group that may remain friendly even as it prevents the teacher from Teaching. At this point the teacher either attempts an authoritarian gambit by trying to get the principal involved (which works but cannot be used repeatedly) or just gives up, either by joining the students in their chats or even by withdrawing to read a book or deal with paperwork. Whereas the latter happens, it is not common and has never escalated into a break in the School frame (rather than the Classroom frame).

4. This is not an analysis of *all* the students' knowledge. It is not necessarily either an analysis of *any one* student's discursive knowledge (though it is probable that an intellectually inclined student might recognize the validity of the analysis). It is an analysis of something that is revealed in the group's behavior, of something that is available to the group and to the individuals in the group. It is an analysis of a social condition.

5. The word "task" is used here to refer to the major segments in the group's activities because one of the participants referred to the final one as a "task for you to do." The word is thus to be understood as a "native," rather than a "theoretical," category.

6. This was not as extraordinary as it may appear to those who have not followed conversation analysis. In recent years, particularly through work by Sacks (1974), Schegloff, Jefferson, and Sacks (1977), Goodwin, C. (1981), Goodwin, M. (1990), Goodwin and Goodwin (1992), it has become quite clear that as body-movement specialists had suggested earlier (Byers 1976; Kendon 1990; Scheflen 1973), the role separation between speaker and hearer is in fact a secondary epiphenomenon of the interactional process. Speakers and hearers always act jointly, not simply by withdrawing and coming back in at the appropriate times but by actively showing they are participating. In simple terms, one cannot address someone who does not perform for the speaker whatever must be done to demonstrate proper listening.

7. In her dissertation, Rizzo-Tolk labels this effect a "shaped utterance" in which speakers complete each other's sentence and echo completion sequences (1990: 155–174).

8. See also McDermott and Hood (1982) and Smith, Gilmore, Goldman and McDermott (1993).

5 Racing in Place

Hervé Varenne, Shelley Goldman, and Ray McDermott

The most powerful of American metaphors for education makes it a race on a field so perfectly level that only individual merit determines the result. The racing metaphor is a pithy summary of an enormous social process of discussion, controversy, action, and institutionalization that is at play in the contemporary United States. If education is a race, is this or that field really level? How might one make it more level? Isn't it terrible that so many children of the more well-to-do get an illegitimate head start at home and in privileged preschools? These worries get argued in various public spheres that help to produce new programs to complement the school and offer legitimate head starts. The new programs get staffed, administered, evaluated, defended, reformed. They get inscribed on the American landscape as new historical facts that change the playing field for both the children of West Side High and those of Allwin Junior High, described in this chapter.

The racing metaphor for education is quite controversial. Many educators as well as parents and politicians explicitly reject it. They argue that talk of head starts, legitimate or not, debases a spiritual and personal process that the proper educator coaxes but does not direct. At sacred moments when fundamental truths have to be reaffirmed in the midst of an uncertain world, the people of the United States tell each other that education is about individuals and their development and that educational practice is legitimate only to the extent that it fosters individual development. In sacred documents, education is about growing, finding one's own way. It is a pilgrim's progress following a different drummer down the road less traveled (to index various powerful metaphors). We find these metaphors more congenial than the metaphor of education as a race. We are also aware of the more subtle ways in which all these metaphors mislead political development as they get institutionalized. For talk of journeys taken under the guidance of a wise elder across treacherous terrains full of temptations and pitfalls can too easily be transformed into talk of races on fields run by precision evaluators.

Over the past 200 years at least, the evolution of these conversations has contributed to making the metaphor of education as race the dominant one for political purposes in Europe and the Americas. It seems to capture a fundamental truth to be extended into myth, discourse, political theater, and, most fatefully, an enormous bureaucracy through which all children must proceed. From Horace Mann to John

Dewey, prophets passionately argued that it was proper to develop special institutions—public schools—to nurture children as they journeyed and grew. These schools had to be carefully designed to help shape the proper citizens of a liberal democracy. Who can seriously question such goals?

But there is a trap here that most could not see. As schools flourished, they were caught by the language of evaluation and individual merit, both for the person and for the particular school. Just as it seemed liberal to wonder about the performance of a person so that the person could be helped, it seemed liberal to wonder about "how well" a school was doing. A democratic polity was certainly entitled, the argument continued to run, to know whether a school was performing as advertised, whether it actually *produced* the educated citizenry it was given the task of producing. And so schools found themselves on a field being compared to other schools. The trick that concerns us most is the one that follows: The success of a school can be evaluated only in terms of the success of the children. The good school is the one where children, more conservatively, learn to read or, more progressively "learn to learn." In either case one must examine children to evaluate the school. And so the full gaze falls on the individual child. The metaphorical journey that started with a child growing and adults lovingly in attendance has been transformed into adults anxiously measuring how far the child has journeyed and arguing endlessly about why there is not more progress to show. In this ideological process the thicket of conflicting people crowding institutions of education with long histories disappears from analysis. Social forces are returned to the background as the child is made to occupy the foreground for extended comparison with other children. It may take a whole village to raise a child, but in America, at the most sacred of times when lives are in balance, the child stands alone for the village to judge. That the village may be responsible for setting the whole thing up is hard to determine and even harder to change.[1]

Since the eighteenth-century republican revolutions, the Euro-American world has convinced itself that descent is not an appropriate method for social reproduction: Lawyers may not, by right, be chosen from among the children of lawyers, and physicians from the children of physicians. Any statistical analysis demonstrating that this may still be the case is taken as an ipso facto critique of the current situation.[2] Lawyers, physicians, and firemen—that is, fire*persons*, abstract human beings with no particular qualities, not even gender—must be chosen on merit alone, on their pure, inner ability to perform the job as described with nothing extraneous taken into consideration. The principle is clear. The problem lies in how to discriminate merit in individuals, and it is taken to be a technical issue amenable to reform through research. Eventually, as philosophy meets politics, the intellectual strivings of John Dewey and other philosophers transform themselves, at the level of educational policy, even against the wishes of their authors, into the altogether desperate—however profitable—search for tests and measurements from Edward Thorndike to Howard Gardiner.[3]

By pointing to the link between the ideological development of powerful metaphors (journeys, races on level playing fields) and a set of overbearing institutions (schools and their bureaucracies, corporations specializing in testing schools and children, etc.), we wish to emphasize the facticity of American democratic culture and thus its external properties vis-à-vis the people who must live in the United States. Democracy is not simply a matter of values or beliefs. It is not simply about the constitution of the self. It is also the environment for local, even private, action and must directly concern anthropologists of education in America and the United States.[4] To the very extent that "merit" as measured by the evaluation of individuals is constitutive of a success officially recognized as success, the ideological imperative that drove Dewey and Thorndike must also lead, at the level of local familial politics, to a desperate struggle to make one's children appear legitimately better. If a university professor can pass a position to an offspring only through the child's merit as measured by tests administered in schools that are themselves ranked, isn't it to be expected that professors will sacrifice much to get their children into the "best" schools, to tutor their children to "do better," particularly if the child may not actually do well on a totally "fair" field? There is a peculiar American reasonableness to a president of the United States supporting public schools for the country and sending his daughter to a private school. To do otherwise would be merely symbolic, and given the understanding of symbolism in American culture, false to the reality of the world, if not hypocritical. Sending an average child to a superior private school can be considered to give unfair advantage, but this very concern is what constitutes democracy. Where competition on level playing fields is upheld as a cultural model both of the way the world is and of the way it should be, getting unfair advantage is what makes sense for people to do. The more fields are leveled, the more the people who race can be seen reconstructing new obstacles for those behind them. Cultural models are always open to human activity that reveals their power and their weakness as all struggle with them. Democracy, it would seem, is about starting equally and ending unequally as quickly as possible.

That the well-to-do will work hard at settling their children in their own position as they struggle with the egalitarian policies of the American School is our concern in this chapter, and it takes us, as an ethnographic inquiry always does, to the concrete everyday performance of people in local circumstances. What do the children of the advantaged do in their schools? The answer may appear surprising: They take tests, they fail many of them, and they continue to be identified as successful students. Like Adam, they may have bad days, but in the long run, they will move on to college and the kind of careers their parents had.

We are not simply being ironical or unnecessarily controversial. Rather we want to emphasize the fundamental character of cultural, rather than psychological, processes in shaping the educational world in which the people of the United States live. Analytically, success in America must be approached as a matter of identification in a complex social scene. To approach it as a matter of personal identity is to fall victim to the very ideology that is the common condition. For a child to be "the best," others must be "second" best, and the rest must be, well, "the rest." This experience of being second best is a common one in Allwin, the "successful" school to which we now turn our attention. Failure in Allwin, as in other American schools, is a cultural fact, a position in a complex field that must always be filled. How is this done? What can people do about it?

The Performance of Success in Everyday Life

Successful children in good schools have always been the reference point in studies of failure, whether personal or institutional. Legitimately identified success is made the ground against which failure stands out as "the problem." In the process, success hides itself, and the intimate dependency of success and failure is difficult to discuss. Even in the anthropology of education, the most powerful work of recent decades has been driven by struggles to offer new understandings of the conditions, rather than the constitution, of politically identified failure. Even in the anthropology of education, for example, in the powerful work of Oscar Lewis, William Labov, Shirley Heath, John Ogbu, and many others, the emphasis has been on finding the best *explanations* of failure. Neglected have been investigations into the *constitution* of failure as an event in the world (McDermott 1987, 1988, 1997). Even when authors complain about the grounds on which some children are identified as failures and eloquently show how successful they would be if the grounds of the discrimination were changed, they end up accepting the reality of the political identification without focusing on the processes that help make such evaluations factual. In the process of explanatory research, bad schools and failing children are separated out. They are made to be "different." They are the target population. They are isolated to the point that the interaction between good and bad schools, successful and failing children, is lost. In the popular political imagination, this difference has been interpreted as evidence for the existence of two worlds, two societies, separate and unequal, a dominant one to be emulated and a colonized other to be explained and transformed. There is another possibility: Both types of schools, and all their children, are part of one differentiated system that is the product of a complex and continuing cultural construction that has been made fact in the history of all concerned. We take the stance that both success and failure proceed from the same principles and that all individuals, families, and localities in the United States struggle with these same facts, American "cultural" facts that open particular social spaces for all (including us) to construct personal lives.

We invoke the concept of "culture" to link ourselves with a long tradition of work in anthropology that started with the recognition that particular historical developments make conditions that enable and limit people in peculiar ways. In culture (and we do not mean in "a" culture), limited aspects of human performances are highlighted, others are erased from the collective memory of all concerned, and people hold each other accountable for that which is highlighted and for forgetting that which must be irrelevant. In the process, some might say persons disappear as particular personae reveal themselves, justify the actions of other personae, and allow uncertainty to be resolved back into cultural order. This is dramatic for some and should be less so for others, particularly the people of Hamden Heights whom we present here. After all, the town is known as "an upper-middle-class community of successful businessmen and professionals." Allwin Junior High School is known to be part of an "excellent" school system. One might expect all to be easy in the best of all American worlds. We show this is not quite so, because in their everyday practice, if not in their ideological pronouncements, the adults and children of Hamden Heights demonstrate an awareness that they are linked to, and in constant competition with, the people of Newark and New York City, whom they rarely meet face-to-face.

Minimally, we want to show they use the same cultural resources available to all "American" schools (that is, all schools accountable to the dominant ideology and political consciousness in the United States). Eventually, the point is to suggest how the people of Hamden Heights, as they actively construct their local world at a suburban distance from New York City, also construct something for the adults and children of Newark, Manhattan, and Brooklyn—even though they cannot be said in any way to control the abundant resources that are put at their disposal.

In the midst of identified success at Allwin, we could trace inconsequential failure in the same manner as we traced inconsequential success in the midst of identified failure. For example, an Allwin teacher gave a class the opportunity to take a test on the same material for a second time because "the majority of the kids in the class shouldn't have failed." Because they "should" not fail, they *could* not fail. This was not merely a case of the self-fulfilling prophecies that have been extensively documented in various "Pygmalion" studies.[5] The teacher had to work hard to erase noticeable failure and inscribe it in her books as legitimate success. She looked for a reason for the failure (the test was given the day before a three-day camping trip), and then she planned a new review period and a second test. Although such a scenario was rare, it was common for a teacher to dismiss a student's failure on a particular test as a significant indicator of the student's eventual success. For example, the failed test would not be averaged or the student would be given makeup work. Students who were caught cheating on an exam might be given a warning with the understanding that "now she will understand that I am watching her." Given an overall identification of success, any single instance of failure was reconstructed as an aberration—in the same manner as a single instance of success at an inner-city school is reconstructed as an aberration within an overall identification of failure.

The central point of this chapter is that most of the tests the children of Allwin were continually taking were not used to do precisely what the myth of testing says they should have been used for, that is, sorting children ever so precisely and mechanically. The sorting that did take place proceeded through less formal mechanisms that rarely limited consideration to an actual performance on a single test score. As admission officers to prestigious colleges like to say, "Test results are only one of the criteria used to select students, and often not the most important." If tests are not directly used for sorting in Allwin, what are they used for? How do they fit within the overall life of the school? We start with this question to explore the linkages between Allwin and West Side.

The Competitions of Everyday Life in Allwin Junior High

The first thing to realize is the ubiquity of tests, measurements, and miscellaneous competitions in the everyday life of the students and teachers of Allwin.[6] There may not have been a day in the life of the students when they were not taking a test, preparing for a forthcoming test or competition, or worrying about the results of an earlier one. On every one of these days the parents participated in one way or another. They helped the children prepare, coached them and supported them, and at every moment worried about the outcomes of the tests even as they were assured, for the moment, of their own identifications as "successful" professionals, managers, entrepreneurs, and so on. In other words, whereas parents had moved to Hamden Heights to a large extent because of the reputation of its schools for producing college-bound students, they did not allow themselves to treat success as a state of being with fixed results. Every child's earlier success was continually put on the line in new competitions and tests that demanded ever more difficult displays of proficiency.

Routine failure on tests was not necessarily consequential; after all, most children on most days failed on most tests in the all-important sense that they did not get to the top of the rankings. What would be more consequential was not taking tests or being caught not performing the test appropriately (through cheating, for example, or not preparing for it or not taking it seriously). A test performed wrongly (which is different from a failure on a test) might lead to escalating interventions from the obligation to take the test again to referrals to the school psychologist. Given all this, it might make sense to think of these tests and competitions as a form of what Geertz called "deep play" in his antifunctionalist interpretation of the Balinese cockfight:

> "Poetry makes nothing happen," Auden says in his elegy of Yeats, "it survives in the valley of its saying . . . a way of happening, a mouth." The cockfight too, in this colloquial sense, makes nothing happen. Men go on allegorically humiliating one another and being allegorically humiliated by one another, day after day, glorying quietly in the experience if they have triumphed, crushed only slightly more openly by it if they have not. *But no one's status really changes.* You cannot ascend the status ladder by winning cockfights; you cannot, as an individual, really ascend it at all. . . . All you can do is enjoy and savor, or suffer and withstand, the concocted sensation of drastic and momentary movements along an aesthetic semblance of that ladder, a kind of behind-the-mirror status jump which has the look of mobility without its actuality. ([1972] 1973a: 443; author's emphasis)

The people of Allwin would likely find this way of talking about their life rather too effete. In their vocabulary, they say simply that the competitions of everyday life are "fun." Competition transforms the boring into the interesting. Like spices on bland food (or drugs), they make the school routine palatable.

There are three kinds of tests at Allwin: classroom-level tests, school- or grade-level competitions, and standardized tests. The first two are routine; the last is strongly marked as special and out of the ordinary. Classroom tests are made up by individual teachers as part of their lesson plans. They take the form of question-and-answer sequences, games, and quizzes. They are slightly formalized instances of what has been repeatedly identified as the fundamental "educational" encounter in American schools.[7] They highlight properties of the pattern that would otherwise remain invisible. Quizzes and tests, for example, function as markers of passage; they punctuate the beginnings and endings of work on units of academic study. They make the class stand out as a class: All students in the class participate in tests and quizzes and no one volunteers for a test. Students are usually competing against their own records or the records of their classmates, and the resulting evaluations usually, but not necessarily, contribute to the student's report card grade. Classroom testing is a frequent activity in almost all of the classes. It is not unusual for a student to have two or more tests in one day, especially toward the end of a marking period. A classroom test grade usually becomes averaged in with other test grades. When teachers do change their opinion about the relative position of a student, an altogether unusual occurrence, they rarely cite a particular test score. They refer rather to patterns in grades over rather long periods.

Classroom games, the other forms of teacher-generated testing occasions, are presented as alternate means of presenting and drilling content. They are presented by teachers and students alike as having to do with learning (rather than testing). As such they are less constrained by ideological strictures and may take other forms than the classical competitions between individuals. At such times, for example, it is permissible to organize groups within the class and to get them to compete against each other. In the process, winners and losers temporarily emerge, possibly confirming a teacher's underlying opinion of individual children. The results of such competitions, like the results of most tests, are not used for any kind of consequential sorting. One is entering here the domain of pure fun, and it is useful to look more closely at one such instance.

An eighth-grade class often played a question-and-answer game called "Screw Thy Neighbor." The official purpose had to do with reviewing content materials for a later and, at least in theory, consequential test. The class was split into two teams. Every student prepared several content questions from readings and notes on his or her humanities unit prior to this occasion. The goal of the game was to "stump" the students on the opposing team by asking them content questions that they could not answer. The students played the game for the entire class period with the teacher moderating and keeping the score. The students laughed, raised hands, and even begged to ask or answer questions during the game. They consistently dramatized that they were playing as if the stakes were high: When they got answers correct, they let out sighs of relief, wiped their brows, and shook each other's hands; when they answered incorrectly, they pouted, cursed, and stomped their feet on the floor. When the game was over, the students on the winning team cheered, clapped, whistled, and "gave each other five." Students on the losing teams smiled, clapped, booed, and asked the teacher when they could have a rematch. In many ways, from the name of the game to the overstylized displays, the message "this is play" was consistently performed (Bateson 1955). "Real" competitions are not officially called

"Screw Thy Neighbor." Still, the structure of this kind of play is not a matter of imaginative happenstance. Everything, including the label, is a symbolic evocation of the times when such performances move out of the play frame. "Screw Thy Neighbor," like the Balinese cockfight, does not do anything: Functionally, it is "just" deep play, and culturally, it is the stuff of life.

"Screw Thy Neighbor" differed from consequential tests in other ways. Most significantly perhaps, it was constructed around teams rather than individual students. Thus it was more like the team sports that are so central to the symbolic life of American schools. It may have also most closely simulated the conditions that would be the most common for Allwin students as they entered adulthood in the private bureaucracies that would later employ them.[8] There too, their individual contributions would eventually count only so much as the success of their companies to survive the marketplace. In the world of IBM or AT&T that their parents inhabited, job security would eventually be more dependent on these companies' bottom line than on the work of any single individual within the company. But in this world, the employee's job performance would also be evaluated individually to affirm that social rewards were granted only according to the merit of the performer rather than on the strength of her group, team, or community.

"Real" tests do not have to do with learning but with evaluation. They are not about teams but about individuals. And they are not fun. As observers, we could see that most tests at Allwin were not radically consequential, but they were still constructed by all participants as something "more serious" than the team games. Tests were less fun, and it was proper for some of the students taking those tests to display, and probably to experience, various levels of anxiety. Eventually those were the tests parents paid attention to, and this attention could lead them to various forms of extraordinary action from extravagant rewards to punishment and various attempts at remediation.

Besides classroom-level tests, there was a set of tests and competitions that involved the whole school either in competition with itself or with other neighboring schools. This was true even outside of sporting events, where that pattern was most elaborately expanded. The interesting thing about these competitions was that they were not directly related to the fundamental democratic requirements about the sorting of individual merit. Again, students were organized into teams, and their individuality was subsumed under that of the team.[9] The Brain Bowl, for example, was a schoolwide contest modeled after a 1960s television show called *The College Bowl.*[10] The Brain Bowl consisted of teams of students competing against each other in tournament fashion on general knowledge and trivia questions. Each year, teachers were asked to construct questions. The questions were made into a test given to any student who wanted to participate in the tournament. Students were then given tournament placements based on their scores on the trivia tests. Next, the play-offs began. Students were verbally asked questions, and each team tried to have a member answer before any members of the opposing team. Points were given for correct answers and deducted for incorrect ones, and at the end of a set time period, the team with the most points advanced to the next round. The testing and tournament play took place over the course of several weeks, and the events culminated in a play-off between the final two teams at a special school assembly.

In such a system, many students do not participate by not volunteering, and most students, that is, all but those on the winning team, experience failure. This does not seem to bother people. Eventually, this is mostly a spectator event, one that most say is an enjoyable activity. Indeed, no particular record is kept of who loses, at what point, or by how much. Once the cathartic final assembly is conducted, the sequence can vanish into a vague memory. Winning or losing such displays is completely inconsequential.[11] Indeed, in most cases at Allwin, there were no surprises as to the identity of the winning team. The team that contained the "top students" generally won. In the process, the emerging organization of the student body was both displayed and justified. The success of these students in inconsequential competitions demonstrated the righteousness of the consequential evaluations. If the students who did well on the "real" tests also did well on the "play" tests, then all must have been right in the best of all American worlds.[12]

There were also schoolwide events that were not officially organized as competitions. They were presented as pure displays designed to be enjoyed rather than evaluated. There was, for example, an arts festival with fashion shows, woodworking exhibitions, and a gallery showing of student art projects and a musical festival with performances by the band and chorus. Students again participated by choice. The competitive frame reemerged through the classroom-based preparation for the events and the students themselves. Even the arts festival became a quite fierce battleground. Indeed, the very fact of choosing not to participate implied a self-evaluation. Among the participants, some worried that their display was not "good enough." A great many class periods went into the design and construction of the displays. Some class groups even kept their ideas secret from other classes. Eventually, an award was indeed given to the best display, and the rest of the results ended in various garbage cans.

In all the competitions, students participated as fully as the teachers and other adults. They and their families, of course, drove the process. Competing was fun. The teachers, in fact, had no problem giving a traditional and commonsense analysis of the situation. Interestingly enough, it was couched in a language that distanced them from what was happening. It was as if, appropriately enough in fact, they placed themselves with the philosophers of education against their own activities as the directors, if not the initiators, of the competitions. Here are a few quotes from a group discussion about competition.

In the classroom: "Give them an activity to get them to practice word skills, and they moan and groan at you. You make it into a contest, and suddenly everyone wants to be an expert at defining vocabulary words."

In the community: "Did you ever see the way these kids do sports? . . . Competition drives them, so why shouldn't we capitalize on it?"

In general: "These kids respond real well to competition. They're geared to it. . . . They're used to seeing their fathers respond to it at work." "They've got to learn how to win and lose. They get chances to do both at some point."

Alfred Kroeber and Clyde Kluckhohn (1953: 357) once noted that there are two ways in which culture impacts the lives of human beings: as a model of behavior and as a model for behavior. The teachers at Allwin invoked both. First, the culture of competition offered a model of behavior: It was an observational fact, there to be seen, that students enjoyed competition. The students at Allwin were full participants in keeping alive what is much more than a myth or belief. Competition is a fact of American culture. It was made and is continually being remade in the history of all involved. Second, competition offered a model for behavior: Students had to get used to winning and losing, and it was the responsibility of teachers to ensure that this happened. Some teachers professed to be disturbed by this, but most used the children's willingness as a resource to push them and make them all, teachers and children, look good.

From our point of view, what is lacking in the adult discourse is an awareness of the processes through which the observation that "students like competing" was made. How did competition become a model of and for behavior? How has it become a "fact" of life in Allwin? Who was involved historically? Who is involved now?

The Ritual Organization of Sorting: Standardized Times

Educational games are fun, but not only fun. Routine tests can be looked at as different levels of deep play, that is, play peculiarly appropriate to demonstrate the validity of the underlying cultural structure. A certain anxiety can surface, and it gets maximized in other tests, extraordinary tests that stand at the opposite extreme from games like "Screw Thy Neighbor." These are the tests that may be most legitimately used for decisions to sort one student from another or to confirm earlier sorting decisions even if the eventual outcome is anything but mechanical. These tests are strongly marked to distinguish them from the routine. First, they are not designed by the school or local school boards. They are state or, more often, national tests designed by educational experts from prestigious universities and corporations. They are presented as based on the most up-to-date understanding of all that is involved in testing, from knowledge of the content area and the design of tests to the mathematics establishing validity and reliability. The local school has no authority to change anything about them. They are "standardized" tests to be treated with proper behavioral respect.

At Allwin, all students (no choice allowed here) take these tests several times during their school careers. When they enter the sixth grade, for example, they are given a battery of diagnostic tests for assessing their reading and math levels. Later in the school year, they take nationally normed achievement tests and statewide competency exams. They are the most formally scheduled and recognized occasions for evaluating student competencies, and they proceed quite differently from other kinds of school and classroom activities. For example, when the Iowa Test of Basic Skills was administered, the school schedule was changed to accommodate the testing in a way that allowed students not to miss more than one period of each subject. Letters were sent to parents during the week prior to the exams to announce the testing schedule, to state the importance of the tests for determining student placement, and to ask the parents to make sure their children had as few absences as possible during the testing week. The actual time for the test was handled formally. The students were seated in rows arranged by the teachers, they used paper and pencil supplied by the test company, and they followed instructions read from the testing manuals. In this as in everything else, a major attempt was made to ensure that every individual student had exactly the same conditions to work in as every other. Every attempt was made to break any social network and to force the individual to stand alone against the prescribed task. In all these ways, "fairness" was established. The field, that day, was as level as educational science could make it; all that mattered was individual talent and preparation, genes and earlier socialization.

In this model, the particular school and its agents can indeed withdraw themselves as actors in the identification of the children. The very fact that the tests are not designed by the school makes the point. The school may be responsible for the preparation the children have received, but it withdraws at the moment the race is actually run. Like the coach in a sporting event, the school and the parents can only watch from the sidelines, giving last-minute advice and admonition before giving the floor to the appointed official arbiters and, through them, to the institutions that design the fields on which the race is to be run.

The Social Organization of Sorting:
Meetings in Uncertainty

When the race has been run, the official score as reported by the testing agency is entered into a permanent record and thus becomes an event in the child's history. One cannot escape the reality that has thus been constructed, but this reality, like any other cultural fact, is not determinant. The score is often consequential, but what the consequences are to be is open to negotiation and interpretation by all the people involved. Like those times when political results interact with the media that will report them, what now becomes important is the "spin" that is given to the story behind the actual scores. The score does not in any way *prescribe* what the school, parents, or child must do with them. In fact, testmakers send various warnings that the scores must indeed not be used "mechanically." They are only items to be used in the process that may eventually lead to an actual transformation in the career of the child.[13]

The sorting process is thus a complex of discussions and meetings involving a large number of people: teachers, counselors, administrators, parents, and others. They meet in corridors and lunchrooms and eventually in formal meeting rooms. They talk in general about their opinions, or they examine in some detail the permanent record of the students, affirm what they have always known about a student, or make a call for more information about her and, eventually perhaps, come to a decision that can involve a redirection in the life of the child. In an occasional case, enough time is spent talking that the problem becomes moot.

Meetings for teachers discussing students are a ubiquitous but somewhat hidden aspect of educational life in Allwin. These are times when decisions are made, and none of the ritual guarantees of fairness are observed. Indeed these are the times when the results of the races are deliberately skewed as some students are handicapped and others given head starts. Let us look, for example, at what happened at a meeting at the end of the school year when teachers were placing the students who were moving into junior high from elementary school. The teachers had never met these students, but they had an abbreviated set of facts before them, in particular the scores on various standardized tests. The committee was supposed to sort the children into five different classes in such a way as not to produce an appearance that the classes were tracked. The solution seems easy: Sort them by using some form of random table. This is not what the teachers did. Their first act was to sort the students according to the five traditional ability groups (gifted, high, average, low average, remedial). It was common sense for those involved that this was necessary to ensure that the students from each group would not get distributed disproportionately into one of the final classes. The ability sorting was not itself performed mechanically: Some students with the same grades and test scores were eventually placed in different ability groups. It seems that the stories that could be made about them by looking at the "whole" of their file were different enough to justify differential placement.[14] Once the ability groupings had been made, the randomization of the students into the five classes could proceed.

It would be easy to criticize the teachers for making a mockery of the requirements for fairness, but the sorting requirement was problematic for them. They had had long experiences with ability groupings, and they had lived through many difficult moments as it emerged that "errors" had been made. As some said, moving a student to a higher group was never a problem, but moving a student down was always complex and involved much more work for the teachers and parents. The solution, for some, was to design a curriculum that would reduce the need for sorting. The problem was how to achieve this. It is worthwhile to quote the conversation regarding this issue at length, for it illustrates the paradox the teachers were caught in: The more information they had about the students, the stronger their decision about placement could be, the more "leveling" there could be, the less "leveling" there should have been, and the more legitimate would be the eventual reproduction of the ranked classrooms:

> S: We have to think about how to do the leveling. For the first time they've provided me with each student's name, IQ score, local percentile ranks on the ITBS, third marking period grades and teacher comments. . . . We want our teachers to use this information to set up the groups.
> R: I want to throw it up for suggestions. I was thinking of taking two sixth-grade blocks and have them meet at the same time. . . . Then we could basically come up with two heterogeneously grouped blocks.
> T: What do you mean?
> R: I'm asking how we should group the kids, how you think it should be done.

S: We have to think about how to do the leveling. For the first time we actually got good recommendations and information from the teachers so we should try to do it carefully.

W: I thought the whole idea of the block was going to be that we would take care of students' needs without singling them out. . . . We should make a commitment to either leveling or total integration . . . just, at least for the sixth grade.

S: Well, then, how would we use Fred?[15]

R: Look, we've been living with leveling. I like what Carol is saying. . . . If we don't level on sixth, what are we saying, that we'll level on seventh?

S: I think Joyce would like to eliminate all remedial seventh graders.
   (All laugh)

J: Low average classes to me is a waste.
   (They continue discussing how they could arrange ability levels at each grade level and decide they could adjust the organization by adjusting schedules.)

W: I think we should have no grouping in a formal way . . . and for the seventh and eighth grade we should eliminate all groupings except for the accelerated kids.

R: O.K. for next year, and then later if we need a remedial group, we can make one.

B: Then there's no stigma. Personally, I'd like to see us get into no grouping.

S: Will the groups be small enough to handle remedial kids next year?

W: Twenty or under certainly seems workable to me.

B: Well, if we group heterogeneously, the level of ability won't be an issue any more in replying with parents' requests for teacher change.

J: Well, how will the parents react? . . . You know they like status.

R: They should like it. The sixth grade becomes transitional and a filtering down process so we can make true levels . . . and it will certainly take away from the demotion problems with the enrichment kids.

R, the reading teacher and testing coordinator, summarized the working compromise that is often resorted to in relevant sorting moments in American education: "Leveling" or ranking is postponed for a year so that teachers can establish legitimate ranks in the next grade.[16]

There is much to notice about American education in this discussion. The teachers emphasized their dissatisfaction with ranking, though the exact reason was not clear. There was the information problem, such as the lack of knowledge about individual children, which was momentarily remedied. Paradoxically, the increase in information was presented as something that would make it less necessary to rank; one might have expected that it would have been seen to be an aid to legitimate ranking. There was the problem of the parents who might protest "because they like status." There was the problem that it was more than probable that leveling would be instituted in the seventh grade; so why postpone it? There was also the unanswered question about Fred, the expert on special children: If everybody was treated the same, then he, his expertise in making legitimate distinctions among children, and all the institutions behind him, became unnecessary. But of course he and they were absolutely necessary, since the whole point of the exercise was "to take care of students' needs." The problem lay in taking care of individual students "without singling them out."

This is the same problem that the great American educators have never solved: How can we treat all children the same while treating them all differently? Separation (because children are different) is not compatible with equality. But equality (because all must be treated alike) does not allow for the respect of difference. This is more than a logical or philosophical problem. It is also an experiential problem for any good teacher, sensitive student, or concerned parent. It is something that people worry about, in general and in particular if, as often happens, one's children do not do quite as well as expected. It is also an opportunity for any callous teacher, scheming student, or aggressive parent. After all, if a child "fails" on some objective tests, one may be able to call a friend of a friend and explain the "special" conditions that led to the failure and to offer arguments legitimizing an exceptional administrative decision.

Like all American schools, Allwin Junior High had a formal setting for discussions on special treatment. They were generally referred to as "team meetings," and they were called irregularly, but quite often, when several teachers, separately at first and then together in informal discussion in the teachers' lounge or corridor, had come to the conclusion that "there was a problem" with a student. The meeting was formally scheduled as an occasion for talking about the student, considering all that was known about her. Let us look at how this was done in the case of "Brian Jones":

S: He's absent so much, how can you pass him? He read an eighth-grade novel and got a 48 on the test . . . and he's content with a D.
B: His mother doesn't make him make up the work he misses.
P: Do you think it would help to hold him back?
C: Can we recommend retention?
P: I don't know.
J: He's a sweet child; it just might help him.
R: He's got schoolitis. . . . He's out when the going gets rough.
P: Maybe we should talk to [the principal]. . . . He may need another year, OK? I'll talk to him and let you know.
R: Ya know, he told me in confidence that the biggest mistake he ever made in his life was allowing his father to remarry.
S: He lives with his mother, and he even pays some of the bills in the house. (More discussion about his job, his enjoyment of working with animals, jokes about his being "like one," how unlikely it is that he will ever be able to become a veterinarian's assistant.)
S.: Maybe he should be in the zoo.

P.: OK, let's do this. . . . We'll try to encourage the kid to come to school and do better in every class. I'll talk to [the principal] about recommending retention to the parents.

Note that in this case, the consequences of the teachers' action could be quite dire: Retention at Allwin is about as public a statement of failure as the school can make. Indeed, the closing statement of this sequence was only about "talking" about "recommending." The evaluation was still not cast in stone, and there were still many ways for the evaluation not to prove radically consequential. The principal might decide not to "recommend" retention, particularly if the parents protested and promised remedial action.

The People of Hamden Heights and Their Activity

When looked at from the angle of the everyday activities of the people, the "success" of Allwin Junior High School reveals itself to be anything but mechanical. This success is accomplished meeting after meeting, test after test, indeed, answer to a question after answer to another question, in a complex of small actions that together and from a distance reproduce the position of the school and of many of the participants in relation to other schools in the United States. But one must not mistake this image as one may perceive it from a certain analytic distance with the activity of the people who together, but probably unknowingly, rebuild—or perhaps better, "repair"—what they inhabit. It is only if we approach the issue from the perspective we have adopted throughout the book that we can understand both the constant presence of tests and competitions in the routine of the school and the underlying anxiety of students and parents.

This anxiety must not be overlooked.[17] In the long run, it looks unnecessary, particularly if one considers the statistics about the extent to which the children of professionals, managers, and small entrepreneurs, what we call the "upper-middle class" for lack of a better term, attain positions similar to that of their parents. In the short run, what looms larger for the parents, for the teachers, and also for many of the students is the possibility they will find themselves among those—a statistically not insignificant number—who will, in one way or another "not make it." Newman (1988) has recently documented "downward mobility" in the lives of adults from the middle classes. Failure is not an abstraction for the people of Hamden Heights. Potentially consequential failure is an integral part of their life. It may even be that, to the extent they have more to lose, it is a more fundamental experience than it is for the people who attend West Side High School.

Paul Willis opened his book about working-class "resistance" to schooling with two puzzles: "The difficult thing to explain about how middle class kids get middle class jobs is why others let them. The difficult thing to explain about how working class kids get working class jobs is why they let themselves" (1977: 1). By implication at least, Willis suggested that social reproduction is something actively performed by those involved. In his analytic practice, he was interested only in the activity of working-class kids who "let" other kids get the middle-class jobs. This concern can be misleading unless a related issue is also raised: Given that working-class kids let middle-class kids get middle-class jobs, why is it that middle-class kids work so hard at getting them? Working-class kids do not simply "let" middle-class kids succeed. They are, eventually, defeated in a generalized, altogether impersonal, and still quite real struggle. The middle-class kids and their parents are not passive. They are intimately engaged in a multipronged struggle that they are not at all sure of winning. There is activity, including resistance, in both groups. This activity uses the same tools on the same social field. The eventual success of one group rather than another is not directly based on the differential constitution of each group. It is, first and foremost, determined by the organization of the social field, by the identification of the actors, routes, and rewards, by the design of the various and other performances one must go through at one point or another.

What is fascinating about Allwin as a social field is precisely the way its daily life is organized around displays of routine failure. As we mentioned, most tests are failed by most kids. This is particularly true of competitions built on the model of sporting events. Indeed, the import of the racing metaphor for education and life is that only one person will win the race, only one person will become "president of the United States." Everyone else will have to play second, third, or even no fiddle at all. Even CEOs can get dismissed. Failure is always possible and increasingly possible for the middle class in America. On tests too, most experience relative failure. A 75 is not an 85 is not a 95, and only a few students will receive the last grade. All the others will know that they did not quite measure up even if some would agree with one student who told his mother: "B is cool, Mom!" Well, a B is not enough to get one into an Ivy League college, and parents are sensitive to the difference a B makes.

Mutualities in Success and Failure

Our discussion of the inconsequential successes of the students of West Side High School emphasized the broader identification of West Side as a school for "students who had failed," and we showed how the students displayed themselves in just the right way to justify their identification. In this chapter, we have made a similar and opposite argument about Allwin; eventually, everyone got organized to justify the identification of the children as successes through routine, but not overwhelming or consequential, failure. In both cases, we also emphasized the activity of the people involved. No one was passive. Everyone was at work with what was given, that is, with what had been made or facted for them.

As we conclude Part 1, we want to restate our main point. Culturally, success and failure are aspects of the same fact. People in the United States do success and failure. They work hard at it. They measure it and relish their findings. They even play at it! They are also willing to risk making life miserable for many children. As cultural fact, the success/failure complex will have its say. It will acquire people to be displayed as a success or failure even if there are only two persons to divide the spoils. Wisdom lies in finding the time to step back and uncover the America that hides behind the very struggles to explain a person's failure or to ensure a person's success.

This America was the same for all the people we have looked at in this book— from Adam to the overachievers of Allwin. The differences among their lives as they experienced them had to do with differences in their initial position within the social organization of the United States, in the resources available to them as they and their parents went on to construct their lives, and, more important, in their relationships to each other as these evolved in the course of their lives.

Adam's problem came from the fact he was noticed as fitting well in an educational category for children who learned more slowly than others. Joe and Sheila were also at constant risk of being noticed, though in fact they were not. What was interesting about their cases was the differences between the resources their families used to deal with their conditions. In a next turn, we might have shown how neighborhoods can differentiate themselves and thus offer new constraints and opportunities with which the people must work. Kingsland is a different place to grow up in than nearby Hasidic Williamsburg or inner-city Bedford-Stuyvesant. And Kingsland was a different place forty years ago than it was when we conducted our work. The overall structure of success and failure allows for diversity by neighborhood, family, and even individual child, but it takes its toll nonetheless. Our descriptive goal was not to catalog contingent and transient diversity. Our goal was to analyze how local particularizing activity articulates with the major constraints that no one who is caught by America can escape.

At the Inn of the Good Shepherd, we saw people working hard to be successful, but we could find no connection between what happened in the choir and any institutionalized attribution of success. It was as if the overall structure of opportunity that dropped these young adults onto the streets of New York was also poised to erase whatever accomplishments they might have performed. It is not so much that culture determines individual behavior as it arranges for the situated interpretation of behavior. At the inn, whatever the success the students could generate, there appeared to be no interpretive materials that could take up success and display it to the world.

At West Side, teachers and students were organized to attempt to mitigate the effects of the result of the success and failure wars that had been fought in the twelve years before the students needed a remedial high school. The teachers were well aware that whatever approaches had been used earlier to teach the students and make them display their knowledge, they had proven insufficient. There was a sense of emergency, if not desperation, as new and more or less experimental approaches got tried, whatever the likelihood they would prove useful. Something had to be done. Rizzo-Tolk focused on homelessness as something that the students knew about and that they might experience in their own lives. They had friends who had joined the ranks, but they initially greeted the topic with hostility and raucous humor. Months later, after a range of interesting experiences with homeless people, they were poised on the verge of displaying that they were successful in ways recognizable by educators assembled for the occasion. Teachers and students put together a small-group discussion of what to do if one were to become homeless. The students worked at it, they completed the task on schedule, but they did it in such a way that their identification in school terms remained ambiguous: Perhaps they did "learn"; perhaps they did not. More important, they performed, among many other signs, the one thing that may be taken to demonstrate that they did not learn much about homelessness: They laughed, and those who listened heard them laughing *at* the homeless. The teachers had set out to cheat the cultural structure, but it was their efforts that were erased. Again, the behavior of the students as it might be identified in an abstract social space is not at issue here. Figuring out through various tests whether the students "really learned" would not have made much difference. What is at issue are the connections of their behavior to ongoing institutional possibilities that brought the overall structure of the society down around their heads. The students were doing their job. They were trying to be successful.

At Allwin, the students were treated to an equally complete immersion in the success and failure attribution games America offered them. These were the same cultural games the students of West Side were obliged to play. There was but one culture, and it was not controlled by any of the participants in any of the localities we entered. The tests that diagnosed Adam's learning disability or Sheila's success were the same tests that were given to the children of Allwin, and the evaluation of individual talent proceeded in much the same manner as at the Inn of the Good Shepherd. Above all, one must realize that nothing that was used with such effect in Hamden Heights had evolved locally. All material objects found there had been bought, all institutions borrowed. "America" is not the culture "of" the people of Hamden Heights. It is not the culture of a group or a class. It is, rather, the pattern that organizes people into groups and classes, landscapes that organize the social field where the people can be found. It is the pattern that links all together.

This is not to say there was a greater fit between what the children of Hamden Heights learned at home and what they were assumed to know at school than there may have been in Manhattan Valley. The students of Allwin were probably quite comfortable in their school, but comfort is not all they experienced when they walk its corridors. As human beings, actors who had to construct their day, they could not simply be who they were identified by others to be. They could not passively rely on the actuarial tables that predicted career success through the background characteristics of their parents. At Allwin, every day, the students were faced with the reverse possibility: Everyone organized their world to reveal how they would fail if they let down their guard for a minute. There may have been wide safety nets to catch them should they fall, but still, day in and day out, they had to always work hard at school and thus make it harder for the students of West Side to catch up.

Work and Resistance in Culture

Our use of the word "work" at this juncture is deliberately multifaceted. As we conclude this first part of the book we must begin to sort out the various paradigms to which it points. First, and most safely perhaps, "work" points to a way of looking at human action that we have learned from a particular tradition within sociology known as ethnomethodology. Work can also point to the commonsense understanding we might find in the phrase "working (rather than "leisure") class." The people of Hamden Heights, adults and children, get up in the morning and then go to work. Work is not play—even if they enjoy their work. It is tiring, if not painful, and the people do a lot of it, however one might want to define it. They may do more work than the students of West Side, whose major problem derives from the fact they and their parents do not have enough work (jobs, careers) to do. The people of Hamden Heights would often blame the people of West Side for not working or not wanting to work. They would point to the many hours of homework and other such activities their own children were accomplishing. In this perspective, material rewards are the legitimate results of "hard work," that is, unpleasant, routine, repetitive work that does not appear to accomplish much—work like, say, the completion of endless sentences in language-comprehension workbooks. This kind of hard work, whatever else it should result in, can result in an increased facility in taking language-comprehension tests. Practice does make perfect, and the continual competitions found in Allwin may help individual students gain a winning edge over those who do not practice quite as much.

Depending on their ideological expansion, statements about the functionality of work can easily become controversial. If the people of West Side worked, it is argued in certain circles, then they would be successful too. This, of course, does not follow, since individual success is dependent on the work that others do. In this sentence, we do mean "work" in a sense that combines the commonsense understanding and the ethnomethodological one. Work, from our perspective, indexes both a determined activity by an actor—whatever the content of the activity—and the factual product of the activity: work "facts." Work produces objects or services in the traditional economic sense. But these are worthless unless they can be made to fit within a social field where they can be used for social purposes.[18] Work also produces social conditions for the actor, for those who work with the actor, and for those who have to work within the conditions they have made. By "working," parents generate the income they spend on their children's education; there is extensive work in the many hours of homework and tedious workbook exercises that the children have to do; the many "educational" (watching *Sesame Street* or *Nova* on TV) or paraeducational (taking trips to foreign lands and such) activities that the parents of Hamden Heights offer their children must also be understood as work. All this is involved in the final product, but we argue it is imperative that the list of work people do must include the interactional work they do with each other. There are the bake sales parents organize or the telephone calls they make to ask advice from teachers. There are also occasions when a laugh, a cry, or any other comment is sequenced to affirm that all is where it should be in a well-ordered world. Eventually, all this work establishes the identification of the child in the collective discourse of the teachers and administrators who give the grades and recommendations that will help the child enter this rather than that college.[19] It is in this sense that we can say that the work of the people in Hamden Heights, because they fear failure and prod their children always to work harder (no matter how senseless the tasks), produces conditions both for themselves and for the students of West Side to be what they are taken to be.

We also framed some aspects of this work in the vocabulary of what Geertz called "deep play" (1973a). We might also have invoked Victor Turner's theories of performance to catch both the symbolic seriousness of what these people were doing and the work involved in actually organizing the games and competitions that best represented the cultural conditions that framed Hamden Heights, its educative institutions, and those of Manhattan Valley, twenty miles away. Theories of symbolic action couched in a nonfunctionalist vocabulary are often taken to be removed from the material life of the people involved. We were led to such theories because of the peculiar place of classroom games and competitions in the overall activity of the people. How else were we to understand the peculiar shape of something like "Screw Thy Neighbor" and its efficacy both as a source of entertainment and as a source of the kind of educational "practice"[20] that helps students learn the content on which they will later be quizzed and tested? In such games, education is made fun, but it is important that it is made fun in precisely the way we indicated. The games may not be functional, but they do function to affirm what the world is like: It is a world in which neighbors screw each other[21] within a controlled field.

The previous sentence can be uttered only in a joking, or politically radical, context. In sacred contexts, these cultural facts must be represented through the extended displays of racing on a fair ground—thus the performative structure of standardized tests and such. The "screwing" is done through the various meetings when test results are transformed into the consequential total identity of the child after being considered with all other available information—including whatever pressure the parents have put on the teachers. Of course, this is not known as "screwing" but as taking into account the special needs of a child, and it is done in ritualized secrecy where privacy is maintained.

Nothing in all this was simple for the people of Hamden Heights. If one suggested to the participants that "screwing" and "taking care" might be structured in equivalent ways, they would be shocked, if not outraged. Parents pressuring teachers, teachers closing their eyes to student misbehavior, school districts manipulating test results—all this may happen, but it should not happen; nor can it easily be said to happen given the consequences of such publicity. The problem is that tests and competitions, and the continual talk that reconstructs their results for future use, are the central cultural forms organizing Allwin, and they are too powerful to be ignored. They are also the most problematic of performances: As Mary Douglas once wrote about the fundamental rituals of any human group, the closer one gets to the sacred, the greater the danger (1966). For the middle class, as for everyone else, a particular act performed at the right moment can have consequences that are all the more radical for being legitimate—they mark the recipient as a particular person of a particular kind within a system of identifications. Such legitimacy, and such identifications, are not the simple property of a class position. They must be worked on in an uncertain future.

We mentioned the anxiety of the parents as a means of stressing their activity and perhaps even what we might call their resistance to their cultural conditions. In the case of Brian Jones, the student threatened with retention, a set of identifications for the child and his mother were constructed by the school. These identifications became a fact for the parents, and their resistance was assumed. If the mother did not resist, this might have been used to demonstrate that the teachers' identification of her as a "woman who does not care" was justified. Still, there were certain things the teachers wanted to do but did not do because they knew through experience that the parents would object. Parents, of course, did object, but objection was only one of the means through which they could resist. The organization of bake sales can also be seen as a means of resistance ("the school will see that we are caring parents and that Joe comes from a good home"), and so should tutoring, paying for a SAT preparation course, and even perhaps voting to raise the real estate taxes on their homes, sending their children to a private school, or otherwise distributing the inheritance that they might otherwise have been building.

When Jules Henry titled his book on American education *Culture Against Man* (1963), he was talking as a humanist appalled at the way a cultural system could silence an individual's self. Our book could have been titled (with due apologies to shifting trends in gender talk) *Man Against Culture* to emphasize our understanding that "man," that is, human beings, are never defeated in this struggle. People are always active and pushing the limits of the conditions they are given. The upper-middle class, like the other "working classes" does not maintain its position by relying on the kind of cultural predestination that theorists of culture know as early socialization. Success is not the inevitable product of the purported fit between family and school environments. Those who win in America do not win because they impose "their" culture on people with "different" cultures. America is imposed on all people in the United States, and all resist it with varying consequences.

NOTES

This chapter is based on Shelley Goldman's dissertation (1982) and on Goldman and McDermott (1987). The high school in the town that is closest to Hamden Heights was studied by Varenne (1983). Related research was conducted by Joyce Canaan in another nearby town (1986, 1990). One might also consult Moffatt's (1989) study of student life at Rutgers, Ortner's work (1993) on remembrances of life in a Newark high school, and Taylor and Dorsey-Gaines (1988) on literacy in inner-city families in Newark to conclude an ethnographic overview of a child's progress through the schools of New Jersey in the 1970s and 1980s.

1. For a more detailed historical interplay between high progressivism (as Dewey attempted to inscribe it) and practical progressivism (as inscribed in the institutional evolution of the American school, its curriculum, tests, and attendants), see Cremin (1961, 1988). Lagemann

(1989, 1992) gives further details about the process that transformed a subtle concern with the individual to be shaped into a citizen into a set of practices intended to measure the extent of the shaping.

2. For a classic statement, see C. Wright Mills (1956).

3. On the development of "objective" testing as a tool against elitism, and for democratization, the discussions by Gould (1981) and others (Jacoby and Glauberman 1995) are interesting. See also Eckstein and Noah (1993).

4. As we have done in other recent publications, and as Varenne justified elsewhere (1986, 1987), we are distinguishing between a political space ("the United States") and the ideology that is dominant there ("America"). Those who must act in any public space in the United States must do so in terms set by America, whether they agree with them or not, whether indeed they are aware of the sources of that which resists them. Whether continued action in such a field makes one an "American" is something which, precisely, we always want to keep problematic.

5. In the most classic of them, Rosenthal and Jacobsen (1968) focused only on the attitudes of individuals arranging more or less unconsciously for prophecies of success and failure to be proven true. Cultural accounts instead focus on the symbolic order in terms of which particular attitudes are made available to individuals in particular settings (Spindler 1959; McDermott and Aron 1978). They must now proceed to show that concrete work must be performed for the prophecy to be seen as having proven true.

6. Lest one think any of this is new or a phenomenon of the 1980s, all that we are reporting here was discussed by Jules Henry for the early 1950s (1963) and by Robert and Helen Lynd for the 1920s ([1929] 1956: 218). Our analysis is an extension of Henry's, though we do not talk about the "absurdity" of the tests and competitions. It is becoming clear that tests are used for many reasons. Page (1991) has shown them being used, for example, as a sign for identification. We generalize this to emphasize their fundamental efficacy as reconstructions of, commentaries on, and resistance to a fundamental cultural pattern.

7. See Mehan (1979, 1982).

8. On the former, see Foley (1990); on the latter, see Jackall (1988).

9. This may be one of the major ways American historical processes have transformed the fundamental structures of democratic ideology: in France, for example, there are almost no occasions for students to organize themselves into teams. The teaming probably has to do with the strength of the community ideology in American culture (Varenne 1977).

10. The label obviously cross-references a supposedly academic activity with sports, particularly football with its "bowls" at the end of the season.

11. Indeed, they are considered dangerous only to the extent that a winner or loser may misinterpret the success. Updike's famous Rabbit series is the story of a man who overinterpreted his success as a high school basketball star. By definition this must be a rare occurrence. More common are the students who interpret their failure as more than what it is culturally constructed to be. For the same problems handled differently in another culture, see Moore (1975) on African marriages and Plath (1980, 1983) and Rohlen (1980, 1983, 1993) for Japanese schooling and career paths.

12. This, of course, parallels what Geertz saw in the Balinese cockfight, namely, an occasion to reaffirm the evolving social organization of the local group.

13. As is well known, an interesting aspect of American education is the absence of the national exams that control in a rather absolute fashion educational results in Europe or Asia (Eckstein and Noah 1993; Miyazaki 1976; Amano 1990). In France, as in most other coun-

tries, individual results on the most ritual of exams, the *baccalauréat*, are not open to educational negotiation: A failure to pass is an absolute event. Admission to the *grandes écoles*, special colleges that almost guarantee entry into the managerial classes, is also based on examinations that leave no room for any consideration of the special circumstances that might mitigate for or against a particular score. Matters are closer to the American pattern at less sacred times (for example, on promotion to the next class or tracking).

14. This is a process that has been observed in other studies. See Cicourel and Kitsuse (1963) and Erickson, F. and Shultz (1982) for a discussion of the role of guidance counselors in the ranking of students.

15. Fred is the reading and exceptional children's specialist.

16. A variation on this process is well documented in Colin Lacey's *Hightown Grammar* (1970). In the English context of a school for the very best of students that can be selected from other schools, he traces the reproduction of academic stratification as they differentiate into top, average, and bottom.

17. Sherry Ortner (1993) has begun to talk about her difficulties in getting adult middle-class informants to talk about anything other than their fears about their children when she wanted them to talk about their own educational experiences.

18. Bourgois (1996) gives the case of an illiterate drug dealer who had purchased three luxury cars but did not have a driver's license and had no legitimate means to get one.

19. Note that this particular set of activities depends on the constitution of the particular culture of schooling. In a system like France's, where national exams are made to be absolute sorting moments when the identity of the child is specifically destroyed, upper-middle-class parents have no reason to get to know the teacher of their children personally to help establish this identity.

20. The word has interesting properties here, since it can index both activity such as playing scales on a piano ("Have you practiced your piano today?") and the general activities theorists like Bourdieu want us to consider when they talk about "theories of practice."

21. Note that the game is named to make an ironic reference to the Biblical injunction "Love thy neighbor." It can be understood as an ironic critique of the kind of Protestant religiosity to which the children and adults were regularly exposed. It was also a reaffirmation of "love" because it emphasized that screwing is precisely what should be mocked. By placing the irony within the context of a game with a joke title, the critique deconstructed itself as critique: It was, after all, done in jest for fun. It was not a serious matter.

PART TWO

Education and the
Making of Cultural Facts

6 Disability as a Cultural Fact

Hervé Varenne and Ray McDermott

In our five stories of people at work in the School America makes, we labored implicitly within a political tradition deeply concerned with democracy in education, a tradition that insists rhetorically that all human beings have similar opportunities to develop themselves. This concern has a social scientific aspect where it takes the form of a charge to offer systematic understandings of what might make it difficult to construct democratic institutions. This charge is an old one, and over the past century, it has developed in such a way as to present current theorists with two problems that we are trying to solve, first through the case studies we presented in the first part of the book and now through a theoretical discussion of the ways the charge has been handled and how it might be handled more powerfully. The first problem is descriptive and the second one theoretical. Actually, they are the same problem twice, but they can be stated quite differently. We emphasize the first in this chapter and the second in the next chapter.

The descriptive problem lives in any account of a person's trajectory through the School. It has two sides:

1. How can such accounts be written without suggesting that this trajectory is the person's sole doing?
2. How can they be written without reducing the person to a mere leaf in the social winds?

Starting an account with the person as subject easily leads to blaming (or pitying) persons for what they cannot do or to celebrating them for what they can do. Starting with the collective and writing of the person as an object of social forces leads to an equally impossible position, descriptively as well as politically. Nothing—neither degradation nor celebration—accrues to the person. Everyone is left without rationality or intelligence, without agency or appreciation—a stance that the kind of descriptive work we have been conducting directly belies.

There is a way around the descriptive problem: Start with historical conditions as structured tools to be carefully accounted for while showing how persons manipulate these conditions and make new ones for each other. This procedure does not turn the person into a cipher. Quite the contrary, it acknowledges that the history of the world, in the most local as well as in the most general sense, is always a "present" (a contemporary given) that cannot be wished away and that must never be analytically ignored. Reforms and revolutions do not abolish history but make new history for future generations to deal with and remake. History does not determine. Even when faced with overwhelming forces in total institutions, people resist; they always do more or less than is required by the institutional context. In so doing, they always inflect the history of their most local conditions. Sometimes, they impact the history of their broader conditions. And often their activity disappears.

Adam and Joe, the children of focus in Chapters 1 and 2, faced a difficult life if they did not get better at school, and the young adults in the choir and the homeless class were already living lives constrained by restricted opportunities. In each case we tried to write accounts that pointed to the active and productive strength people bring to their local conditions while also showing how much they are forced to deal with what is already there in the world around them. We offered accounts affirming the political and moral point that they are not restricted people even though they may have restricted lives. They are indubitably people at work, taking careful account of their actual conditions. They are full agents, if not "free" agents.

All people in the world face restrictions to the extent they live their lives with others. There is no humanity to single human beings except through interaction with other human beings—even if the interaction is indirect, painful, and most of the relevant others are dead.[1] No one, whatever the conditions, is a free agent with the right to name the time and place of activity. Agency is always limited in its initial conditions and process, and the restrictions are always particular to a time and place. They are historical, constructed, "cultural" in our sense. They are also fully real and consequential, often dramatically so. To paraphrase David Plath, the particular tools with which all people must author their lives limit them in particular ways, and these tools include the people who authorize their lives. In the American context, few tools are more powerful in what they allow people to author than the sorting apparatus visibly at work at Allwin Junior High. The students had fun taking tests they did not design. But they did not think much about the extent to which this placed them under the authority of people far removed from them, their parents, and any "community" to which they might have belonged. They accepted the fields that had been leveled for them and then competed on them. They did not seem to care overly about failing most of the tests or about becoming the object of those who authorized the tests—perhaps because they expected soon to join their ranks. Mostly, they behaved as if all this was the most natural thing to do. As anthropologists, we have to take the stance that all this activity is not the most natural thing for human beings to do. The whole institution of Testing is a product, a tool that shapes what people who use it can themselves produce. Our theoretical task is to lay the tool on the table for analysis, "from the outside," so to speak—even as we continue to use the tool. We are quite aware that as human beings in America, we too live our lives with sorting and Testing, but we can struggle with it.

We opened our work with Maxine Hong Kingston because she can stand for any "successful" person—a person no one would be ashamed to have as a child. Staying with others like her would have kept the political problem of inequality at bay, but this could not have lasted for long. As soon as we introduced her sister, we brought the problem of differential performance to the fore: How could we *not* ask why Maxine did better than her sister (according to the normal tenets of those who authorize such questions)? Why did the sister *not* become a famous author? This question is patently unfair, particularly if framed within the failure vocabulary one cannot escape when working with educationists. It is the fundamental question of educational psychology, and one we struggle to escape. The problem is not solved by shifting our attention from the Kingston family and its individual members to the ethnic group with which Maxine identifies herself. Shifting the analysis to Maxine Hong Kingston's ethnicity leads by a strange fatality to a comparison of the "success" of the Chinese to that of other groups and the celebration of what "voluntary migrants" (Ogbu 1987, 1991a, 1991b) can do in the United States that others cannot do. This comparative conversation brings us back to competition (between teams rather than individuals), and this does not represent much progress.

We refuse to enter into this conversation even as we examine its mechanisms. We do not want to explain success and failure. We do want to figure out what people are talking about when they try to explain success or failure. We want to trace the consequences of this very attempt at explaining. In Part 1, we did this by focusing on the details of the lives of various people in various situations. In Part 2, we do this by examining the ways of writing among theorists caught in the same conversation. Maxine Hong Kingston may not have competed with her sister, but others can set them against each other nonetheless. Similarly, the Chinese in California may not have thought of themselves as competing with other kinds of migrants, but others have been doing the comparison for them. Social scientists have defined the parameters of the competition (income, educational level, status, etc.), and they have been keeping score. The competition Maxine Hong Kingston and her Chinese neighbors have not been able to escape has also dominated the theoretical writing of social scientists working on the School. On a moment-to-moment basis, to be in America is to be always on call for a relative ranking in some kind of competition. There is no way we can describe anyone's trajectory through the American maze without taking into account that the maze is *always already there* before the people show up and that they are always at work with it, diem ex die, hour to hour, and moment to moment. In Part 1 of the book we showed how the competitive frame dominated the organization of any setting accountable to the School. In Part 2, we try to make the same case for the social sciences that study children working their way through school by focusing first on descriptions of this work and then on theories.

The descriptive problem overlaps with a central concern in contemporary social theory, namely, the relationship between culture (that which is always already there) and person (that which has never been there), between human products (e.g., the American School) and the productive human being (e.g., Adam wondering how to make it a good day). In our accounts of the five settings that make up Part 1, we often invoked culture (rather than community or identity) as the conceptual key we would need to describe both the complexity of the individuals under analysis and the complexity of the situation that the American School organized for them. So the three chapters of Part 2 take up the theoretical complexities of using any concept of culture.

Raymond Williams (1977) has described culture as one of the most difficult words to define in this century. No one definition can clarify the situation, but our concern is not definitional. This is not a work in culture theory, at least not directly. Any use of the term has definite consequences for description and analysis. Each use of the term directs attention to certain phenomena, allows certain analyses, and likely hides aspect of humanity that should be highlighted. Different uses of the term are differently consequential, and it is the relationship between types of use and types of potential consequences that we want to explore in these three chapters. Eventually, we hope to have justified an understanding of culture that is both grounded in the history of the use of the term and yet, we hope, more careful in its implications. It is an understanding that emphasizes human beings as constrained and constraining agents: people in culture making culture for their peers in the present and the future in proportion to their current position and the authority that comes with it.

The current chapter proceeds as follows. We begin the discussion of theories of culture and their use in the ethnography of the American School by offering two brief examples from the literature on physical disability. These should complement our five case studies by suggesting how the same approach can be used to analyze other situations when possibly difficult personal characteristics, such as deafness or blindness, are expanded culturally into major social problems while potentialities inherent in the very characteristic are blocked. The cases should thus help us sketch more starkly our fundamental argument about the impact of cultural facts on the lives of all. What Adam suffers at the hands of others when he has to read and write in school is nothing compared to the treatment of people with more constant physical disabilities.

When the esteemed anthropologist Robert Murphy found himself in a wheelchair due to a tumor around his spinal column, he went to a meeting at his local political club and met there an up and coming politico who at first did not recognize Murphy in his new circumstances. When Murphy reintroduced himself, the man looked quite shocked and wondered how a thing like that could happen to a person of such stature. "A thing like," "a person of"—what could he have been talking about? Was Murphy too successful to get a tumor? Was he too enabled intellectually by his surroundings to be disabled by a disease? Being squeezed into a wheelchair was one kind of problem. Being squeezed out of full participation from the various institutions he had been so successful in was a far greater problem (Murphy 1987).

We focus on people without sight and then people without hearing to show how their problems stem only incidentally from what they cannot do and much more radically from the ways others further limit their movement and participation. This is the same theme struck throughout our earlier chapters, namely, that the problems many people have in the American School stem only incidentally from what they can or cannot do and much more radically from the way they are treated by others in relation to the designation, assignment, and distribution of more or less temporary or partial difficulties interpreted as success or failure and responded to in the terms of the Testing world.

The examples from studies of physical difficulties help us to frame Disability as a major trope in the institutionalized ups and downs of success and failure in the American School. Over the past forty years, there has been a tremendous rise in the number of categories for describing children as disabled, and our descriptive problems have become even more complex. As a cultural fact, learning disabilities seem to have moved front and center as more and more children fill the new slots opened for them. Although designed at first to mediate the strength of the division between successful and failing children in school, and despite the goodwill of many people, the LD (Learning Disabled) designation is becoming a handicap to those who bear the label; they now have a new way to fail in school. Learning disabilities have moved from personal characteristics to become the foundation and justification for a major institution that has expanded the reach of Testing in the School and must now acquire children and instructors in ever larger crowds—with more and more radical consequences for the children, and indeed the professional adults, who are caught.

In the second part of this chapter, we model two uses of "culture" and their different understandings of development and disability. First, we use early attempts by Erik Erikson and Oscar Lewis to account, descriptively and theoretically, for the difficulties of growing up in the wrong environment. Second, we consider current efforts by Shirley Heath and John Ogbu to deal with what they deem to be the learning problems of the disenfranchised. In each case, we find a use of the concept of culture that, more or less wittingly, delivers a psychology that obscures the role of cultural facts in the organization of problems. In the process of this critique, we develop the presentation of our own attempts at confronting similar issues in such a way as to deliver a social science that preserves the agency of the person.

In Chapter 7, we continue the same exercise, but in relation to a wider range of issues than the ethnography of schooling in the United States. More specifically, we try to show that social thought in America has always been overly invested in a psychology that leaves little room for a social and cultural imagination, and we point to two current movements, the emergence of a cultural psychology and the Americanization of the work of Pierre Bourdieu, to make our case. Next (in Chapter 8), Varenne focuses on the close-grained descriptive work originally done by McDermott without use of a concept of culture, and he translates it into the language of this book as a way of illustrating how one might describe a child in difficulty while emphasizing both her agency and the conditions she finds and makes for herself and her peers.

Describing Difficulties as Disabilities: Sightedness

In his short story "The Country of the Blind," H. G. Wells ([1904] 1979) tells of a man by the name of Nunez who finds himself on a peak in the Andes. He falls to

what should have been his death and finds himself miraculously dropped into an isolated valley populated exclusively by congenitally blind persons. Nunez is not particularly nice, and he senses only opportunities. He can see, and they cannot. The
world is his, for, he figures, "in the Country of the Blind, the One-eyed Man is
King" ([1904] 1979: 129). Almost instantly, Nunez runs into trouble. The Country
of the Blind is, of course, wired for people who cannot see:

> It was marvelous with what confidence and precision they went about their ordered
> world. Everything, you see, had been made to fit their needs; each of the radiating paths
> of the valley area had a constant angle to the others, and was distinguished by a special
> notch upon its curbing; all obstacles and irregularities or path or meadow had long since
> been cleared away; all their methods and procedures arose naturally from their special
> needs (135).

"Everything, you *see*," writes Wells, showing the difficulty of a seeing person explaining a Country of the Blind, where there was no word for "see" or any words for
things that could be seen. If Wells had written, "Everything, you hear" or "Everything, you smell," he might have made more sense, but not to Nunez: "Four days
passed, and the fifth found the King of the Blind still incognito, as a clumsy and useless stranger among his subjects" (134). From bad, things get worse until the people
of the valley decide on a definition of the problem and a solution. Their surgeon says
that his eyes are diseased: "They are greatly distended, he has eyelashes, and his eye-
lids move, and consequently his brain is in a state of constant irritation and destruc-
tion" (142). The only solution is to cut them out of his head, and Nunez finds himself with little choice but to flee up the mountain.

The perfect unit for displaying the wisdom of the people (and the stupidity of the
visitor) in the Country of the Blind is what anthropologists call "culture," a term
most commonly used to gloss particular and localized sets of rules for mutual understanding and then to argue that human populations are separated from each other by
their particular ways of making sense and meaning. In the Country of the Blind, a
one-eyed man is confused and confusing. This is what it is like to be in another culture. With time, perhaps if he had been a decent person or if he had been an anthropologist, Nunez could have learned their ways well enough to fit in and perhaps to
write an ethnography of their particular version of wisdom.

There is a downside to the use of the term "culture" as a set of rules for understanding. Even a century ago, it was rare for a people to be as isolated as H. G. Wells
imagined. Conditions of the anthropologist's arrival have usually been worked out in
advance, if not by actual contact with the people being visited, then by the visitor
and the visited having somehow been brought together by their respective places in
the wider world order. Margaret Mead never fell down a mountain into a new tribe;
a retinue of colonial officials, porters, and secretaries eased her way. Even H. G.
Wells had to build a point of contact into his fiction: The people in the Country of
the Blind, isolated for fourteen generations before Nunez's arrival, spoke an old ver-

sion of Spanish that, minus the visual vocabulary, Nunez could use to figure out where he stood.

There is a second problem. To talk about a country of the blind is to make a hypothesis about the coherence of institutions particularly well suited to one interpretation of blindness. Is it also, in much of the literature that uses the concept of culture, in anthropology and even more so in related disciplines that are now discovering the concept, to make a hypothesis about the people who must live in this country. It seems to make sense to assume that cultural coherence is the result and cause of people being the same psychologically or experientially. It makes common sense to write phrases about people "being members of a culture," of their "belonging to a culture," and even of their owning a culture that is said to be "theirs." The language of sharing, consensus, community, is so powerful it is easy to miss everything else that is significant to the people described. One can understand why we say this by looking at what happens "at home," among neighbors. At home, it is not similarity that stands out but discord and disagreement. From our point of view, the coherence of a culture is crafted from the partial and mutually dependent knowledge of each person caught in the process. It is constituted, in the long run, by the work they do together. Human life, Bakhtin ([1940] 1984) reminds us, is polyphonous and multivocalic; it is made of the voices of many, each one brought to life and made significant by the others, only sometimes by being the same, more often by being different, more dramatically by being contradictory. This world is the temporary product of people placing each other with the well-structured tools already available. Whether they become "the same" in this process is open to debate. We can think of culture as the very process of shaping a world. It may still be appropriate to write about "a culture" as a pattern of institutions more or less linked and coherent with each other, but one must fear this use when it leads to hypotheses about individuals struggling with these institutions. Thick brushstroke accounts of Samoans or Balinese, to stay with Margaret Mead, may give some hints as to what Samoans and Balinese must deal with in their daily lives, but they can greatly distort the complexity of Samoans and Balinese as people.

This is more than an obscure theoretical point. One's more or less explicit position on these matters can have serious consequences when dealing with the apparent "exceptions" to some generalizations (like being sighted in the Country of the Blind). Fifty years of experience in the social sciences and psychology as it applies to disabilities, physical and otherwise, demonstrate the ease with which having personal access to exceptional and special properties can become a lack to be remedied. Before entering the Country of the Blind, Nunez thought that sight was essential to being fully human and that having sight in a world of people who could not see would net him the cultural capital of a king. He was wrong. A culture that coheres around blindness is a distinct human possibility, and in such a culture, sightedness could always be treated as a problem caused by the sighted. We do not want to suggest either that the Country of the Blind had only one way to be, and there is some suggestion that H. G. Wells knew that too. He writes of Nunez's betrothed, a blind woman who enjoyed his illusions of sightedness and who could well understand his marginal position given that she too had been pushed aside by an appearance that included eye sockets that to the hand seemed to be full. In the Country of the Blind, even a sightless woman can be made disabled.[2]

The Fabrication of a Cultural Disability: Deafness

For the two centuries before our own, the people on Martha's Vineyard, a small island off the coast of Cape Cod, Massachusetts, suffered, or some might say were privileged by, a high rate of genetically inherited deafness—approximately 1 person in every 155. It is easy to use the word "suffered" to evoke sympathy from hearing persons for the plight of the deaf. It is a physical difference that can count, and it is not unusual for deaf people to suffer terribly because of the way it is made to count in various social settings. It is not clear that the people of Martha's Vineyard would share the horror with which most hearing Americans approach deafness. Although it was definitely the case that the Vineyard deaf could not hear, it was also the case that they had the means to turn not hearing into something that everyone in the community could easily work with, work around, and turn into a strength. In Nora Groce's (1985) history, we are given a picture of deaf persons thoroughly integrated into the life of their community and the hearing thoroughly integrated into the communicational intricacies of sign. When surviving older members of the community were asked to remember deaf neighbors, they could not always remember who among them had been deaf, for everyone there spoke sign language, sometimes even hearing people with other hearing people.

The case of the Vineyard deaf raises questions about the nature of disability, the same questions forced on Nunez and confronted daily by the Israeli sightless (Deshen 1992), questions that go beyond etiology to function and circumstance: *When does a physical difference count, under what conditions and in what ways and for what reasons?* When, how, and why: These are, of course, the questions anthropologists have learned must always be asked of any act by a person or quality that this person might sometimes be said to have. From the accounts we summarized, it is clear that, depending on how a physical difference is noticed, identified, and made consequential, the lives of those unable to do something can be either enabled or disabled by those around them. From Martha's Vineyard, there is good news: It is possible to organize a culture in which deafness does not isolate a person from a full round in the life of a community; not being able to hear can cut off behavioral possibilities that can be taken care of in other ways, and by everyone speaking sign, other possibilities can be explored. There is also bad news: Martha's Vineyard was not an island unto itself but a peripheral area in a larger social field within which deafness was made into an appalling affliction.

On Martha's Vineyard, people had jobs to do, and they did them. That one person could do them faster or better than another was likely less important than that the jobs got done. In such a world, it was not important to sort out the deaf institutionally from the hearing. By almost every social measure, for example, rates of marriage and propinquity, economic success, and mastery of a trade, deaf persons were indistinguishable from hearing persons on Martha's Vineyard. There is a record of an unbalanced deaf person in the community, but the order to have him committed to an institution did not emphasize his deafness as part of his problem and was, in fact, signed by a deaf person. It is possible to organize a culture in which the deaf play an equal and unremarkable role in most parts of life. On Martha's Vineyard, when it was time to hospitalize a troubled person, a deaf person could be asked to play either side of the culturally constructed divide between the unbalanced and the incarcerator, but not either side of the culturally irrelevant divide between hearing and deaf.

Unfortunately, deaf persons on Martha's Vineyard were not treated well by outsiders who could not sign, and the fortunes of the deaf declined as the island opened up to extensive tourism. That they could not hear was made worse by outsiders who pitied them, wrote them up in Boston newspapers, explained their origin in scientific tracts (one popular claim was that their deafness was a result of a melancholy suffered by their mothers), called for a remedy for their situation, and suggested a eugenics program for their erasure. An irony can be found in the fact that perhaps the people best able on Martha's Vineyard to read such reports were deaf. Although most Vineyarders went to school for only five years in the 1800s, by mandate of the state educational system, the deaf were supported through ten years of school, and when faced with a difficult reading and writing task, the hearing would often go to a deaf person for help.

In a study from inside deaf culture, Padden and Humphries state the case: "Being able or unable to hear does not emerge as significant in itself; instead it takes on significance in the context of other sets of meaning to which the child has been exposed" (1988: 22). It is one kind of problem to have a behavioral range different from that of most people; it is another kind of problem to make a life in a culture when that difference is used by others for degradation. The second problem is by far the worse.

Three Ways to Write About Difficulties in School

For the past thirty years, the anthropology of education has been dominated by the question of how to talk with rigor and respect about children, particularly minority children, who fail in school. There must be something wrong with their life, goes the mainstream story—how else to talk about their not having learned to read or gained the basics of elementary mathematics. Yes, there must be something wrong here, but is it useful to insist that what is wrong is "their" life? What if the very act of saying there is something wrong, if improperly contextualized, makes their situation worse?

Two general modes of contextualization show up in the literature that concerns us. The first answers the question of what is wrong with their life by focusing on what is "wrong" (not working right) with the children and often their families. Much in the name of helping, of course, these answers specify nonetheless that something is in fact not working up to some par inside the children, that something went wrong in their cognitive, linguistic, and social development. More unwittingly perhaps than not, the explanation becomes a new tool for degradation as the child becomes known and treated as "someone special." Those who find themselves in this special position, whether because of physical, mental, economic, or neighborhood characteristics, have to put up not only with missing out on certain developments that come easily to many of their peers; they have to be doubly cursed and taunted by researchers focusing on them, separating them from their peers, making them special and then explaining why they do not have what others have and what should be done about it. This is the "Deprivation approach." As Nunez would put it, "I have eyes, you don't, let me help you with your problem."

That this version of the situation would allow him to become king (or to receive large grants from the government in order to research the problem) is clearly a side benefit that no sane Nunez would refuse even if he happened to feel somewhat embarrassed by it, for, after all, he is trying to help.

The second contextualization instead answers the question of what is wrong with their life by focusing on what others do to them that makes their life so seemingly, or at least so documentably, miserable and unproductive. Instead of focusing solely on what is wrong inside the child, the second effort focuses on what is wrong outside the child in the world given to him. This effort is an improvement over the first approach. It has the advantage of self-criticism in the acknowledgment that the world given to children, the part that does not work for some of them in school, includes everyone involved in constructing School in America: school personnel, of course, and parents, and let us not forget the philosophers, curriculum designers, textbook publishers, testers, and educational researchers, including anthropologists, in other words, "US."

Over the course of the past fifty years, it has been rather easy for social scientists to identify conditions that put some children at some risk. Besides conditions that have directly to do with the internal wiring of a child (including blindness or deafness, various kinds of profound troubles like autism and various retardations, and possibly less serious ones such as dyslexia), a long range of other conditions were also identified: the mother's nutrition during pregnancy, the quality of talk around the child, the number of books in the house, the quality of the schools, whether they were racially integrated, whether the curriculum or pedagogy was or was not adapted to the child's familial or ethnic background. This list is miscellaneous, and sociologists are hard at work trying to weigh the relative contribution of this or that "variable" to the eventual success of the child. Nunez might have argued: "Our world is blinding and deafening. We are working on fixing those things which cause the blinding and deafening. In the meantime, let me help you with your problem."

Anthropologists have insisted on a distinct version of this approach. It is worth investigating in some detail—even though it may be more dangerous than the sociological version precisely because of its greater attractiveness. We call this the Difference approach because of our concern with culture. It is probably the case that people are more commonsensically attuned to the exigencies of their customary culture than they are attuned to the exigencies of other cultures, and it makes sense to assume that persons projected into other cultures would have difficulties. Furthermore, certain cultures might develop certain skills (for example, quantity estimation skills among African farmers and Baltimore milk truck dispatchers, calculation skills among African tailors, mnemonic strategies among Micronesian navigators using the skies for direction) that are of no concern to other cultures. If one had trained Nunez in anthropology, he might have said: "You have developed a beautiful Country of the Blind, we have developed a beautiful Country of the Sighted. In this country we can now do much that you cannot do. Let me help you by teaching you in the ways of my country, since this is where you will inevitably want to be."

In explanations of school failure, the Difference account maintains that children from a minority cultural background mixed with teachers from a more dominant cultural background suffer enough miscommunication and alienation to give up on school, this despite the fact that they are, at least potentially, fully capable. This is by far the most popular language among anthropologists for theorizing about learning and schooling because it harks back to the Boasian classical strictures about the "psychic" (that is, neurological and biological) unity of mankind.

Against a flood of Deprivationist thinking in the early 1960s, the Difference stand took shape to honor the lives of those who had been left out of the system and who were in turn being blamed for their failings. Where the Deprivationist saw a poverty in the language development of Black children, sociolinguists (e.g., William Labov, Roger Shuy) saw only a different dialect, grammatically as complex as any other language and lacking nothing but the respect of mainstream speakers of English. Where the Deprivationist saw cognitive delays in the behavior of inner-city children, ethnographic psychologists (e.g., Michael Cole) showed how thinking was invariably complex once it was studied in relation to ongoing social situations. Where Deprivationists saw immorality and the breakdown of the family among the poor, anthropologists (e.g., Elliot Liebow, Carol Stack) found caring behavior set against a breakdown in the opportunities available in the job market. Where Deprivationists saw mayhem in classrooms, ethnographers (e.g., Frederick Erickson, Peg Griffin, Ray McDermott, Hugh Mehan) looked closely and saw tremendous order, some of it oppositional but order nonetheless.

The gradual replacement of the Deprivationist stand by a Difference theory of why children from minority cultural groups fail in school represents a considerable achievement but a temporary one. There is a delicate line that separates saying that minority children are missing enough of mainstream culture to be constantly in trouble at school and saying that minority children are missing culture period. It has been interesting to read how ethnographers with an allegiance to appreciating children from other cultures gradually begin to use terms and phrases directly borrowed from the Deprivationist discourse. Anthropologists have also often resisted this evolution, but rarely with much success, particularly when they presented their work as if it were another answer to the question of why more members of one group fail in school. This is the evolution we resist as we try not to be caught answering. Since we cannot ignore it, the task is one of investigating the logic of the question and the very structure of the argument. Whatever one's starting point or intentions, we fear that attempting to "explain" success or failures obliges analysts to treat consequences (the actual difficulties a child encounters in particular situations) as if they were causes on a par with biological characteristics. On the model of a phrase about a child being "visually handicapped," it is too easy to write about children who are "socially disadvantaged" or "linguistically deprived" or, even worse, "culturally" deprived. The categories are multiplying, and so are the euphemisms. For us, the matter is one of grammar and not of vocabulary. It makes little difference whether one writes of a child being "blind," "visually handicapped," or even visually "challenged." In all cases the attention is placed on a characteristic of the child rather than on the processes that might make this characteristic consequential.

Our own attempt at contextualization, one we label the "culture *As* disability" approach, deliberately focuses on the mechanisms of failure, including the mechanisms for the justification of failure. We are less concerned with whether a child is blind, deaf, dyslexic or the native speaker of a language other than Standard English as with why this characteristic might make a difference and for what purposes. Blindness is obviously a fact of neurology, but it becomes of human relevance only after has been transformed into a cultural category fitting in a particular manner with other cultural categories. Such "facts," as Pirandello (1922) warned, are like empty sacks until they are filled with "reason and sentiment" that transform facts of nature into *social* facts, into objects of institutional expertise and budget lines that belong to a different realm of reality. If, as we believe, the success/failure complex is a fundamental structure of American culture and if child-centered explanations of either success or failure are really parts of the justification and rationalization of the workings of this structure, then, of course, any suggestion about the direction reform should take must point at this structure rather than at the child. Congenital blindness may be always with us. Perhaps human beings will always be born with neurological conditions that make spelling difficult. What a future culture might do with these must remain an open question. For what American culture does with them is in no way the most "natural." It is "most" cultural.

Anthropologists and many others have always wanted to celebrate culture as that which constitutes the humanity of human beings and allows them to build worlds that were not given by their biological endowments: Neither the pyramids nor the Bill of Rights nor the Chicago blues sprang fully formed from human muscles, neural networks, or hearts. The collective movements that produce such events in the evolution of the universe are what the concept of culture attempts to catch. But culture also produces slavery, pogroms, and the atomic bomb. Culture, the great enabler of humanity, is also and in the same movement the great disabler. Culture, as we say in our lectures, gives all we know and all the tools with which to learn more. Very nice, but culture also gives, often daily and eventually always, a blind side, a deaf ear, a learning deficit. For every skill people gain, there is another not developed; for every focus of attention, something is passed by; for every specialty, there is a corresponding lack. People use established cultural forms to define what they should work on, work for, in what way, and with what consequences; being in culture is a great occasion for developing new abilities. Being in culture is also a great occasion for developing new disabilities with farther-reaching consequences. Every person's problem is eventually everyone's concern. As neither Nunez nor H. G. Wells could have said, "Your Country of the Blind will soon be invaded by the Country of the Sighted. Let's try to see how we can reorganize the Country of the Sighted so that your blindness does not become an occasion for the sighted to humiliate you."

It takes a whole village to raise a child, but the concerns of the village are not necessarily congruent with one or another of a child's characteristics. Cultural abilities are controlled by the collectivity, and so are cultural disabilities. One's neighbors will always use the established cultural forms at their disposal to construct their own lives and, often without noticing it or intending to do so, disable others to the extent they enable themselves. By established cultural forms, we mean anything from built physical structures that leave some people locked out even as they make others more comfortable to school assessment systems that discourage people from learning what is in some way needed even as they allow others to go far beyond what they might otherwise have done. Notice that in each case, there are two sides to the same story: Those who are *locked out* of the building suffer because others are *inside*; those who are *shut off* from learning suffer because being *in the know* is used in a meritocracy for much more than knowledge. As Louis Dumont ([1966] 1970) once starkly argued, racism is a correlate of liberal democracy: If "all men are created equal," then evidence of inequality must be so unsettling and unexplainable that it requires the dehumanization of many who appear not to perform equally. We might just as well say that culture fashions problems for us and, from the same sources, expects us to construct solutions. It is from life inside this trap that we often get the feeling that working on problems can make things worse. Without a culture we would not know what our problems are; culture, or better, the people around us in culture, help to define the situation-specific, emotionally demanding, and sensuous problems that we must confront. There is a significant sense in which—or at least, there is much analytic leverage to be gained by thinking as if—

without a money system, there is no debt;
without a kinship system, no orphans;
without a class system, no deprivation;
without schools, no learning disabilities.

The concept of culture has always had a utility for those with a sense for the patterns in the work people do in organizing their lives together. This phrasing displays an insistence that culture is not a property of individuals-as-conditioned; rather a culture is an account of the world, built over centuries, for people to inhabit, to employ, to celebrate, and to contest. This shift from personal trait to agency, from *habi-*

tus to *inhabitation*, is essential when working in complex, divided societies. Careful work with those locked in "special" identifications always reveals the ingenuity of the ways they resist constraints they cannot ignore. It makes present their resistance to being made into less than they could be or less than they are. Anthropological work must begin with, but not stop with, a celebration of this resistance. The resistance to what the "special" among us cannot ignore also reveals the hegemony of the institutions that originally constructed their problems. Indeed, those who were made special can tell us about the world we have all inherited. Money is best understood by examining the bankrupt. What is most significant in family life is highlighted most clearly in the life of the orphan, and so on and so forth. In the ethnographic study of disability, the subject shifts from THEM to US, from what is wrong with them to what is wrong with the culture that evolved a THEM separate from an US.

Cultural Explanations of Poverty and Other Disabilities

The Deprivation and Difference theories of the relation of culture to learning have a deep history, and they are not easy to escape, particularly when the authors are driven by an abiding political concern with Democracy in Education. Many anthropologists have had such a concern. Although directly struggling against the suggestion that the source of the problems lies in the persons who exhibit them, anthropologists continue to produce analyses that recenter their audience's attention precisely on the person. In this chapter, we continue to focus on the descriptive traps that America makes available to authors working on the School. We start with two works from the classical period in anthropology. They can be taken as archetypes of the many that shaped the evolution of a concern with human activity as an environment for learning. These are Erik Erikson's *Childhood and Society* ([1950] 1970) and Oscar Lewis's *The Children of Sanchez* (1961). While neither is directly about "education" in the American School, each is about understanding the fate of children like Adam, Sheila, and the others we encountered earlier. Erikson studied how being a child in different cultures would lead to the development of different adult personalities and different "identities." Lewis started with a theory of active adaptation to particular economic and historical conditions but linked his observations to personality theories of the type offered by Erikson to argue that once a particular pattern of adaptation has institutionalized itself, it will then perpetuate itself through education, learning, and the modeling of adult personalities.

Erikson starts where we also start, though we would of course modernize his vocabulary. He is concerned with the conditions of life in the United States:

> This dynamic country subjects its inhabitants to more extreme contrasts and abrupt changes during a lifetime or a generation than is normally the case with other great nations. Most of her inhabitants are faced, in their own lives or within the orbit of their closest relatives, with alternatives presented by such polarities as: open roads of immigration and jealous islands of tradition; outgoing internationalism and defiant isolationism, boisterous competition and self-effacing co-operation; and many others ([1950] 1970: 285).

He does not seem to wonder about the adequacy of such a description of American conditions, and he immediately moves to what really interests him:

> The influence of the resulting contradictory slogans on the development of an individual ego probably depends on . . .
> The process of American identity formation seems to support an individual's ego identity. . . . Thus the functioning American, as the heir to a history of extreme contrasts and abrupt changes, bases his final ego identity . . . (1970 [1950]: 285–286)

An interest in America thus becomes an interest in Americans. The intellectual problem is that this progression is not simply typical of someone who identifies himself specifically as a psychoanalyst and therapist. It is also the prescribed rhetorical device behavioral scientists use to demonstrate a "concern for the individual." But the descriptive consequences of this rhetorical movement are profound. Erikson says repeatedly that he is interested in culture, but this interest proves to concern only the impact of culture on individuals. He spends infinitely more time investigating this impact, and this has the consequence that he ends up radically shortchanging the cultural analysis itself. By insisting on the individual as a unit of analysis, even as he appears to study culture, he gives up the possibility of studying culture.

The problem is not of purely academic interest. We have no choice but to distinguish carefully among the philosophical, moral, political, indeed religious, issues that move all of us to worry about Democracy in Education. Individuals must be the units of concern and justice, but they are misleading units of analysis and reform. The greater our concern with individuals, the greater must be our efforts to document carefully the social conditions in which they must always express themselves. We must look away from individuals to preserve them. To confuse the descriptive and political agendas may bring about exactly the kinds of problems that Adam, Joe, and the others constantly encounter. Treating them as subjects in our descriptions highlights everything that they cannot do and hides the rhetorical moves that identify, among all the things that they, like us, cannot do, some particular ones to be treated. In the process, the erstwhile subject has become an object of professional activity.

Oscar Lewis is a good example of such a confusion that ends in a particularly unfortunate place. After twenty years of anguished work among the poorest of the poor in Mexico and the Caribbean, Lewis coined the "culture of poverty" phrase that continues to haunt the field. There is no doubt that, initially, Lewis was searching for a way to celebrate the work that the people he studied did under the most difficult of economic and political circumstances. He wanted to do this without sentimentalizing their work and perhaps thereby discounting it. In a celebrated dispute with Robert Redfield about the best way of telling of the life of peasants in a small Mexican village,[3] he comes down squarely on the side of presenting Tepoztlán in the wider context of its ties with a complex national economy and in the context of the social discontinuities and tensions that, among other things, fueled the Mexican Revolution. As Redfield summarized the issue later, he himself painted a picture of a "relatively homogeneous, isolated, smoothly functioning and well-integrated society," whereas Lewis offered a picture emphasizing "the underlying individualism of Tepoztecan institutions and character, the lack of cooperation, the tensions between villages . . . , the schisms . . . , and the pervading quality of fear, envy and distrust" (Lewis [1951] 1960: 428–429; as quoted in Redfield [1956] 1960: 134).

Given the need to silence neither what ails human beings (poverty and all that it entails) nor what they may do that we must treat as somehow destructive (theft, familial violence, murder, addiction), how are analysts to present their work, particularly if they want to acknowledge that people are active participants in a life that they build moment to moment, day by day, year in and year out? For Boas and the people around him as they determinedly challenged evolutionary theories, ethnographic and empirical investigation demonstrated that, everywhere, human beings work with their particular environments and, in the process, develop in wonderful and different ways particular, local institutions (customs, mores, ways of handling themselves and their relevant others, etc.) that must be understood in terms of their historically constructed specificity. This specificity was presented in a relentlessly optimistic fashion and thus appeared as a progressive frame: What people do in culture can always be described as orderly rather than chaotic, constructive rather than disorganized, human rather than brutish. Culture springs out of humanity in joint action. By the 1930s and 1940s, as Ruth Benedict and Margaret Mead took the symbolic lead of the Boasians, a new twist was added. As they got interested in psychology and started to read Freud and others, the later Boasians wondered about enculturation in the context of a theory of culture and personality.

In *The Children of Sanchez,* following the classical cultural anthropology of his time, Lewis started with a sentence emphasizing the positive, structured, stable, and persistent: "[Poverty] is also something positive in the sense that it has a structure, a rationale, and defense mechanisms without which the poor could hardly carry on. In short, it is a way of life, remarkably stable and persistent" (1961: xxiv).

But by working with the concept of culture, he then had to move to talk about the constitution of the person. Culture, the "culture of poverty," became an overwhelming determinant of a person's behavior. The people Lewis had spent so much time with stopped being "in poverty" (as a system); they were now "poor"—on the same model as people in instituted blindness or learning disability become "blind" and "disabled" in the language of those who now wish to help them. In the process, Lewis highlighted the limitations of the culture and personality model. He expanded his observation of the activity of people in difficult circumstances into a discussion of the ways this activity shaped their personality, their child-rearing practices, and what their children learned and, above all, of what they could not learn except through the deliberate remedial effort of the enlightened middle class. He was led to assert that once a personality has been shaped, further change is difficult: "[Poverty] is a way of life . . . passed down from generation to generation along family lines. The culture of poverty has its modalities and distinctive social and psychological consequences for its members" (1961: xxiv).

In a later work he further expanded on the issue of transmission and learning:

> The culture of poverty, however, is not only an adaptation to a set of objective condi-
> tions of the larger society. Once it comes into existence it tends to perpetuate itself from
> generation to generation because of its effect on the children. By the time slum children
> are age six or seven they have usually absorbed the basic values and attitudes of their
> subculture and are not psychologically geared to take full advantage of changing condi-
> tions or increased opportunities which may occur in their lifetime. (1965: xlv)[4]

It is as if, once enculturated through particular experiences in particular conditions,
one stopped being able to adapt to new conditions in different ways. It is as if, once
enculturated, a human being ceased being capable of culture and thereby lost some
humanity.

That "culture" is internalized is common sense and is also a major perversion of
the Boasian intuition about the central character of culture in humanity—even
though many Boasians were great theoreticians of internalization. As we understand
the original intuition, it attempts to focus us both on historical inheritance and on
the continued work of those who receive this inheritance. In America, this intuition
was melded with another intuition first systematically explored by social psychologists who saw that individual personality is shaped more powerfully by social experiences than by biology. The "self" is always socially constructed. But cultural anthropologists, particularly when they pay attention to Durkheimian insights, must also
insist that enculturation is not destiny. We will return to all this in Chapter 7. What
is important at this point is to note how Lewis's evolution underscores the limitations of the model of culture as learned ways of being. For poverty, as a condition,
cannot be said to constitute a culture. Certainly, it can be shown that local action in
poverty can pattern itself in particular manners, possibly different here and there, as
different groups move into American poverty from various parts of the world and are
partially isolated from each other. The development of such particularities within the
United States cannot be taken to mean, however, that the general condition of
poverty constitutes a distinct culture, since it is itself an aspect of the wider cultural
pattern and will thus vary across time and place (Dean 1991; Green 1982). Poverty
is a position within a field of positions within which people in complex societies
construct their lives. For some, in the middle classes, for example, this means an easier life because they can get services they might not otherwise be able to afford; for
the others, in poverty, it means a more difficult life.[5] For both, it makes a situation in
which further concerted action across a wider range of circumstances—those involving rich people, caretakers, and many other poor people—is always necessary.

Education and Difference

Within a few years of the first publication of Lewis's arguments and of such related
arguments as Daniel Moynihan's on the "deterioration of the Negro family" ([1965]

1967: 51), a flurry of critiques was published (for example, Cazden, John, and Hymes 1972; Leacock 1971 or Valentine 1968).[6] More important, a series of studies was published that directly confronted stereotyped disabilities apparent in the activities of people in dire circumstances.[7] Through that work and work that had been done earlier but could now be seen in a different light, it became clear that whereas poverty is always an immediate problem for those who live in it, "deterioration" is not, at least not systemically. There is as much, if not more, reason to highlight the stories of success in adversity that can be found in poverty as there is to highlight the stories of addiction and death that may exercise the pity of the more fortunate while also silencing the productive work of the poor.

Part of our goal in the first five chapters of this book was precisely to highlight the productive work of fully human children and their parents or teachers in difficult circumstances. Our goal now is to warn those who continue to find the concept of "culture" useful against the unwitting reproduction of the intellectual conditions that led to the development of the "culture of poverty" analysis. Certainly, few social scientists now talk about the "culture of poverty." The attempt to celebrate the local activity of people in difficult circumstances is now commonly framed in various other languages, most prominently, for a while at least, in the language of "difference" and, more recently, in various versions of the language of adaptive refusal.

By the "difference" perspective, people would fail in school (and remain poor) mostly because schools would not be adapted to what is again identified as "the people's own culture" with purportedly specifiable traits that children would absorb early in childhood and in such a manner that they are prevented from learning any different pattern in the normal course of interaction. In this tradition, there is less discussion of the historical origin of a culture or of its evolution. At most, there is a vague reference to some pre-American origin that survives in the unconscious habits of the present generation.

In its most commonsensical phrasing, this is in fact a throwback to the worst interpretation of cultural anthropology. Lewis, Moynihan, and others at least attempted to deal with the social conditions of the people about whom they wrote. Poverty and difficulty in school, from their point of view, are not simply a historical accident produced by migration and the inability to integrate. Rather they are a systemic condition to which one cannot help but adapt because one is human. The drama of poverty as a condition derives from the interpretive power of human educative action. The people placed in poverty survive, and in the process develop local patterns of expression and identifications that are worth studying. Where Lewis, Moynihan, and others stumbled was in assuming that temporary adaptations to conditions are transformed into psychological syndromes that can then be considered a proximate "cause" of the poverty. This error is further compounded when it is suggested that these adaptations are then passed on to children who appear to have lost their own ability to adapt and learn.

For the critics, to talk about "adaptation" to poverty and then enculturation into it appeared to be a form of "blaming the victim." Why this should be is an interesting question we do not have to address at length. In its connotations, the symbol of "culture" may be so powerfully associated with a person's ownership—as in "one's own culture"—that "culture" must be attributed only to the most positive aspect of a group's work over its history. In any event, the reaction—at least among those who remained committed to the concept of culture—was a recentering of the ways Lewis suggested culture and poverty were related. He suggested, and this was widely expanded in various theories of "cultural deficit," that the cultural forms found among the poor were maladaptive given a goal of mobility into the middle classes. The underlying hypothesis was "Change the culture of the poor, and they will be able to move out of poverty." In the evolution of the work critiquing this hypothesis, the underlying hypothesis—at least at its most formal—became "Teach the poor and the middle class each other's culture, and the cultures of the poor will cease being an obstacle to economic success." The emphasis was placed on pure "difference." This work demonstrated that the poor could be different in ways infinitely more complex and varied than had been thought. The status of this difference was considered problematic, and a lot of interpretive energy was spent arguing that the trouble the poor experience derives from the response given to their difference by nonpoor people with authority, for example, teachers or counselors.[8]

The Difference hypothesis has been successful academically and politically. It has become the empirical justification for most forms of multiculturalism. Many have suggested that whatever the limitations of the hypothesis, it is more enlightened to argue that people are "different" than to say they are "deprived" or the victim of some "deficit." From our point of view, a fundamental problem remains. Theories of cultural difference again place the onus on the enculturated individuals who, by implication at least, are made to appear just as passive as they are made in the culture-of-poverty argument. The Difference argument easily moves from careful description of a local pattern to a set of hypotheses, first about the independence of this pattern from other patterns and then about the constitution of the person who is born and raised with the pattern. In the process, it becomes difficult to trace the tie between the poor and prosperous in a systematic fashion. And it becomes even more difficult to understand the activity of the individual among and between all the patterns because, as usual, we are led away from historical institutions and into psychological constitution. Let us look how this approach operates in one of the most successful texts of the present generation, Shirley Brice Heath's *Ways with Words* (1983).

Patterns of Southern Cultures

Heath's setting is late-twentieth-century southern Piedmont country. Slavery, the Civil War, Reconstruction, the depression, a limited form of industrial development, the civil rights era, all have passed and a landscape remains of

> black and white communities, tied to the textile mills in different ways, [that] in the
> decades of the 1960s and 1970s, [were] caught between their families and the school,

between community and classroom in their urge to be "on the rise." Two such communities are Roadville and Trackton. Roadville is a white working-class community of families who have been a part of mill life for four generations. . . . Trackton is a working-
class black community whose older generations have been brought up on the land,
either farming their own land or working for other landowners. (1983: 28–29)

In the background a third entity, "the townspeople," looms; they hold the political power in general and the school power in particular.

Heath focuses on Roadville and Trackton. The core of the book is a description of
the differences between the two, focusing particularly on the way parents and young
children interact linguistically. This difference is starkly summarized by the chapter
headings that Heath used when presenting her analysis: "Learning how to talk in
Trackton" (chap. 3) versus "Teaching how to talk in Roadville" (chap. 4). In Trackton, "children are not expected to *be* information-givers; they are expected to *become*
information-knowers by 'being keen'" (1983: 86). The children are expected to *learn*
on their own. In Roadville, "adults see themselves as the child's teacher at the
preschool stage, and teachers ask and answer questions" (1983: 129). The children
must be *taught* what they need to know. Heath then goes more rapidly over a third
"way" (her word for what Ruth Benedict (1934) would have called a "pattern") of
approaching speech and writing—that of the "townspeople." She does not offer the
same kind of pithy summary of this way that she did for the others. She speaks of an
emphasis on reading and writing for information about objects that are not physically present, and she shows how this corresponds to the organization of work in fac-
tories and bureaucracies.

The punch line is as starkly differentiating as the chapter headings: "The two
communities [Trackton and Roadville] hold different concepts of childhood" (1983:
145); "the ways of the black and white townspeople are different from the ways of either Trackton or Roadville" (1983: 265). The differences are important because
"these concepts of childhood and parenthood determine the kinds of talk and play
adults provide Roadville and Trackton children" (1983: 146); "townspeople carry
with them, as an unconscious part of their self-identity, these numerous subtle and
covert norms, habits, and values" (1983: 262). And this has the consequence that
"for the children of Trackton and Roadville . . . the townspeople's ways are far from
natural and they seem strange indeed" (1983: 262). The second part of the book
concentrates on what happens in classrooms dominated by these "townspeople"
when the children of Trackton and Roadville take tests, write essays, and otherwise
participate in their schools. In brief, teachers are "puzzled," and they make "invidi-
ous comparisons." The children "meet different notions of truth, style and language"
(1983: 294). Their "conceptions of stories affect their response to performance of
stories in school" (1983: 297), and this has serious consequences for them both edu-
cationally and as they enter the workforce.

As is usual in the anthropology of education, the analysis is unabashedly political
in what it tries to explain and in what it explicitly suggests. Heath ends with recom-

mendations about what students and teachers should do about this situation, and
these clearly show the limitations of her working model. In brief, she recommends
that teachers be aware of the differences she discovered and that Trackton's schools
design programs that specifically teach the children what they did not learn at home.
It is an argument for a multicultural curriculum that derives its power from theoretical arguments about the relationship between the individual and the internalized
culture. This is fundamentally the social psychological theory once used by Oscar
Lewis: A difference in "ways with words," a more modern version of what Lewis
called "culture," produces concrete difficulties when people who have acquired different "conceptions," "norms," "habits," or "values" interact. The "differences" between various "ways" are absolute rather than relative to each other (that is, they are
not generated by the interaction and cannot be expected to change if the organization of the interaction changes). After they are acquired, "ways with words" become
part of the fundamental personality structure ("identity") of individuals, and people
with different personality structures have difficulty interacting with each other. Improving this interaction must proceed through the specific training of all individuals
involved in the ways of the other.

There is much in this formulation that is an advance on Lewis's formulations.
Heath encourages us to look at the poor not as failed versions of the middle class but
rather in their own terms, as actors who have transformed their conditions. There
are also major theoretical problems. First, Heath implicitly operates within a classical
"enculturation" model that, from our point of view, collapses the social and interactional back into the personal and thus conspires to hide the specific organization of
the conditions persons find as they build their lives. Second, and more specific to all
theories of cultures *within* the United States, is the problem of boundaries and historical contact. In what ways and for what purposes is it useful to speak of "difference" about people who have spent two or three hundred years together in the same
valley, who have lived the same history, and who have worked with each other? If
there are observable differences on this or that aspect of language use, what is the
source of these differences? Couldn't they just as well be the historical *product* of interaction within a common cultural evolution? Even if one is to accept that an individual is the product of his community, what are the boundaries of that community?
To us, the boundaries are the product of the people who must pay attention to them,
of both those who enforce them and those who try to sneak through them. Such
boundaries and the different spaces that are thereby constructed are artifacts of history, the product of culture as it makes rules and conditions for human action to
take into account.

Adaptive Withdrawal

One of the least-examined assumptions of the "difference" argument is that all children try equally to succeed in school. Ogbu, among others, has been presenting evidence that there is no reason to assume that all students in fact do equally try. In a

series of publications (1974, 1978, 1987, 1991a, 1991b) that predate the related "resistance" argument, he pointed out that many students from what he calls "involuntary minorities"[9] do not demonstrate active involvement in the day-to-day activities that must eventually constitute instruction. Their attendance is spotty, their attention wonders, they do not do homework. Why? Because they, and their parents, have come to the conclusion that the system of segregation within which they live will not allow them to attain the fruits of education even if they exert themselves. Ogbu strongly emphasizes the following: "Burghersiders do not fail in school because, although they try, they cannot do the work; that is, they do not fail because they do not have the ability. Rather, Burghersiders fail in school because they do not even try to do the work. They are not serious about their school work, and therefore make no serious effort to try to succeed in school" (1974: 97).

If the education path is indeed blocked, then there is no need to follow it. Working at school is at best misguided and at worst, treasonous: Only "Uncle Toms" and "Oreos" do so.

As far as we can tell from his study of schooling in Stockton, California, Ogbu (1974) is focusing centrally on the kind of experiences one can have in schools like West Side High, which appeared in Chapter 4. Ogbu anchors the school in a specific locality that he explores in some socioeconomic and political detail. The picture that emerges is of an area that may be even more strongly differentiated on racial and class lines than Heath's. There are Whites and Blacks, Mexican Americans, and other immigrant groups. Many of these people have come into the area from different parts of the United States more or less recently. There is much more reason than in Heath's case to expect major "cultural" differences between groups because these people had little direct contact until they settled next to each other. Ogbu does not even begin to make a difference argument. He goes in another direction that he later expands into a specific critique of the difference argument: Not all "different" groups do equally badly in school (Ogbu 1987). Pure cultural difference need not make a difference. There must be an intermediate variable.

Ogbu spends a lot of time exploring the complex set of attitudes that Blacks or Mexicans express toward education and argues that these attitudes constitute the variable. He balances what many informants told him about the "importance of education" with other statements about the uselessness of "trying to work as hard as whites in school when school success would not qualify them to succeed in society because they are blacks or Mexican-Americans" (1974: 12). In other words, many of Ogbu's informants were aware that they did not actively compete with Whites. They were convinced that exerting oneself in school would be useless. If the race is rigged, why run? Ogbu developed his argument in later publications, and it is most completely presented in *Minority Status and Schooling* (Gibson and Ogbu 1991), in which the authors compare the success of various minority groups in American schools and show how common it is for some of the most "culturally different" groups not only to succeed but often to succeed more thoroughly than the majority groups. In the race to enter the most prestigious universities, some people from

"Asian" groups easily outrun the pack. How can this be if cultural difference, or even implicit discrimination, is mechanistically deterministic of formal success?

Things are obviously more complex than the mechanical operation of communicational mismatches. What else is at work is not quite as obvious as Ogbu indicates. His interpretation has features that make it hard to evaluate. Not surprisingly, and like all critics of American education, Ogbu blames a history of segregation, discrimination, and continuing racism as compounding the effect of poverty, itself produced by a class-based capitalistic system. Oscar Lewis would have agreed. And Ogbu, like Lewis, like us and all other social scientists interested in finding out how race and class actually come to make a difference, does not stop with the gross correlation between social position and success in school. Something is going on, but Ogbu, eventually, offers something that is not so far removed from what Lewis offered. When he talks about the refusal to try at school, he talks of an "an adaptation that has developed over a long period of time" and is now self-reproducing: "In spite of the recent increase in the desire of Burghersiders for more education, the pattern of behavior that underlies their adaptation has not changed" (1974: 102). The chapter introduced by this statement explores the means through which "this adaptation . . . is maintained." The means include absenteeism, interschool mobility, work habits in the classroom and at home, and so on. In the very rhetoric of these statements, the proximate source of the problem is the individual student who stops trying and, worse, stops learning. The eventual practical, day-to-day responsibility for the students' failure is placed on the shoulders of parents and children as they actively do not try. The emphasis on "adaptation" as a personal characteristic is even stronger when Ogbu directly compares "immigrant" and "involuntary" minorities: "The more academically successful minorities differ from the less academically successful minorities in the type of cultural model that guides them, that is, in the type of understanding they have of the workings of the larger society and of their place as minorities in that working order" (1974: 8). In so doing, Ogbu has removed any continuing interactional aspect to children's failure. At times, particularly when discussing a remedial program in Stockton, Ogbu does suggest that perhaps the problem is not so much that students do not try as that teachers do not teach. He talks about disagreements on the nature of learning and instruction between reformists in charge of the program and the parents. The reformists emphasized play and self-esteem; the parents expected reading, writing, and arithmetic. The parents suspected, and we tend to agree with them, that while their children were being "prepared to learn" through play and self-building exercises, they were not in fact learning anything while their peers in the White middle-class schools across town were increasing their head start. Still, Ogbu has not explored these leads much as his work has developed over the past twenty-five years. On the contrary, in general summaries, it is the unmotivated and psychologically alienated individual who is placed at the center of the causes of school failure. Having internalized not trying in school, a mass of unmotivated individuals do not learn, and the School, ever ready to help anyone who might try, is simply there to record, with disappointment, another generation of failure.

Things can certainly look that way, particularly to dedicated, experienced, highly trained teachers confronted with a room of unwilling teenagers and young adults. It can look as if the teenagers of Stockton or West Side High refuse to learn or refuse to display their knowledge, but there is no reason to interpret this refusal as an oversocialized reaction or confused adaptation to misunderstood conditions. These adolescents, in the long run, must be understood in terms of what they do learn as they cultivate their own conditions while participating in the complex rituals of success and failure that link them, willy-nilly, with the adolescents of Allwin. For the past twenty years, the adolescents of Stockton may have evolved a pattern of aggressive refusal to participation in a charade, a pattern perhaps best expressed in various rap genres. Whether this is the more effective political response to a difficult situation for all involved, including full participation in the School, remains to be seen. Analytically one thing is certain: Any theory that starts with politically active participants will go further, and is less likely to be co-opted by dominant ideological interpretations in an American context, than theories that start with encultured, socialized individuals overwhelmed by their early experiences.

American Education as a Culture

In Chapter 7, we argue that the continued reconstruction of human difficulties into psychological ones is consistent with an American individualistic focus embedded in the work of the pragmatist philosophers and social psychologists. As a culture, the individualistic discourse will do two things, the first magnificent, the other dramatic. First, it will enable any human being who uses it (whether an American citizen or not) to see individual achievements and travails in a way not surpassed by any other discourse. Second, it will disable the same human beings from easily confronting the social conditions that give individuals the material for their work. As we conclude this chapter, we want to reaffirm something implicit in this understanding of what culture is all about. By fundamental postulate, a philosopher of education must start from the point of view that education is not about enculturation (though it probably always leads to the shaping of personalities). Nor is it about instruction in particular skills that may come more or less easily to people. Education is cultivation, not enculturation. It is about discovering, taming, and transforming our humanity. It is not about becoming the acquiescent member of any culture. By the same token, education is a fundamental aspect of humanity. All children get educated, and all adults end up with an education that springs from their resources, their circumstances, and what they made of them. This trust in the power of the human person is fundamental to all great philosophies of education, and there is something marvelous in a political system attempting to base its solution to a major social problem on such philosophies. What philosophers of education and political actors have forgotten is that as people cultivate themselves, they make culture for themselves and others in the present and the future. This is where things get complicated.

It is said the devil is in the details. In culture, the devil manifests itself when broad philosophical orientations are institutionalized. Historical and cross-cultural evidence demonstrates clearly that humanity has progressed far without overloading either education, enculturation, or instruction with formal concerns about success or failure. It is equally clear that European and American polities took a fateful step when they gave schools and universities, which earlier served the few for limited purposes, the major political task of freeing the person, equalizing chances, and building a more just community. Over the past 300 years, the political history of Euro-America can be seen as a massive and continuing struggle against the injustices accompanying feudal, family-based systems of social stratification. Everywhere, one can see the attempt to ground legitimacy in the individual with private and unique qualities and needs. In this political process, a massive fact was built over the American landscape: the School as a specialized institution dedicated to instruction by specifically authorized personnel. With the School came laws, regulations, certifications, teachers, classrooms, administrators, counselors, an industrial-academic testing complex—all tightly framed so that their presence echoes far beyond the areas one might expect to find them, in the everyday lives of all in the United States. Most fatefully for an educator, getting particular jobs and surviving economically has been linked with the exact performance of carefully drawn but altogether irrelevant tasks. This is the cultural process that must be not so much explained as carefully *described* and confronted in its organizations and consequences.

As personal actors and citizens, we must all work within the School however much we yearn for other methods to build Democracy. We must all do it, whatever our personal adaptation to local conditions in poverty or prosperity, whether we "understand" analytically, passionately, or emotionally what the School is all about. But it is our responsibility to move further aside to see more clearly the School as historically constructed, *always already there*, and always consequential. Above all, we must struggle against the ideological underpinning of this system when it tells us to center our gaze on the person as self-constituted individual. As one focuses on the learner, the focusing mechanism—America—disappears. Worse, the "individual" that appears alone, standing in isolation, thereby overwhelms the landscape and is yet subverted. The more attention paid to the individual, the more "determined" and the more restricted the person. To respect the individual, politically and morally, one must analytically cast one's eyes away.

NOTES

Sections of this chapter are adapted from McDermott and Varenne (1995, 1996).

1. This is an inflected version of an insight affirmed eloquently by Geertz: "Without men, no culture, certainly; but equally, and more significantly, without culture, no men" (Geertz [1972] 1973: 49). As Boon (1982: 146) noted, this statement is an eerie echo of another statement often presented as the antithesis to a theoretical position emphasizing agency and emotional involvement. When Lévi-Strauss (1964: 20) wrote that *"les mythes se pensent dans les*

hommes, et à leur insu" (myths think themselves in men, and without them being aware of it), he was not simply refusing agency to human beings as if all you could say about them is that they are caught in a web of myths transforming themselves through them. Rather, he was pointing unblinkingly to an aspect of the human condition that philosophical humanists and individualists may find dramatic: All human beings are born into a *cultural* world that is as relatively overwhelming to individual agency as the physical world often is. Boon talks about the different pictures of the relationship between culture and humanity that emerge out of the recognition of the centrality of culture to humanity. Some of the pictures are optimistic; some are pessimistic or dramatic. Our sense is that the suggested picture must be optimistic, pessimistic, and dramatic: Culture makes humanity; it is also its downfall, and therein lies the drama.

2. In a gentle ethnography of the sightless of Tel Aviv, Deshen (1992) showed how much the troubles of the blind are forced on them not by their disability but by those around them.

3. Redfield published his *Tepoztlán, a Mexican Village* first (1930). Lewis conducted a restudy seventeen years later (1951). The contrast between the pictures could not be more sharply sketched. A good discussion of this contrast is to be found in Redfield's *The Little Community* ([1956] 1960). Philip Bock conducted a third study that showed at least some of the differences between Redfield and Lewis had to do with a gradual incorporation of the village into Mexico City (1980).

4. See also his statement in *Scientific American* (1966).

5. We are here generalizing Drummond's analysis of the interdependence between those who hire nannies or baby-sitters and the nannies and baby-sitters (1978).

6. In 1969, *Current Anthropology* devoted a forum to a discussion of Valentine's critique. It includes responses from Lewis, Margaret Mead, Moynihan, and others.

7. Exemplary here is the work of Hannerz (1969); Stack (1975); Holloman and Lewis, F. (1978); Shimkin, Louie, and Frate (1978); Susser (1982); and many others.

8. The work by Schneider and Smith (1973) exemplifies an alternate approach.

9. For Ogbu, such minorities are made up of people who did not come to the United States voluntarily, who were integrated into the country against their will, or who have existed in poverty for many generations. Such are African Americans, Latinos (particularly Mexicans and Puerto Ricans), and American Indians.

7 Ways with Theoretical Words

Hervé Varenne
and Ray McDermott

In the preceding chapter, we focused on the descriptive problems facing all who take up the general charge of understanding social and cultural constraints on the development of democracy in education. We showed how the charge has been interpreted as a simple call for explanations of differential success and failure across groups, and we argued that this interpretation is fraught with descriptive problems. In this chapter, we argue that it is also fraught with theoretical problems, and we move to specify the alternative that has guided us throughout the book.

The most powerful political voices do state the charge as a search for causes: Why can't Johnny read? The question is not responsive to the more fundamental charge: What is going on here such that we, democrats and humanists, have so many difficulties with the institutions developed in the name of democracy and humanism? This second charge frees analysis from the popular questions and allows us to consider the possibility that the very shape of these questions limits understanding and slows reform. We have stated repeatedly that we refuse to search for causes of success or failure as if either were objects in a natural world. For us, they are mutually defined cultural categories that are used as tools for broad social purposes. We look at them as tools with particular formal properties that have profound impact in all situations where they are used.

Trying to "explain" "failure" in "schools" prevents any understanding of what is to be explained, namely, the very patterning of education in America with its requirement that the performance of individuals be explained using prescribed tools. The focus of research must shift to this underlying patterning. To do so, we have turned to the concept of "culture," though we understand it differently from the more commonsense ways used in "Difference" explanations of school failure. For more than a century, the social sciences have used the concept to account for social patterns so overpowering that they are unavailable for direct attention. "Culture" can help focus analytic attention on the processes that make teachers, parents, and researchers spend so much energy worrying about their children failing while ignoring the conditions that make school failure something to worry about. These are complex processes. By tracing them along with the collective activity that enforces them, we hope to bring the pattern to analytic light.

We have critiqued "explanations" of school "failure" that mention "culture" as a causative factor because they radically weaken what has always been most powerful about the concept: the insistence that humanity makes conditions for itself in a process that transforms its biological endowment and ecological environment. This process inevitably has consequences for the makeup of the individual, of the self or identity, as Erikson understood it. But the process itself is not a psychological one. It is, fundamentally, an interactional one. It is about millions of human beings living *together*, most of whom do not know each other but all of whom are linked to each other. In recent years, researchers from various fields (anthropology, ethnomethodology, Marxism, and other critical studies) have shown an increasing awareness of the need to understand human action in terms of its context. In the midst of a theoretical bias in educational research that remains relentlessly focused on the individual, this awareness is welcome. Our work builds on this move to context, but with trepidation: In educational discourse, context has often become another cause of the constitution of the individual. By the magic of this mistake, the concept of culture is refocused analytically on what children internalize, and research finds itself back where it started. This chapter is concerned with the cultural process through which intuitions about the joint construction of conditions for future action are transformed back into the commonsense cliché that "everything depends on what each participant knows or feels." We are searching for a way to escape what has been the usual fate of such theories in America. The first step in this search takes us back to early intuitions about the need to account for human behavior in terms of joint activity rather than individual constitution. In the process we start to outline what remained a major difficulty in the early accounts, the apparent necessity, or at least the good common sense, to place the characteristics of a situation back into the heads of participants in joint action as a condition of their continuing to act together. In a second step, we show how recent attempts to recapture the intuitions have been falling into the same traps. In a third step we point at a possible way around the trap, one that preserves agency, paradoxically perhaps, by emphasizing how much of the social world is *always already there* and *always to be there* in the conditions people find and in the responses of others to what they do. This is followed, in Chapter 8, by a reanalysis, based on the theoretical framework we are building and illustrating in this book, of a case one of us has worked on for many years..

Our concern with the Person in Culture is inherited from a long conversation. We accept a literal reading of Ruth Benedict's account of the individual as a center of action when she wrote that as an anthropologist, she was interested in "the manner in which the customs of any people function in the lives of the individuals who compose them" (1934: 2). "Customs" are what we call historical, cultural facts, what is *always already there* when we enter the human world. They function in the lives of individuals, and individuals in turn "compose," constitute, reproduce, and resist them. We are not the first to notice that such phrasings are almost as dangerous as they can be useful. We are particularly concerned with the rhetorical transformations of the principle that we must be "concerned with the individual." Some of these transformations yield a view of the world in which it makes sense to talk about "impoverished selves" to be helped by professional intervention. In Chapter 6, we traced this transformation in the work of researchers who clearly started with the intention of building up the reality of social conditions and ended with explanations that identified the problem with the emotive, conscious, and decisionmaking individual, millions of them at a time. Perhaps, go the arguments, the impoverished were shocked into immobility by their deprivation; perhaps they adapted too well to impoverished conditions, and they became impoverished persons; perhaps they just do not understand or are just not understood; or perhaps they just refuse to play a game at which they have always lost. In the process social conditions become shadowy causes that normal psychological and sociological research continually breaks down into always narrower "variables" said to account for tinier gradations in the variability in outcomes.

We think this process of atomization in research writing about education is an unwitting product of the larger process that dichotomizes individual from social in American culture. Of course, the individual must remain the unit of contestation and concern. But the individual cannot be made an analytic unit of inquiry or an explanation for any cultural pattern without precisely destroying individuality and agency. In this chapter, we locate the struggle with individualistic discourse in early-twentieth-century American texts, particularly in philosophical pragmatism and cultural anthropology. There we can find clear evidence of a helpful understanding of the analytic relationship between individual and social conditions, a relationship we want to help develop. We can also find the seeds of a rhetorical turn that reduced the insights of the pragmatist concern with interaction into a view of society as another variable explaining individual behavior. Many took this turn even as they claimed the pragmatist inheritance. Behind this turn is a communicative situation that George Herbert Mead, a major figure in pragmatism, described well: Addressing an audience requires taking the position of the audience and using its words and rhetorical forms, sometimes to the point of the address being recast by the response of the audience. In America, an author must demonstrate a practical, recognizable, and identifiable "concern with the individual." Otherwise the text will be dismissed, if it is read at all. Unfortunately, demonstrating a rhetorical concern with the individual often invites a response that constitutes the individual as the unit of analysis. This has the confusing effect of erasing a consideration not only of the social forces in the lives of the individuals under study but of the social forces that have made the individual the point of rhetorical focus in research. By this logic, the source of the problem is not that the authors or audiences "are" American but that they write and read with America in America. In America certain things are hard to say. Understanding how hard they are to say and finding a way to say what needs to be said are our goals here. We start this process by reconstructing something that was extremely powerful in the writings of three major figures of intellectual America: Arthur Bentley, G. H. Mead, and Ruth Benedict.

We return to nascent cultural inquiries, long abandoned in American intellectual life, to show how early intuitions about the central place of interaction and history as the product of interaction were erased by the next generations of authors (and sometimes by the original authors as well). Over the past thirty years, many have attempted to revive some of the early intuitions, but the obstacles that faced Bentley, Mead, and Benedict are still with us, particularly the tendency to see social reality only to the extent that it has been internalized in the individual who knows, feels, thinks, and decides. There may be a world out there, external to humanity, but its relevance is dependent on personal meanings. As Herbert Blumer put it at the end of a long career fighting all theories of the external social fact, "Even though [a joint action] may be well established and repetitive each instance of it has to be formed anew. ... The participants still have to build their lines of actions and fit them to one another. . . . They do this . . . by using the same recurrent and constant meanings. If we recognize this, we are forced to realize that the play and fate of meaning are what is important, not the joint action in its established form" (1969: 17, 18).

We chose this quote to summarize the position we are most directly struggling with because Blumer claimed, and succeeded in claiming, that his "symbolic interactionism" was the direct and most legitimate successor of Mead's social psychology.[1] We too claim Mead, but we read him differently and think his struggle against psychological behaviorism was also a struggle against psychologization in general. Almost a century ago, he complained that his peers in psychology and sociology continued to study the relation between the social and individual as if they were separate events "in the same manner one might investigate the psychology of mountain tribes because they are subject to the influence of high altitude and rugged landscape" ([1909] 1964 : 94). Mead preferred something more interactive, transactional, and reflexive. How to arrive at it carefully and systematically so as not to mislead readers was then and is now the difficulty. The ease with which Blumer could transform Mead back into a psychologist of the self is a problem we can study at the distance given by half a century of retellings.

Let us start with a text written long before Mead, Thomas Paine's foundational version of the origin myth of society: "Let us suppose a small number of persons settled in some sequestered part of the earth, unconnected with the rest, they will represent the first peopling of any country, or of the world. In this state of natural liberty, society will be their first thought" ([1776] 1976: 66).

First the thinking persons, then society. The image is an old one, embroidered on earlier versions by Hobbes and Rousseau, and it keeps striking many as apt. It reappears in various guises, in Chomsky (1966), for example, as he defined the theoretical problem of linguistics as the description of how two speakers of a language can understand each other. It reappears in Berger and Luckmann's *Social Construction of Reality* as "two persons from entirely different worlds [beginning] to interact" (1966: 56). Paine knew, and Berger and Luckmann emphasize, that the people who settle in a "sequestered part of the earth" come from much less sequestered parts and that such parts are never quite "unconnected with the rest." In most versions of constructionism, the strollers reach a new consensus as if they were the only people in the world and without acknowledging that the language they speak was borrowed from generations before, that they are walking on lands invariably claimed by others, that their developing agreements must be legitimated with still others who only appear absent at the time of the meeting. Human beings were never so inherently, naturally, or completely in control of their community. They are even less in control of their selves.

We start with the early pragmatists because they moved further than most toward understanding that one's self is partially the construct of others and partially under one's control. In most every case, the people we quote had a more complex position. But in every case, if only for easy communication in an American nexus, they all return to make statements that, one, systematically overstate the powers of the individual to define conditions and, two, simultaneously recreate the conditions for not taking any one individual too seriously because having internalized the same culture, having been oversocialized as a member of the same consensual community, each one is just like the rest. The early pragmatists understood that the self, though never in complete control, also resists. Even as they searched for interactional theories of the active though constrained self, sometimes in their own writings and almost always in that of their students and followers, they presented theories of the self *becoming* the other.

Having sketched this dilemma in pragmatist writings of the first half of the century, we next examine three recent efforts to develop a more cultural account of human agency. We start with a version of cultural psychology that shows, despite a contemporary rhetoric about culture and human agency, how easy it is to fall back into the most discredited approaches to culture and personality. Our second and third foci move us closer to what we seek. First, we point at the limitations of Bourdieu's theorizing about culture, *"habitus,"* and education ([1972] 1977, 1994). Whereas his emphasis on practice and strategies within "objective structures" would seem to point to an active agent struggling with conditions that are *always already there*, his continued use of the concept of *habitus* ("incorporated structures"), or habits acquired early in life, rekindle the socially internalized self that has dominated American social thought. A little psychologizing may have been useful in the context of a French sociology locked in an arthritic Durkheimian prestructuralism, but it is proving to be extremely dangerous when read in America. As part of this context, Bourdieu's work can too easily be seen as a new call for a social psychology that can again mask the continuing power of all those around the habituated self. Finally, we focus on what has come to be known as various "constructionist" traditions, particularly in the work of Berger and Luckmann (1966). Here too, dangers lurk, but the possible gains are considerable.

The Intuition of Culture

We are not the first to call for the version of cultural analysis we are illustrating in this book.[2] In the first half of this century, others, even other Americans, stated important parts of our argument, and in every case their words have been swallowed into the mainstream of American social thought. We can open with an astounding text from Arthur Bentley (1908), who devoted the opening third of his book on government to a diatribe against the causal and explanatory power of individual feelings and ideas:

> "Feelings," "faculties," "ideas," and "ideals" are not definite "things" in or behind society, working upon it as causes. . . . Many refined theories exist which state these psychic elements not as "things" but as process. I am not concerned with such theories, but with the practical use made of the elements themselves in interpretations of society; and in that use they always present themselves as "things," however much that fact may appear to be veiled. Their very statement as phases of individual life throws them concretely into opposition to the society which they are used to explain, and makes concrete causes out of them in the bad sense (1908: 165).

It is important to note that Bentley is not arguing against the existence of feelings and ideas or against their usefulness in an inquiry into people's lives or even against the occasional use of a mental image as a "shorthand expression indicating briefly causal connections we have already worked out, which would take many words to state otherwise" (1908: 169). And so it is that we could not have presented the stories about Adam and Joe having a difficult time learning to read without being attentive to what they must have been feeling and thinking. But none of these uses, either Bentley's or our own, turns the individual into a Promethean force making a world without regard for what is *always already there*. None of these uses turn isolated individuals into an explanation for the ways their behavior is segmented and made consequential by others. "The minute we plant ourselves on feelings and ideas as solid facts, that minute we open the way to all confusions" (169). In lieu of focusing on the individual actor, Bentley calls for an account of the person as "a center of activity" rather than as a "point of view" for an account of the "psychic process" without the "concreted mental type" (1908: 256; 1926: 457). In lieu of focusing on the individual actor, Bentley calls for an understanding of the cultural world served by that focus. Instead of asking only about individual action, he asks about the world that organizes that action and makes it relevant. Instead of asking about individual school failure, Bentley would ask about the educational process that would make such a systematic and lethal, big deal of small performances. Why not instead, he would ask, focus on what everyone might be able to do, on what every citizen might be able to contribute.

It is often the case that Bentley-like appeals to not forget the worlds in which individuals must make their way are dismissed for leaving the individual out of the action. No matter how much a Bentley then or a Varenne and McDermott now temper their social and cultural arguments with an insistence that the worlds they are interested in must be and must be shown to be composed, constituted, reproduced, and resisted by individuals as "centers of activity" more than as "concreted mental types," they are always confronted with the American dichotomy: either society or the individual. Bentley was wonderfully aware of this danger and faced it directly:

> We may well expect difficulty with interpretations based on a fundamental split between the idea and the outer world [read also: individual and social, subjective and objective, micro and macro, etc.]. If we throw emphasis on either one of the two to the exclusion of the other, and deny the complement, we are constructing a world out of stuff that has definition only in terms of the very opposition we attempt to deny. If we take both concretely—the subjective and the objective—and attempt to function them together in a causal system, we are putting two halves together which never possibly on causal lines can make one whole; for the excellent reason that the original analysis which produced the two parts was not made on adequate causal lines. (Bentley 1908: 171)

So it is that we are not trying to pit a social account of schooling against a psychological one as traditionally conceived. Against the claim that African Americans fail in school because of restricted cognitive or linguistic growth, it is only a small advance, for us, to argue that they fail in school because they are alienated by socially perceivable job ceilings and prejudice. Either way, African Americans are still organized and perceived as failing, and we are helping to build that fact by documenting and explaining that failure's relation to individual decisionmaking. If we must choose between psychological and social, between one or the other, we would prefer to follow James Joyce (1939), who preferred to confront all dichotomies by taking "one aneither." With Bentley, we would prefer not having to make the choice. Instead, we are trying to locate the cultural order that has Americans turning school performance into an ever ready institutional tool for the creation of success and failure as an event to which everyone in the culture must somehow orient, with which everyone must struggle, and about which everyone must seemingly make a decision.

For its first forty years, Bentley's early work had little impact on American letters. After World War II, he was rediscovered as the founding father of interest group theory, and the line of argument we have been quoting was held up, illegitimately, as a classic call for a static behaviorist approach to politics.[3] Having directed his attention to transcending the social and individual dichotomy in favor of an account of activity, including an account of the activity of isolated individuals as the explanation of all behavior, he was caught in the related and equally lethal dichotomy between subjective and objective methods of analysis and hailed, despite his position to the contrary, as an objectivist, empiricist behaviorist. Although his work in philosophy is cited occasionally, and that likely because of his association with John Dewey, Bentley's cultural intuition remains on the wayside of American social science.

Almost the opposite story can be told of G. H. Mead's effort to understand the *always already there* that not only confronts individual activity but helps to constitute the very fact of the individual. This strong social position aside, by midcentury, Mead was hailed as a psychologist who argued for the self as a solitary figure in interaction with but essentially separate from others. In the hands of symbolic interactionism of the type associated with Herbert Blumer, Mead was understood as a student of the effects of outside social forces on the inside subjective self. Although Mead's fate was the opposite of Bentley's, the difference is only partially, or mistakenly, warranted by their main texts. From his earliest essays on, Mead wrote of consciousness, the self, and perspective, each a possible center for the feelings and ideas that Bentley wanted not to call "things" as real things with all the properties of real objects. Although this is a difference that would make them sound terribly divided, they were exploring quite different arguments to the same end.

Although they argued their points with different words, both Mead and Bentley were opposed to any conception of an isolated, internalized, available-upon-introspection-only, causal self. They were similarly opposed, as we are, both to any account of a solitary, passive self buffeted by the world outside and to any account of the world as if it were driven solely by individuals imposing their will. For Mead, we can go back to a definition of the self as a social reality in mutually constitutive relations with others in processes such as consciousness, learning, and communication:

> There is a persistent tendency among present-day psychologists to use consciousness as the older rationalistic psychology used the soul. It is spoken of as something that appears at a certain point, it is something into which the object of knowledge in some sense enters from without. . . . The way out of these crude psychological conceptions, in my mind, lies in the recognition that psychical consciousness is a particular phase in development of reality, not an islanded phase of reality connected with the rest of it by a one to one relationship of parallel series ([1910b] 1964: 105–106).

> So far as education is concerned, the child does not become social by learning. He must be social in order to learn ([1910a] 1964: 122).

> In the process of communication, the individual is an other before he is a self. It is in addressing himself in the role of another that his self arises in experience. . . . Social beings are things as definitely as psychical things are social. . . . The others and the self arise in the social act together ([1927] 1964: 313–314).

For Mead, the reality of the self is relational, *in situ*, in activity, in work with others, just as, for Bentley, feelings and ideas are best understood at the center of activity. They are where the action is, and in that sense, they are real.

Ruth Benedict was also interested in the perspectives, feelings, and ideas of individuals in action with others. Unlike Bentley and Mead, she had a word that was supposedly able to capture that interest: As an anthropologist, Benedict could rely on culture. But the idea of culture available to her kept splitting her intuition into two parts. On the one hand, by culture she means something quite separate from what the individual can control. In her book on Japanese culture and behavior, *The Chrysanthemum and the Sword* (1946), she describes the principles of reciprocity by which Japanese order their interactions with each other. She explains their ideas and their emotions, and she sometimes proceeds as if a thorough account of any Japanese individual would reveal the emotional patterning of Japanese. In contrast, at significant places she resists and asks us to remember that if no Japanese person behaves in a way consistent with her description of the emotional patterning of all Japanese, it does not mean that she has not provided a good description. No one has to behave according to the rules of Japanese culture for her description to be adequate; it only has to be the case that some people—particularly those with authority—worry about people not behaving according to the rules.

It is interesting to see how an absolutist account of the individual psyche ("this is the way a Japanese person thinks, feels, and therefore behaves") goes hand and hand with an absolutist account of the cultural environment ("this is the wider culture that is uniform enough to produce so many of the same individuals"). In Benedict's writing, she even gave this account a physical image: The person is a piece of film that lit up and enlarged on a blank wall, becomes the culture, the individual writ large. And so it is that no sooner are we told that no one has to be drum-roll-driven lockstep into idealized patterns of Japanese behavior for the whole system to work that Benedict gives us the detail on how the Japanese are inescapably socialized and entrained, like so many mountain tribes to their high altitudes, into the performance of what is recognizable Japanese behavior. From the opening pages of *Patterns of Culture* (1934) to the closing pages of *The Chrysanthemum and the Sword* (1946), she delivers a focus on overly socialized individuals ready to do for themselves what the culture demands because from the very moment of a child's birth,

> The customs into which he is born shape his experience and behavior. By the time he can talk, he is the little creature of his culture, and by the time he is grown and able to take part in its activities, its habits are his habits, its beliefs his beliefs, its impossibilities his impossibilities. Every child that is born into his group will share them with him, and no child born into one on the opposite side of the globe will share them with him, and no child born into one on the opposite side of the globe can ever achieve the thousandth part (1934: 3).

There is something reasonable about such an argument, and we are certainly not arguing that it is not true that children are socialized into their culture. A better diagnosis is that the argument is true, of course, but misleading as stated, for it leaves us with overdetermined individuals and a sense of culture as uniform; it leaves us back with what Bentley and Mead were resisting; it leaves us without individual agency and with culture as pap. When applied to the problems of schooling, it leaves us with the successful (those who were properly and completely socialized) and the failing (those who are missing the essentials of socialization) and neither with an account of how the wider system might be filled with instructions for coordinating the mutual construction of success and failure. It leaves us without a possibility of successful failure.

Intuitions Denied

The struggle to keep both culture and person alive, interactive, and mutually constitutive is blatant in Ruth Benedict's anthropology. She loses the battle in most of her own texts, and posterity remembers her mostly in terms of a culture-as-individual-personality-writ-large theory of socialization (although see Varenne 1984). Bentley and Mead win the battle more consistently in their own texts, but their precision is mostly ignored or remembered for the wrong reason. It certainly seems possible to read them without being forced to take their intuition of culture into account. Consider the following instances of American common sense from Mead's most popular, and textual scholars tell us (Miller, D. 1973; Joas 1985) least representative, posthumous book:

> Social or group attitudes are brought within the individual's field of direct experience, and are included as elements in the structure or constitution of his self, in the same way that the attitudes of particular other individuals are. . . . So the self reaches its full development . . . by thus becoming an individual reflection of the general systematic pattern of social or group behavior in which it and the others are all involved. ...
>
> The getting of this social response into the individual constitutes the process of education which takes over the cultural media of the community in a more or less abstract way. Education is definitely the process of taking over a certain organized set of responses to one's own stimulation; and until one can respond to himself as the community responds to him, he does not genuinely belong to the community (1934: 158, 264–265).

There we have it all: the individual gradually internalizing a community and getting an education that determines how much the individual "genuinely belongs." Ruth Benedict could have said it, and there is hardly a class in educational psychology or the sociology of education that would not buy into it.

The plot thickens when we turn to John Dewey, who spent seventy years fighting against every dichotomy that clogs the American mind.[4] For every dichotomy that posits this against that, the body against the mind, the inside against the outside, the past against the future, and even the individual and the social, Dewey would raise the flags of context, communication, interaction, transaction, of things only in relation to things in relation to purposes and outcomes. And yet even Dewey, especially in his writing on education, is not immune to giving us a text that redivides social and individual, culture and learner, embedded participant and reflective decision-maker: "[When a child] really shares or participates in the common activity . . . his original impulse is modified. He not merely acts in a way agreeing with the actions of others, but, in so acting, the same ideas and emotions are aroused in him that animate the others. A tribe, let us say is warlike" ([1916] 1966 :13–14).

This is followed by a parable illustrating how the children of a warlike tribe become warlike themselves. This parable is preceded by a strong statement about the centrality of communication and consensus, that is, shared patterns, in the establishment of communities ([1916[1966: 4–5). The culture exists. The child enters, and the culture molds the child. The child, already a self complete with impulses, is taught to agree, to build consensus, and to fade into the culture.

If John Dewey can slip this far off his own assertions about the centrality and the precariousness of activity in human affairs, imagine the difficulty of lesser thinkers resisting the temptation of treating individual and culture as two dead trees that fall on each other. When Dewey tackles the social world, he thinks about individuals who already share a culture reaching consensus on a difficult issue and thus expanding its consensus. There is little appreciation for the complex social fields that feed difference and competition over sharing and, ironically, sometimes cruelly arrange for the appearance of consensus to be a charade, a mere mystifying comment on what is always already there and for the most part beyond the control of participants. Although Dewey at his best offered, now almost a century ago, a critique of schooling (1899) that remains vital and current, Dewey at his weakest, Dewey in his consensus model of citizenship, is dangerous fodder for the education mill. Making nice along the road to consensus in a society is not a model of schooling that America can afford, not when that society is already constructed in ways lethal to many of its citizens. (See Feffer [1993] on the crashed hopes of early-twentieth-century progressivism; see Dewey [1938] and McDermott [1973] for an account of a later Dewey who was much more wary of impacted inequalities built into the American consensus; see Manicas [1993] for a Dewey that presses beyond a methodological individualism.)

While Dewey was writing, there were certainly available more complex formulations of the workings of the social world, but even in the most sweeping theories of social action, there was little advance in the search for a theory of agency and culture. Consider the following from Talcott Parsons and Edward Shils:

> Without the organization [of the basic alternatives of selective orientation], the stable system of expectations which are essential to any system of action could not exist. Not only does the child receive the major organization of his own selective orientations from adults through the socialization process, but consensus with respect to the same fundamental selections among alternatives is vital to a stable social system. In all societies the stabler and more effective patterns of culture are *those which are shared in common* . . . by the members of societies and by groups of societies (1951: 21, our emphasis).

Again it is the consenting decisionmaker who is the unit of culture. Nothing could be more obvious to the American reader. This is what makes us nervous, for as obviously true as it is in some sense, it does not insist that readers consider the conditions under which it is less true or in some sense patently false.

Although Parsons knew a great deal about social structure, he theorized about personalities and failed to take into account all the people who build the system and keep it going. Because his analysis starts with the individual actor making up a mind, there is a limit to how much he can take into account the full range of constraints that shape the events about which no decisions can be made: "An actor in a situation is confronted with a series of major dilemmas of orientation, a series of choices that the actor must make before the situation has a determined meaning for him" (1951: 76). In other words, at the moment of action, the actor is alone and must look inward to decide what to do next. This thereby renders problematic what social theory attempts to explain: how collective action proceeds. Parsons and Shils resolve the problem by invoking communication and the similarity among the individuals produced in secondary steps through a process of communication: "In interaction, ego and alter are each objects of orientation for the other. . . . Communication through a common system of symbols is the precondition of this reciprocity or complementarity of expectations. . . . When such generalization occurs, and actions, gestures, or symbols have more or less the *same* meaning for both ego and alter, we may speak of a common culture existing between them, through which their interaction is mediated" (1951: 105, authors' emphasis).

What makes for continuity, then, is that the same people keep showing up and finding out that they share enough to move ahead. Similarity is so central here that Parsons and Shils emphasize the word "same," which appears as a leitmotif in their "general theory," whether they are talking about personality, action in society, or culture. In an account of the School, it would lead to a claim that schools produce the kinds of failure and success rates that they do because the same people keep showing up and making decisions about whether or not to fail or succeed. What is left out is an account of how success and failure came to be the only pathways to which school people could orient, and actively and relentlessly so.

Current Common Senses of Culture

Given the pedigree of a way of talking about individual action that makes it the product of an internalization of "culture," it may not be surprising that it should seem common sense. By the 1980s, Shirley Brice Heath could assume, when writing *Ways with Words*, for example, that the word "culture" would be so clear as not to need definition or discussion. The word occurs repeatedly in the book. The closest to a definition is a phrase that warns readers against missing "the central point of the focus on culture as learned behavior and on language habits as part of that shared learning" (1983: 11). The word is used extensively as an adjective, as in "cultural milieu," "cultural life of a social group," "culturally different communities," (11, 343), "cultural background" (2), "cultural habits" (7), "cultural groups" (13), "cultural difference" (266, 271), "cultural patterns" (344, 367, 369), "cultural features" (366), "cultural change" (416). It also occurs as a noun as in "community cultures" (3). We have not conducted an exhaustive analysis of the occurrence of "culture" in the book, but it is clear that these occurrences are well ordered. The paradigm of "culture" includes concepts such as "patterns," "habits," "difference," and "group," not to mention "learning." They are all modified by the "effects" of "culture" on "individuals."

None of this is surprising given the power of a culture (such as America as we have been talking about it) as it is institutionalized in the history of a particular intellectual tradition. The culture of "Culture in America," like the culture of "Education in America," consists in the pattern of a conversation, the structure of a collective discourse, within which all new participants must fit if they want to be heard and through which what may be a truly different personal voice gets co-opted. One might trace with some amazement what happened when Durkheim or Freud was read by Parsons and Erikson as they recognized and recast the power of their insights into the native idiom. One might also trace the resistance of many cultural anthropologists as they criticized the first generation of cultural and personality and then reconstructed it, seemingly without awareness, into orthodoxy.[5] In the past decade, psychology has again discovered culture, and the struggle to weigh the respective roles of the social and the individual and their interconnection is again front and center. We look at two sophisticated versions of this struggle, one focusing on intentionality, in the work of Richard Shweder and Shirley Brice Heath, and the other on practice, in the work of Pierre Bourdieu.

Cultural Psychologies of Intentionality

In America, there may be something inevitable in the regular reaffirmation of the central character of what Richard Shweder—one of the "authors" of a new cultural psychology—calls "intentionality":[6] "Culture refers to the intentional world. Intentional persons and intentional worlds are interdependent things that get dialectically constituted and reconstituted through the intentional activities and practices that are their products, yet make them up" (1991: 26).

Given the ideological framing of the theoretical conversation, this concern with the intentional actor has an interesting twist: In order to deal with the "cultural" aspect of the self, the conversation appears to produce a more oversocialized view of the individual than anything Durkheim and other sociologists would have dared suggest.[7] In Shweder's writing, typically, the individual is a heroic actor. But he is also utterly defeated:

> Culture is the constituted scheme of things for intending persons, or at least that part of the scheme that is inherited or received from the past. Culture refers to persons, society, and nature as lit up, and made possible by some already-there intentional world, an intentional world composed of conceptions, evaluations, judgments, goals, and other mental representations already embodied in socially inherited institutions, practices, artifacts, technologies, art forms, texts, and modes of discourse. It is those inherited conceptions, evaluations . . . about which the intending think, out of which the intending build their lives, and with respect to which the intending give substance to their minds, souls, and directed actions.
>
> Psyche and culture are thus seamlessly interconnected. A person's psychic organization is largely made possible by, and expressive of, a conception of itself, society, and nature; and the best ways to understand cultural conceptions of self, society, and nature is to examine the way those conceptions organize . . . the subjective life of intending individuals. (1991: 26)

The individual is at the center, but his "substance" is completely made up by what he has "inherited." In order to get out of the trap, Shweder (1991, chap. 1) attempts to co-opt postmodern strictures about irony and what he calls "casuistry": The individual may be defeated, but he can laugh.

Whether one is convinced or not by such arguments, our concern is, first, with the kind of empirical work that Shweder points to as central to cultural psychology and, second, with the implication of this work for the analysis of educational processes. The stylistic formulas implying radical socialization are everywhere, as in the following paragraph: "Oriyas adults do not subscribe to a mechanistic-physicalist conception of nature. Rather they believe . . . For Oriyas, there are . . . Oriyas believe . . . Every informant can cite . . . " (1991: 157–158).

Who knows that Shweder might be right about the Oriyas being all essentially alike on such important issues as a conception of their universe? Given what we know about human beings in general and the history of India in particular, one must be skeptical of Shweder's claims. Hindus in late-twentieth-century India have been in contact with Muslims for many centuries, with Christians for at least two, with modern liberal democrats for more than fifty years. Hinduism itself is a complex religion with few mechanisms for enforcing orthodoxy. Could the unanimity of the informants be the artifact of Shweder's collection mechanisms? And beyond the methodological problems, *must* he treat them as unanimous to explain why they can act together?

When one examines the grounds on which Shweder talks about "Americans," the methodological difficulties become glaring. In one study he says that "the seventeen informants in the American sample came from three separate groups: counseling psychologists . . . , a college fraternity . . . , and nursery school teachers, . . . All lived in or around Chicago and were predominantly middle class" (1991: 129). Of another study he says: "The American sample includes [60] children and [60] adults. . . . [The adults], predominantly white, and of middle-class or upper middle-class background, are descendants of the reformed to secularized branches of the Christian or Jewish traditions. . . . [The children] were recruited from schools in Hyde Park, the residential community surrounding the University of Chicago" (Shweder, Mahapatra, and Miller 1990: 161).

There are stock questions to put against such claims, questions about sampling procedures and the like, that personality psychologists would easily ask and then answer. They would carefully stratify a stronger sample using gross sociodemographic data (place of birth, citizenship, a rough measure of income or education, of religious identification), and they would tell us with confidence who is "American" and what their personality structure is like.

But such questions are not ours. We are sympathetic to Shweder's goal of distinguishing America from Oriya cultures—our way of stating his problem. For anyone thinking development is a set of stages through which all children pass, Shweder's Oriya data are a necessary disruption. That he performs this service admirably does not mean that he has produced a theory of culture that disrupts the mind-set that brought us theories of stages in the first place. Given this purpose, it might make initial sense to let the reader assume uniformity among informants of the same type. For our purpose this is a trap. To allow uniformity and consensus to stand in for variation and discord may be a place to argue from, but it soon invites the erasure of the active person from the lifelong struggle with what is *always already there*.

If Shweder's theoretical framework was applied to the problem of minorities, he could sound much like Erikson or Lewis minus the latter's understanding of the institutional world the poor and the not-so-poor occupy with equal presence. Shweder summarizes his approach in a stark statement that radically denies the importance of copresence on which we insist: "It is a presupposition of cultural psychology that when people live in the world differently, it may be that they live in different worlds" (1991: 23). If this is read from the obvious observation that the poor and the prosperous do live differently, then the poor are left in a separate, deprived world that shapes them and from which they cannot escape. Shweder is not applying his framework to American minorities, and he might alter it if he were.[8] A possible result of approaching the poor as the enculturated product of a separate world may be illustrated by Heath's pessimistic account of "the children of Trackton's children" (1991). In *Ways with Words* she had painted a comparatively optimistic picture of local enculturation practices in Trackton, a small, rural southern community. Years later, she visited one of the children she had met in Trackton after the child, grown into a woman, moved into inner-Atlanta housing with her own children. She wrote of this woman's life as a fall from rural grace into urban poverty. In the inner city, the community collapses, the individual falls into anomic depression, and the children are left to themselves to reproduce what their parents have made:

> For Sissy and Zinnia Mae, in the absence of such associations of sustenance and reinforcement of cultural membership, the intimate symbols of connectedness, pride, and perseverance have left them seemingly unable to adapt their own socialization for that of the next generation or to recreate new foundations of togetherness. . . . An absence of shared work and leisure set mother and daughter apart in the shared background fundamental to leisure talk, and Sissy's continued socialization from womanhood and motherhood comes less and less from her own mother, but from other young women as adrift as she from either a past or a future. (1991: 514–515)

E. Franklin Frazier sounded the same theme when he used Chicago social psychology to analyze what happened as blacks moved from rural areas to urban enclaves: "In the foregoing picture of Negro illegitimacy in a southern city we have all the factors involved in the general problem: poverty, ignorance, the absence of family traditions and community controls, and finally the sexual exploitation of the subordinate race by the dominant race. . . . But of course, such cases of illegitimacy, involving the degree of poverty, social disorganization, and personal demoralization represented in the description are not typical" ([1948] 1966: 257).

The story Frazier quotes before this paragraph is an eerie echo of the tale Heath weaves, and it is used for about the same rhetorical purposes: It is an interesting, pathetic, human case, apparently intended to move us to pity. It is also a case relevant to our theoretical concerns. It appears as proof of the eventual analysis: Urban poverty leads to personal disorganization. In poverty, people are "adrift" with no methods for connecting. They are, it would appear, people in need of our help because they can no longer help themselves.[9]

Heath finishes her paper with the now required bow to the rhetorical dangers of ethnographic writing, a possible occasion to warn, as Frazier did, against assuming "typicality" of the children of Trackton's children. Such a warning is itself paradoxical, since it establishes as relevant what it tells us not to pay attention to: If such stories are not typical, what stories would be, and what is the relevance of the story actually told? Are these the stories sociological audiences "want" to read? Just what is the status of the story being told? And what would give warrant to move from a telling of the story to a conclusion about minority culture. Heath offers an explosive conclusion: "We must run the risk of demonstrating that fewer and fewer individuals in some minority groups define themselves in terms of webs of significance they themselves spin, and many may be caught without understanding, interpreting, or transmitting anything like the cultural patterns into which they themselves were socialized" (1991: 517).

"Fewer and fewer" may be the key words, for they keep us focused on the constitution of individuals and their failings: "They" are unable to adapt, "they" don't understand, "they" do not interpret, "they" do not transmit. Thirty years of work that has attempted to demonstrate the wealth of productive action in the most difficult of circumstances—the work of Labov, Liebow, Stack, and so on—has been canceled. Heath may even be canceling that part of her work that represented the vibrant cultural activity of the black poor in the South.[10]

There may be policy reasons for Heath's dismissal that would bring us back to the issues we raised earlier and to which we return in the concluding chapter. At this stage, we want to continue the theoretical discussion. Our intuition is that the detailed ethnographic work of the past two decades, including the work in Part 1, must not be dismissed. The actions of various young people from the mean streets of New York, as they do classroom or choir, like the actions of Adam or the children of privilege in New Jersey, reveal their active sensitivity to the world, and we suspect that so would the characters in Heath's morality tale if their conditions were confronted more directly. There is cultural power in poverty, and it has little to do with how much mainstream ways with words are learned or internalized. Poverty is both a cultural product and a condition for further cultural elaboration. It is a cultural product in that it evolves into particular forms through the history of the total society of which the poor are a part. It is a condition for further cultural elaboration because it requires, like all social conditions do, a constructive response by the people placed in the condition. Even a response that may appear to an observer "objectively" destructive—if the goal is a move to the middle class, for example—must also be analyzed for its sensitivity to the actual conditions of the people involved.

A Sociology of Educational Practices and Habits

If Ogbu (1991b) makes us wonder at the refusal of some to succeed at school, Bourdieu marvels at the reverse: Why should the working classes of France be so profoundly attached to Education, its rituals and practices? Why should it be that politically progressive forces are so adamant about expanding the reach of the School even in the face of continual demonstrations that the School is a major institution reproducing the position of people within the class structure of industrial societies?

Bourdieu's answer is *méconnaissance*, a specifically developed misknowing about the School that is fostered by the School itself among those whom it captures, whether parents, students, or teachers: "Given that it explicitly raises the question of its own legitimacy . . . every [institutionalized education system] must produce and reproduce, by the means proper to the institution, the institutional conditions for misrecognition (*méconnaissance*) of the symbolic violence which it exerts, i.e., recognition (*reconnaissance*) of its legitimacy as a pedagogic institution" ([1970] 1977b: 61).

The argument proceeds in several steps that emphasize the "arbitrariness" of the School: The specific organization of School is not made necessary by some universal aspect of educational processes. The School is a cultural institution but with the proviso that the legitimacy of its practices not be seen as the historical product of a cultural process. If the School were recognized as only one of the many ways through which human beings get educated, then its legitimacy could be questioned. How could a modern democratic nation-state legitimately oblige all children to attend its schools if it was not generally agreed that these schools are a universal field within which all human beings, without regard to sex, race, religion, and so on, can compete equally? Bourdieu insists that this cultural arbitrariness operates at all levels of educational practice from the most general, national levels to the most local, as, for example, when a teacher asks a child a testing question to which the teacher already knows the answer. What are the grounds that make this a legitimate question for the teacher to ask? Why is it that the child is obliged to answer it (and is legitimately punished for giving the "wrong" answer or, worse, for not answering it at all)?

Bourdieu is less interested in the first question than the second. He does not explore in any detail the actual organization of the School as a cultural system. He spends most of his empirical time demonstrating that the School does not operate as a level, universal field and then focuses his theoretical action on the student or parent who acts in terms of the School's definition. In all his writings, Bourdieu has emphasized his concern with "practice" and "strategies" and has systematically criticized various forms of social structuralism in the French tradition for talking in general terms about the constraining power of various conditions without paying attention to the actual mechanisms through which these made a difference in the everyday life of actual human beings. The criticism is somewhat overdrawn but is not without its merits. Bourdieu's solution is that individuals operate within arbitrary cultural systems because, in the process, they "habituate" to them. In his words: "Insofar as it is the arbitrary imposition of a cultural arbitrary . . . , [pedagogical action] entails *pedagogical work*, a process of inculcation which must last long enough to produce a durable training, i.e. a *habitus*, the product of internalization of the principles of a cultural arbitrary capable of perpetuating itself after [pedagogical action] has ceased and thereby perpetuating in practices the principles of the internalized arbitrary" (Bourdieu and Passaron [1970] 1977: 31).

The people captured by the School end up "misknowing" their conditions; they fail to understand the source of their difficulties and thus participate in and eventually reproduce them. This is particularly true of professors and students at the ideological core of the School, where constraints other than purely educational ones disappear ([1970] 1977: 67).

There is little evidence that Bourdieu followed in any detail the history of Bentley, G. H. Mead, Benedict, and how they were "adopted on the collective mode," to paraphrase Lévi-Strauss ([1971] 1981: 627). Nor does he discuss the "culture of poverty" controversies or how the concept of *habitus* might be recast to not take us back to deprivation accounts. He certainly does not take up our argument that by placing cultural arbitrariness within the habituated individual, he has already robbed the person of all agency, including the possibility of seeing through conditions that remain there as concrete obstacles even after one's consciousness has been raised. As de Certeau points out (1984: 56–60), the *habitus* is a kind of theoretical black hole postulated to complete the theory but essentially metaempirical. Bourdieu does not directly investigate the *habitus*; he invokes it to resolve a theoretical problem. *Habitus* holds the place of "personality as learned and shared" in early culture and personality theory. In fact, the theory fails to take into account his own activity (and that of many other intellectual critics of Euro-American Education).

Bourdieu must end with *habitus* because he could not imagine a situation where people could be shown to submit themselves practically, in their everyday life, to a cultural arbitrary that they either understood and accepted or (mis) understood and resisted. Paradoxically, he seems to accept the pedagogical notion that knowledge (both substantive and cultural) is "inculcated" in schools, that is, that knowledge moves from outside into a person through education. There are other solutions, out of the ethnomethodological literature,[11] that start with the idea that rules of conduct, that is, a "cultural arbitrary," are not so much "followed" by well-encultured individuals as they are practically performed by agents. This performance allows analysts to talk about "rules" (structures, cultures) but not to project the source of the rules to an initial psychic state of the actors. The actors re-cognize the features of their social world in the real time of their performance. They un-cover these features for the analyst to dis-cover. They are always at productive, cultural work. Whether they have an analytic discourse available about their condition (and thus demonstrate their "unconsciousness") is beside the point. "True" (rather than "false" or "mistaken") consciousness is irrelevant for action, that is, for "faction," the kind of action that makes, constructs, cultural facts for others to deal with.

Constructive Agency in Cultural Conditions: Problems and Possibilities

The last sentence of the preceding paragraph summarizes the stance we take when analyzing specific cases. The stance is rooted in the original intuition of pragmatist theorizing in its insistence that *all* action must proceed through the protagonists engaging in what G. H. Mead called a "conversation of gestures" (1934). It is also rooted in the Boasian premise emphasizing the historical *particularity* of all conversations: The pattern of conversations is never purely determined by the functional requirements of the conversation and its participants. *All* human action is susceptible to a cultural activity that transforms the functional requirements and in the process externalizes itself. These statements are not presented as applying only to *some* action in some settings. They are general theoretical statements about humanity. They are not functionalist statements about what should happen for social life to proceed. They are descriptive statements about what does happen. Survival, that is, production and reproduction, is based on active cooperation and a mutual dependency that makes something new.

We have traced how this tradition got caught in debates about learning, sharing, and the formation of the self or identity, debates that had the paradoxical effect of constructing the image of an oversocialized, essentially passive individual shaped to the core by external conditions. It is not surprising that one can trace, starting in the 1960s and continuing to this day, the development of new attempts to center on human activity. These come wrapped in various theoretical languages derived from pragmatism, phenomenology, Marxism, and anthropologies of action. Despite the variation, we can sketch a general impulse to understand "action" as "joint construction" "in specific contexts" in the course of "reproducing" social conditions. In pragmatism, individual agency was central, but it may have remained somewhat abstract. In more recent developments, partly under the influence of Marxism and partly under the goad of those who seek to look most determinedly and inductively at humans in action, the understanding of agency has shifted to emphasize the concreteness of what is accomplished. Through their activity human beings reproduce themselves, socially as well as biologically, and the very acts of reproduction as concretely performed may be what "culture" is all about.

Problems remain. The same forces that dulled earlier insights are still with us. To illustrate this, we start with Peter Berger and Thomas Luckmann's *Social Construction of Reality* (1966), an important alternative to any view of human beings as "oversocialized" and analytically unappreciated as agents at work transforming their world. The problem we see is easily made explicit. Berger and Luckmann present their work as a "treatise in the sociology of *knowledge*." They understand knowledge, quite commonsensically, to be an attribute of individual consciousness: "The world of everyday life is not only taken for granted as reality by the ordinary members of society in the subjectively meaningful conduct of their lives. It is a world that originates in their thoughts and actions, and is maintained as real by these" (19–20).

In a stroke of the pen, they have equated "thought" and "action," and though we find it problematic, many found liberating their insistence on the subjective agent as the "originator" of the world of everyday life. And yet along with this freedom from sociological determinism did come a confusion between "action" and "knowledge," whether knowledge is understood as a matter of cognition or as a matter of consciousness and subjective meaning. This is another instance, à la Mead, Benedict, Shweder, or Bourdieu, of the slide from agency into enculturation. Berger and Luckmann perform the slide from the former to the latter as they move from an introduction in which they mostly talk about "knowledge" to a first chapter that they start with "Since our purpose in this treatise is a sociological analysis of the reality of everyday life, more precisely, of knowledge that guides conduct in everyday life . . . " (1966: 19).

As "sociologists," it is in fact fully proper that they should be interested in *conduct*, but behind the conduct, there is a knowledge, the real reality steering, guiding, and shaping what is "subjectively meaningful" and "maintained as real." No sooner does theory rush into the head than we have apparent grounds for pitying or condemning those with wrong things in their heads. No sooner is the social made real only as it is internalized than we have apparent grounds for noting what the children of Trackton's children are missing without having to notice that someone else is taking it away.

If one can resist the slide from agency into enculturation, major possibilities for theoretical development remain. The revolt against the kind of Parsonian sociologies that had formalized the earlier versions of the slide, a revolt in which Berger and Luckmann were major figures, did produce much that developed early pragmatist insights, and it continues to promise much. In this generation of work, analytic currency was given to such words as "work," "accomplishment," "reproduction," "performance," "emergence," and "reflexivity," words that in different ways, for different purposes, and from different theoretical perspectives all focus attention on a property of "action" that was buried in earlier paradigms of sociological metaphors: Human interaction with other human beings always does something concrete. It makes something, a thing, a fact. It "constructs" an objective world for all involved. Action, in other words, is not a product of conditions; it is a transformer of conditions.

These difficult propositions may be summarized in two ways. First, taking seriously that all joint action is productive focuses attention on historical consequences: In the real time of face-to-face interaction, everyone has to deal with the past constructions of other persons, often absent and perhaps long dead. Everyday, a teacher must deal with last week's outburst by a student, a principal's decision to assign this rather than that teacher to a particular classroom, New York State regulations about the qualification of teachers, and even, however indirectly, such cultural constructions as the Constitution of the United States. These are not causes, not even after they are memorized and put in everyone's head, but they are powerful conditions.

Second, taking seriously that joint action is always productive focuses attention in a new way on the identification of the "subject" of action: who or what is to be made responsible as the originator of a specified act. We began the introduction to this book raising questions about whom to make responsible for the "success" of a famous author and for the obscurity of her sister. Clearly, Maxine Hong Kingston is a person who went to school, grew up in a Chinese enclave in California, wrote a book that sold many copies, and can commonsensically be said to "be successful"—as a property of her personal self. Similar things could be said about her sister, who also grew up in a Chinese enclave in California but did not write a book and did not become successful in the same manner. We could have written a book about why

Kingston became famous and her sister did not, but our concern is elsewhere. We wonder about who made the category "Chinese," who bounded "California," who evolved the "book" as one physical shape a text can take, and who constituted the category "success" and its pair, "failure." Berger and Luckmann, like many others, ask these questions as if they are easily answerable: "What remains sociologically essential is the recognition that all symbolic universes and all legitimations are human products; their existence has its base in the lives of concrete individuals, and has no empirical status apart from these lives" (1966: 128).

In short, everything is a "social construction": "China," "California," "book," "success/failure." But such an answer is no more than a restatement of the problem we are confronting: Who are these "concrete individuals"? How could we locate the "men" who made the social world "and therefore, can remake it" (Berger and Luckmann 1966: 89)? Easy answers about "men" are confusing because they conflate two incommensurate concerns: Locating the activity of individuals in a local setting is one thing; tracing collective processes over many years of joint history, and the consequences of the products of this history for local action, is another thing altogether. Writing a sentence may be one thing; having it taken as meaningful and then as worthy of publication and applause is something else altogether. In Chapter 1, Adam may have been doing many different things when he warned his peers that all they could do was "try to make it good day." By this act, he proposed something that was taken as another sign that he had a disability of some sort. The young adults in Chapters 3 and 4 of the book could be shown to be quite sensitive to the conditions of their settings and quite active in their use of the possibilities the settings were offering. But the analyses also had to show that most of this activity was erased and made inconsequential as matters specifically not to be taken into account when time came to mete academic rewards.

A century ago, Durkheim gave sociology the charge to confront not the immediate precursors of individual suicides but rather the rates of these suicides as they varied. We have picked up this charge as we have tried to confront not the reasons for individual success or failure but rather the very collective understandings of what is to count as success and failure as well as the massive social constructions that maintain success and failure as realities for all in America. The charge is certainly a more complex one than Durkheim envisioned, particularly to the extent we cannot answer it without directly confronting individual agency. Yes, we must wonder about the "social construction" of subjective reality. But we must wonder also about the construction of social objective realities, the construction of these cultural objects that "I," that is, 我 as an agent, encounters as 我 conducts a life. But "construction" as a concept intended to highlight the centrality of practical activity by concrete individuals is too central to be used imprecisely. It is not easy to catch people in the real time of their practice. When we perform practical research tasks (without which we cannot say that we are interested in practice), apparently paradoxical things happen as we notice how actors are both continually sensitive to matters they cannot be said to have constructed and also continually slightly "off" the most conventional version of what they could have been expected to do. It might be more accurate to speak, along with recent theorists of resistance,[12] of a social deconstruction of reality when one is primarily interested in the actor as subject. Certainly, as we hope emerges in the foregoing discussion of what a child once upon a time built in an American classroom, what subjects construct in the real time of their activity can never be said to be what it would be easiest to say it is. What subjects construct may never be any particular thing that any audience may label it to be. We, as analysts, must always take the position that it is something more, something other, something that cannot be named without replacing it within the very frame the act attempted to escape.

Constructing Walls and Other Boundaries

To draw (construct, inscribe) this argument in its sharpest form, let us start with a famous account of the making of a wall, a social boundary between "neighbors." In the following chapter, we discuss in more detail the context of moments in the making of classrooms. We are told by a great American poet struggling to express the conditions of his human experiences that "at spring mending-time,"

> *I let my neighbor know beyond the hill;*
> *And on a day we meet to walk the line*
> *And set the wall between us once again.*

And so Robert Frost tells of the work the speaker and his neighbor "beyond the hill" must perform to make right a wall that was attacked over the year by the "something there is that doesn't love a wall." This is a poem (Frost 1949: 47), but it is also an account of a human activity that quite literally "constructs" ("mends") a physical object (a stone wall) with social consequences ("good fences make good neighbors"). The "I" in the poem "wonders":

> *It comes to little more:*
> *There where it is we do not need the wall:*
> *He is all pine and I am apple orchard.*
> *My apple trees will never get across*
> *And eat the cones under his pines,*

There is no "need" for this wall, no cows that might wander where they could cause mischief, and "I" wonders further:

> *Before I built a wall I'd ask to know*
> *What I was walling in or walling out,*
> *And to whom I was like to give offense.*

If there is no economic need, there may be something else that has to do with "giving offense," something that Frost does not name but describes quite graphically:

> *I see him there*
> *Bringing a stone grasped firmly by the top*
> *In each hand, like an old-stone savage armed.*
> *He moves in darkness as it seems to me,*
> *Not of woods only and the shade of trees.*

The suggested need is dark indeed, and the darkness does not have to do with the trees of the wood that are blocking the light. "Good fences make good neighbors" repeats the neighbor in an atmosphere that has become ominous.

Later in the poem, the "I" repeats the line "Something there is that doesn't love a wall" and talks of something "that wants it down." Earlier, we had been presented with a list of these things: The "frozen-ground-swell" and other physical forces, the hunters and other social forces who "work" at leaving "not one stone on a stone" "to please the yelping dogs." But the wall is there to be (re)constructed and demolished again in a process that remains mysterious to the "I" of the poem.

Many, from Lévi-Strauss to Gregory Bateson, have seen human wisdom at work in the recognition of lines (boundaries, walls). For Lévi-Strauss, the injunctions that the wall represents physically, injunctions such as "thou shalt not marry thy sister," are the fundamental cultural act (Lévi-Strauss [1949] 1969). They are the realization of our humanity, and one should glory rather than despair in all the evidence that demonstrates there is always "more" in human constructions than one would expect from an examination of "needs" based in economic or sociobiological rationality. The wall has little to do with wandering cows or even with darker offenses; it has to do with the transformation of a vague physical divide ("beyond the hill") into a sharp cultural one. Thus *neighbors* are made, constructed, neighbors who are "good" to think, communicate with, and about (Lévi-Strauss [1962] 1963b).

Much has been written about the actual wisdom of a structuralist stance, which many find as uncomfortable as the "I" of Frost's poem found the need to mend the wall. This "I" is far from the only subject that doesn't love a wall. There are many hunters out there who are destroying what stands in the way of their enjoyment. This destructive activity is as much something to be accounted for in our social theories as the wall constructing activities that fascinate various structuralists. Our goal is to explore the various relationships people can have with "actual" walls, walls that are the product of someone's *action*, action in the sense most respectful of the independent agency of the people who participated.

Actual walls are undoubtedly "social constructions of reality." Putting up a stone wall is a deliberate act that involves a whole society, the neighbors first and then a crowd of others: the workers in stone quarries, the masons who cement the stones, the truck drivers who deliver them, the bankers who lend the money, the lawyers who check old deeds and trace the exact line on a map, and even the poets who warn people about the ambiguous nature of these cultural constructions. But then the wall is up. Something happened, and a new social process is instituted. All further action around the wall will be of a different order. Some will, from now on, do the "mending" that is the occasion of Frost's musings. Others, like the hunters, will try to take some of it down. And there may be the children who, perhaps on the model of Charlie Brown and Linus in *Peanuts*, will use it as a leaning surface whence to ponder the mysteries of life and little red-headed girls.

The wall, it has been said many times in various traditions of work on humanity, will not be quite "the same" wall for each of these people. They will be using different aspects of its properties for a range of miscellaneous possibilities that were not inscribed either in the acts that made the wall or in the physical properties of the wall itself. It would thus seem permissible to say that those who will act around the wall, once it has appeared in history, construct (what) the wall (means to them). From this point of view, the wall, like a tree falling in the forest, does not have any "reality" if it is not specifically constructed in social actions that take it into account. It remains an empty potentiality, a meaningless feature of a physical environment.

We want to challenge the exact phrasing of this expansion of the understanding of construction to focus on the local specification of an object as it is temporarily used for particular purposes. For us, a distinction has to be made between what are two different processes: First, there is a literal construction, the making of something that wasn't there before. Then, once the wall is up, human interaction around the wall changes character. The further acts that people take are not quite "constructions of the wall" in the same manner. It is certainly the case that as long as the wall stands physically or in the memory of the people concerned after it has been bulldozed, what these people are doing is *taking the wall into account* in their action—in their talk and all other behavioral displays.

While it may not be farfetched to talk of this activity as a "construction of a reality," it is still important to realize that the word "construction" is now used in a metaphorical sense. Charlie Brown and Linus are not literally constructing the wall on which they lean, although they are constructing something—a conversation— that takes the wall into account. They are in a similar situation to the one that was the builders' situation because they themselves took into account some properties of stones to transform them into something else, a "something" that can safely be labeled "a wall." In a vocabulary taken from conversation analysis, we might say that for people who confront a historical wall, this wall is an "accountable" event. Clearly the participants are not absolutely constrained by the wall any more than the builders were constrained by the stones. Participants may even be able to tear it down, but they cannot ignore it. The wall is external to them, it precedes them, and as they run into it, it is imposed on them. It is, in brief, a "social fact" in the most classical sense: It was "facted" by a social group. Still, the historical act is never absolutely binding, and we must acknowledge the contribution of the "constructivist" tradition when it reminded us that roles and statuses are never simply "things" that might be described in the absence of the activities that originally made them, maintain their relevance, and in the long run reproduce them.[13] The historical act can never be abolished either, as the very activities that are necessary to destroy it reveal. Formally, one must look at human beings as continually in the business not only of taking into account an object that stands in their way (a wall, a choir, a law that all children must take standardized tests) but of literally building in real time the more or less temporary objects (acts such mending the wall, singing together, preparing for tests) that demonstrate their active accountability to a wider system of constraints. These are the objects that the constructivist tradition has helped us see and that concern us most in this work.

NOTES

1. Blumer's intellectual relation to Mead has been disputed by Fisher and Strauss (1979).

2. In pointing to the "intuition of culture" in Bentley and Mead, we do not mean to imply that they used the word "culture." We prefer to use "cultural" where they said "social" because the word emphasizes the many possible shapes human-made worlds can take.

3. See Lavine (1995) for a clarifying statement.

4. There is little record of intellectual contact between the pragmatists and the Boasians. Dewey and Boas shared the same campus and many political commitments for thirty-eight years but had little direct contact. When Dewey needed to talk about the primitive world, he would cite Malinowski (1923). In *Patterns of Culture*, Benedict does cite Dewey (1934: 2, 271).

5. For a discussion of the process that allowed symbolic anthropology, understood as a critique of culture and personality theories, to be recast into a theory of socially constructed identity, see Varenne (1984).

6. The world "intentionality" is relatively new in the tradition; it appears in the same contexts as "orientation" and "meaning" used to appear in Parsonian social science.

7. In *Suicide* ([1897] 1951), Durkheim repeatedly and specifically rejected any explanation of social facts such as the rate of suicide that would invoke internalization by any individual of the fact. The probability that anyone will commit suicide is too small to drive anyone to suicide. Thus the individual act cannot be explained sociologically. Implicitly, the individual is independent from society, though society cannot be ignored. The formal example is a fact such as the *rate* of suicide typical of a society. We have no grounds to assume that any individual has acquired this rate. The rate reveals the existence of an external force. The illustrative example is a social movement—a war or revolution—that grabs everyone, even those who refuse to move in the direction they are carried toward.

8. For a cultural psychology that does address the struggles of minorities and employs a framework appropriate to that cause, see Cole (1996). It is no accident that the roots of Cole's cultural psychology are in the Soviet psychology of Vygotsky (1978, 1987) and Luria (1979) and not American psychology.

9. The power of these narrative tropes in ethnographic work in black communities is painfully revealed in Duneier's study of working-class black men at the Valois cafeteria in Chicago (1992). He discusses in detail how the general frame of "innocent sociologist (anthropologist) breaking prejudices through in depth observation" can nonetheless reproduce stereotypes when groups specifically chosen for their marginality (street-corner winos, blues singers, etc.) are presented as central to the black experience in ghettos and become the basis for blanket interpretations. The stereotypes may even be credited by someone like Richard Wright as the "scientific" source for a novel like *Native Son* (in the introduction to St. Clair Drake and Horace Cayton's *Black Metropolis* (1945: xvii–xviii).

10. Heath establishes a more positive tone and theoretical verve in subsequent work on urban community organizations (Heath and McLaughlin 1993).

11. The ethnomethodological critique of the social actor as a role and status robot following collective rules is particularly relevant. After Harold Garfinkel (1967), the work of D. L. Wieder (1974) on "telling the code" in halfway houses is particularly powerful.

12. See Willis (1977) or MacLeod (1994). We discussed some related incidents in Chapter 4.

13. Like Frost's wall, all these constructions— marriages, divorces, schools, and other social contracts—are threatened, and one must take care of them, for "something there is that doesn't love a social boundary."

8 Local Constructions of Educational Facts

Hervé Varenne

Emergence and Accountability in Real Time

At the end of the preceding chapter we sketched the theoretical tensions inherent in the phrase "emerging constructions." One can talk about walls as emerging constructions, but one must also talk about them as architectural and jural remnants of older, and completed, activities that are made up for future actors to inhabit. Besides such massive facts as walls, one must also consider temporary constructions such as "cooking classes," "choir rehearsals," "classroom discussions," and "Screw Thy Neighbor" games that both embody the performance of major social structural forces and are the actual "object-ive" product of a local construction. The School (a remnant of centuries-long construction) and the school building (a remnant of a particular construction) require of people who "inhabit" them that they organize themselves to make many well-specified interactional sequences. In the course of a day or year, the inhabitants will have to show that they constructed "classroom discussion," "LD," "smart and dumb," "success and failure"—objects that will then stand in their common history. And they will participate in this construction whether or not they understand what is involved, like it, or resist its consequences. Without activity on the part of the inhabitants, the room, building, or institution would not exist as classroom, school, or School—except perhaps as ruins, half-forgotten remnants in the memories of a few old men and scholars. At the beginning of any day, a class (as a summary term for a great variety of pedagogical scenes such as discussions, reading lessons, or games) does not yet exist as a scene, the organization of which local participants will then become accountable for—just as, at the onset of Frost's poem, the wall has not yet been mended. But what the people make as they go through their day is highly constrained, and therein lies a paradox that all social science has confronted at least since Durkheim talked about the persistence and difference of suicide rates in and across various kinds of social groups ([1897] 1951). Without people the School does not exist. But the School is factual enough that the behavior of people, singly or in groups, cannot ignore its requirement. By the end of the day, if the School, through its enforcers and interpreters, has not recognized what people made as a class, then the people may be in trouble. If School does, then there is no problem even if what is constructed is something some might say should not have been so recognized.[1] A class identified as "bad" on any number of criteria is still a class, and an interaction shown to be highly educational may remain for all concerned not a class.

Or is it? Even as a bounded setting, a class cannot start in the absence of specific acts (reorganization of focus, synchronization, greetings, etc.), but the inhabitants have little choice about the performance of the acts. More exactly, they have no choice about their acts—whatever they are—being accountable to "the beginning of class."[2] If, for example, the teacher is absent, the prototypical class activities will not start, since they can be initiated only by the teacher. After a few minutes the absence will be noticed, and things will then proceed on the basis of "class with absent teacher," which implies that even though no one has performed the prescribed acts, they have, *in their practical consequences, in (cultural) fact,* been performed. The class frame is "on" and must be taken into account. Even to go home, the students will now have to perform an ending: "The teacher is not coming. We can leave."

Further distinctions between "construction," "deconstruction," and "reconstruction" are necessary. We use again Frost's "North of Boston" wall.[3] Up to now, we have contrasted the neighbors' reconstructive activity with the hunters' accounting of this earlier activity as they (de)construct the wall to help their dogs. Neither the hunters nor the neighbors are the initiators of the wall. The neighbors cannot be understood as two free adults meeting for the first time in the wilderness and consensually deciding to construct a wall. Frost even suggests the two have *different* motives for mending it. "I" definitely questions the need for the wall. His neighbor does not seem to ask the same question, and his motives may be dark: He may be scared, of himself as potentially a violent man, of the resistance against the wall. The prescription "Good fences make good neighbors" is an impersonal one. This is the way it is whatever the personal reservations. There is no consensus, only the need to maintain the peace by not questioning categorical distinctions that may not make sense anymore.

At this point, we have returned to the domain of culture as we understand it. We have returned analytically to what makes it necessary and appropriate to build walls between agricultural lands or between classrooms and schools, where people meet each other not as neighbors mending walls but as teachers teaching and students learning. Our structuralist stance is that something like walls and boundaries is ubiquitous in all human activities. But the exact placement of these boundaries, the exact nature of the activities that constitute them, and myriad details about the qualities of the performance can vary. New England is not western Ireland or southern Europe. Thus the neighbors in Frost's poem are mending a wall rather than a stone marker, a stone wall rather than a barbed-wire one, a wall of a particular height rather than another one, and so on. Everywhere, neither the need for boundaries nor the need for particular kinds of boundaries are consensually agreed upon. The need for walls with well-defined characteristics is preconstructed by a larger social group.[4]

Classrooms—or the ensemble of features that mark an interactional sequence as "relevant to Classroom"—are preconstructed by much earlier activities than those performed at the temporal "beginning" of concrete classes. The relevance of the School and Classroom frames is not established by the actual participants, and initially at least, there is little they have to do to find themselves under School and Classroom constraints. Children may simply have to walk into a school building to find themselves accountable to both. The architecture is probably enough to establish the frame of relevance, to make the statement "This is School, this is Classroom" that marks everything that is to happen there until the symmetrical closing message (performed as the ringing of a bell, perhaps) "turns off" the marker.[5] The participant does not have to "know" what is involved or even that a marker is at some moment relevant. Participant "errors" are always possible. A three-year-old entering a preschool for the first time and wandering off into spaces he identifies as something he knows from home is as much "in school" as a senior fourteen years later. They are both in school, in School, whether or not their parents' culture prepares them for what they find there. The process is not cognitive but social. It is the significant Others and their activities that determine the relevance of a person's act (including the identification of an act as an "error"). As Erving Goffman said, "Regardless of whether a person intends to take a line, he will find that he has done so in effect" (1967: 5). Strictly speaking, a classroom is not *constructed* solely or even mainly by the teacher and students who are momentarily present. What marks an interactional sequence as Classroom was constructed by those who are responsible for the School as a jural and architectural setting—and most of those people are dead. The person who takes a line, in our case, the person who orients to the Teacher or Student role that others have assigned, may protest, attempt to shift if ever so slightly what is required, or otherwise destroy the frame. Other persons may move in another direction and further reconstruct the defining features. Still others may critique their situation in a movement of deconstruction. All are involved in the cultural process that in the long run transforms the conditions human beings find themselves in. They are all at work culturing what they find *always already there*.

Even though markers that say "classroom is now on" are always constructed by other than the actual participants in an actual classroom, they still have to live the time when the classroom marker is "on." They have to construct something jointly. But what they construct is not strictly speaking "a classroom"; *that* task has already been done for them. What they will construct is something-that-is-relevant-to-Classroom, a *particular* instance of Classroom. It is this particularity that does not exist at the beginning. It is the particularity that will allow someone to say at the end of the session, "This was a good class" or "I wonder what was wrong with them today, I just couldn't get anything out of them." This local construction may create a fact that will have to be taken into account the next time the participants meet, whether because something extraordinary happened ("That was the time when so-and-so did such-and-such, and things have never been the same since") or simply because classes often cross-reference themselves ("as we discussed last time").

If the markers of Classroom are *always already there* as the participants enter a school building, then one cannot say literally that they create or even construct a classroom or that the classroom is a joint achievement of the participants. The constructing marker "This will be a classroom" is performed in another time and place, in other constructions in which the local participants may and probably may not have participated.[6] The local participants do actively *construct* other things. Let us now further explore this in some detail by looking at the very moment of local construction.

A Particular Instance

We approach the issue of local construction through a reanalysis of McDermott's study of "????"—it is essential for our argument that the "it" of his ethnographic study is glossed as question marks. Our goal is to rephrase some statements that, however well described for an interactional analysis, may now be reshaped to take culture into account. To do this, we build on one of the more technical papers (Dore and McDermott 1982).[7] This paper provides a blow-by-blow account of a moment from the point of view of the emergence of an organization in ambiguity. This is the analysis of a transitional moment when, by all accounts, the participants do not display a clear personal understanding of what they are together accountable for doing next. Each (individually and as subjective agent) could be doing something different. For a brief moment, the participants have the interactional time to externalize, perform, or incorporate aspects of their own personal agency. For this moment, theories of resistance and deconstruction might be helpful. One person in particular, "R" (whose personal qualities—gender, age, status, psychological makeup, etc.—we will not mention at this point) externalizes something that appears as a problem for the other participants as they respond to it, in their own action, as one more historical remnant to take into account.

Such externalizations of apparently inappropriate performances are a problem for any analyst convinced that the units of analysis of human interaction must be derived from an observation of the behavior and not through a deductive process. In brief, for us, "the analyst must first DISCOVER (a) the units of behavior to which the participants are oriented; (b) the particular contexts, frames, or constraints which are most immediately in effect; and (c) the ways in which the most immediate contexts are embedded in more inclusive social and institutional contexts (also available in the behavior of the participants)" (Dore and McDermott 1982: 375).[8]

Implicit in this statement is an acknowledgment of the epistemological reality, or at least the usefulness, of "units of behavior" that have the property of being discoverable, which must mean, in the actual historical practice of our analysis, that we can find systematic *labels* for these units. I return to the matter in the conclusion to this chapter. Temporarily, let it simply be noted that the act of discovery can be easier or more difficult depending on the moment when one enters a social interaction (either as a participant or analyst) and depending on the amount of information to which one has immediate access. For example, Dore and McDermott base their analysis almost solely on the speech of the participants even though McDermott spent a year in the classroom, videotaped hours of interaction, and had conducted extensive analyses of movement communication among the participants. This is an experiment in sensory deprivation that is defensible because it models various informational deprivations from which we must assume the participants were also suffering.

The temporal matter is most relevant: Organizationally, the participants had been left hanging and they had to arrange themselves for one of the several things that could happen next. They had to "discover," just as analysts have to discover, the unit of behavior to which to orient. But this leaves the analyst with a major problem: If the participants do not "know," "have not agreed," "have not reached a working consensus," or even simply "have not organized themselves into a particular thing," then how can one label this(these) thing(s) that they are (not) doing?

One point of their paper is to argue that, precisely, at certain times one cannot label the thing(s) that the participants are doing (saying) because they are at work trying to make first one and then another thing. And yet the participants are hard at work on something: They are not sleeping or even simply being pushed around by a social structure requiring them to do "????." In the real time of everyday life, they have to construct something that is not yet there, an event in history that can then serve as a unit of behavior to orient toward. What they do is shown in Figure 8.1.

There may appear little here out of which to make general statements about the construction of social scenes, but this is not so. At the most local of settings, when issues are emerging, being constructed with earlier constructions for future consumption, the central social problem is being played out, and we must pay attention. Some people are doing something together; what is "it"? How do they demonstrate to each other first (and secondarily to an observer) what "it" might be? How are we to know? To answer these questions, we must bring to bear all we have learned about human beings and test it.

An initial analysis can argue that apparently (if we trust that the participants are not lying or playacting) during the first four seconds, the matters of concern are "Perry (and A and perhaps M but not J) being ready," "going," and "reading." The ambiguity rests only in the exact nature of the organization of "reading" and has to do with what is implied by T's question ("Who else is ready?"). Dore and McDermott offer the following list of propositions about what is to happen next (based on what has happened regularly in the past):

(Perry/who else) is ready . . .

[1] to read next/
[2] to call for a turn to read next/
[3] to read along silently with the designated reader/
[4] to read together in chorus. (1982: 381)

Given that Perry indicates paraverbally[9] in his next two utterances that he is reading, we have good grounds to argue that locally and for the immediate participants, "one person being ready to read and reading while others read along silently" is the unit that

FIGURE 8.1
Transcript

sec.	R	A	J	Perry	M	R	T
1	~ ~	~ ~	~ ~	~ ~	~ ~	All right,	Perry's ready ~ Who
2	~ ~	~ ~	~ ~	~ ~	~ ~	~ ~	else is ready? ~
3	~ ~	~ Me.	~ ~	~ ~	~ ~	~ ~	~ ~
4	~ YOU::	~ ~	Not me. ~	~ CA- ——	~ Can I go?	~ ~	~ ~
5	~ ~	~ ~	~ ~	~ ~	~ ~	~ ~	~ ~
6	~ ~	~ ~	~ ~	~ CAN-	~ ~	~ ~	~ ~
7	I could	~ ~	~ ~	~ ~	~ ~	~ ~	~ ~
8	read it ~	~ Can't we	~ ~	~ ~	~ ~	~ ~	~ ~
9	I wanna go	please go	~ ~	No ~	~ ~	~ ~	~ ~
10	around	over it with	~ ~	~ ~	~ ~	~ ~	~ ~
11	~ ~	everybody	~ ~	~ ~	~ ~	~ ~	~ ~
12	~ ~	~ ~	~ ~	~ ~	~ ~	~ ~	That's the word
13	~ ~	~ ~	~ ~	~ ~	~ ~	~ ~	you drew a line under
14	~ ~	~ ~	~ ~	~ ~	~ ~	~ ~	~ ~
15	~ ~	xx in the xx	~ ~	~ ~	~ ~	~ ~	~ ~
16	~ ~	Ahhh YOU::	~ ~	~ ~	~ ~	~ ~	~ ~
17	~ ~	~ ~	~ ~	~ YOU.	~ ~	~ ~	~ ~
18	~ ~	~ ~	~ ~	~ CAN	~ ~	~ ~	Right. You.
19	~ ~	~ ~	~ ~	YOU~ CAN	~ ~	~ ~	~ ~
20	~ ~	~ ~	~ ~	YOU ~	~ ~	~ ~	~ ~

is being constructed. At the beginning (sec. 1), no one is reading, and at the end (sec. 6), someone (Perry) is reading. A boundary has been marked, something specific has happened. But "something there is that doesn't love a turn to read," and thirteen more seconds pass before Perry is given the behavioral space to read. The turning point that specifically delays the reading by taking into account the boundary just constructed is R's utterance "I could read it" because it makes explicit that reading by an individual is what is relevant to future action—it places the final stone on the interactional wall— because it reopens the question of who this individual is, and because it eventually establishes Perry's turn through one aspect of the utterance being ignored (that R might be the one to read). Nobody, possibly not even R, picks up on the possibility that R might actually read, and so the event gets performed: the social framing of R into a particular box (as someone who could, hypothetically, read but who, in fact, cannot read cognitively or emotionally) with possibly major institutional consequences.

In this sequence, we have (at least) two sets of events emerging in human history. One concerns R and his or her fate as "one who cannot read" and the other, the fate of the group as it transforms itself from "getting a turn to read" to "reading." Let us focus on the second set of events, particularly on the misleading nature of the labels. Whereas we could provisionally trust the participants not to be lying or playing and can assume that they know specific things relevant to the moment, in the long run this provisional trust and these assumptions have to be grounded on a more delicate analysis that does not confuse what emerges in the verbal flow produced by some members with the "actual" activity that is being performed or to which all participants orient themselves knowingly and consensually or, perhaps better, "collusion-ally," to use the qualifier proposed by McDermott and Tylbor (1983) to deal with the coming together of people around an activity. At no point did the analysis rely on the knowledge or perception of the participants. It always relied on their behavior. And it is in their behavior or, more exactly, in the *change* in their behavior, that one can see a wall, boundary, sociosemiotic marker, being constructed. At one point in time they were in state A, concerned with matters of state A that included a concern with state B. And then they were in state B.

McDermott arrived at this analysis primarily through an analysis of the postural behavior of the participants (rather than through their talk). He demonstrated that in the segment he looked at, there are four basic states, what he calls "positionings," into which participants can shape their bodily postures (see Figure 8.2). The analysis was based on the work participants had to perform in order to establish the relevance of a positioning and then to display that they were indeed doing what they had staged. In Dore and McDermott, for example, we are shown people organizing themselves into one State (Positioning II in McDermott's scheme) that allowed them to move into another State (Positioning I). First, like the "I" of Frost's poem, they had to "let their neighbors know" it was time to engage in one state and then that it was time to mend the wall, which would get them into the next state.

One advantage of the positioning analysis is that it does not rely on possibly misleading verbal labels. Whether the people were playing or lying, whether they knew

FIGURE 8.2
Main Positionings

POSITIONING I
Reading

POSITIONING II
Getting a turn to read

POSITIONING IV
Waiting for the teachers

Note: These are reproductions of illustrations in McDermott, Gospodinoff, and Aron (1978, figs. 1, 2, 3). They depict the structural features of each positioning.

what they were doing or not, the shift in their behavior could be monitored. The shifts in their positions could be seen. The discontinuity within the historical flow was observable and could be accounted for even in the absence of an analyst's hypothesis about what it could be. That the discontinuity was marked verbally obviously reinforces the analysis, not because it offers the ultimate explanatory label but because it allows us to generalize its relevance.

Constructing Labels

Up to now we have intentionally not used most of the labels McDermott used to refer to his observations in previously published papers. We argued instead only that the grounds on which we can distinguish between the two states the group deals with in the segment have little to do with the verbally signaled propositional content of either state. The analysis depends on the behavioral *difference* between the states, a difference revealing an isomorphic organization between propositional content and postural organization. There is no reason to label one state (Positioning I) on its own terms as if it were inherently "reading" rather than "looking at a book." The latter is less misleading in that it implies less about what is going on in each child's head. But the former makes more common sense in the context of the American School that the participants, we the analysts, and you the readers inhabit.

The relative commonsensicality of labels is an important matter because it brings us back to our initial concern with local control. In the previous pages, we established that, literally, the participants in the interaction dealt with, first, a state and then (though somewhat concurrently and after some resistance) the boundary marker that placed the group in another state. The locally relevant issues were these states and the relative positions of the participants within these states. The analysis could be performed even in the absence of any labeling of the participants. In the quoted talk of the participants, only one person is labeled in speech (Perry). All the others are defined deictically through the exophoric use of pronouns ("me," "I," "you"). Anything else we might want to say about these people is not performed locally. For example, there is no explicit performance in the text of, among many other things, the sex of the speakers, their age, or their relative status. It is as if these things were not locally relevant, and the fact that we could conduct the analysis without knowing the sex of R or the status of T demonstrates that these things did not have to be performed.

In earlier published pieces, McDermott did do some labeling work. In introductory paragraphs, he said that these were "six first-grade children and their teacher" and that they were taped "while sitting around a table during a reading lesson" (Dore and McDermott 1982: 377). He said in passing that "T" was "Teacher," "A" was "Anna," "J" was "Jimmy," "M" was "Maria," and "R" was "Rosa." In this fashion, he performed for us the context of *his* work, a context where people can be distinguished between "persons-to-be-known-by-their-first-names" and "persons-to-be-known-by-a-status-label" (and also "persons-whose-gender-must-be-marked" vs. "persons-whose-gender-does-not-have-to-be-marked").[10]

We can trust McDermott not to be lying to and playing with us. His account of who the people were and what they were doing is probably the same account that we would give in commonsense conversation or introductory comments. Having participated in many conversations with many people who have read McDermott's work and seen the visual material, we know that to say anything else would be controversial. The characterization can be accepted as "true." Still, it is important to note that "reading group," "teacher," "Rosa," and so on were literally performed *by McDermott* and are performed only now *by us* as we construct something that must be consequential in the interactions we are having around the earlier research. The performance of the label in a published paper has to do with the construction of an audience of people who "do not know" in different ways. The readers are made into people who, on one hand, do not know what the setting is but can be trusted to add the necessary commonsense information after having been provided with a convenient label and who, on the other hand, must be painstakingly taught something else (the point of the paper). McDermott was not adding random information about the participants that came with giving them names and status markers. Instead, he took the opposite risk: Because the labels disambiguate the original event and identify it as a "kind" of event, we may end up knowing less about it as a particular case. McDermott did something that must be done because of his concrete situation as the author of social scientific papers in the anthropological tradition. He, like us now, was not "free" to construct the rhetorical tools he needed to make his point about joint constructions and positionings. These tools were constructed elsewhere and are implied in the very physical object that a paper or a book constitute.

Similarly, the teacher and students on the tape did not have to make up the markers of School or even Classroom on which they may have at certain times relied to establish what they were doing. Those tools had been made for them. They were available all around them as remnants to be picked up whenever the need might arise. The segment analyzed by Dore and McDermott is ambiguous only under conditions of sensory deprivation. On the video itself, everything is displayed architecturally: the blackboard behind the group, the size of the table in relation to the size of the people, the dress of the participants, the pigmentation of their skin; all this and more immediately disambiguate the setting and the personae. One knows their approximate age, sex, and ethnic group almost before one has had time to wonder. In a cultural process that hides as much about the people as it reveals, one loses the ability to focus on society for analysis to the very extent one settles within the boundaries it provides.

The only solution to the problem is to realize concretely that the labels, signs, symbols, and propositions that litter the landscape of any interaction are material for local construction. They are remnants of earlier constructions. They may be "live" in the same sense as an electrical wire can be, safe only so long as it is not picked up.[11] Gender, for example, is not at issue in the video segment, but it is eminently usable, constantly available for further interactional work. The fact it *could be* used does not mean that it *has been* used. Whether it has is a matter for the analysis to determine.

Similarly, it is for the analysis to determine whether and how the use of a particular cultural remnant has shaped the interaction.

Social Constructions and Cultural Reality

Dore and McDermott write: "The second analysis begins with an *easily recognized setting* within American culture (a grade-school reading group), develops methods for describing the group's concerted activities as *mutually constituted frames* of interpretation, and then attempts a statement of how linguistic form and social negotiation mutually organize utterance interpretation" (1982: 375, my emphasis).

The key phrases here are "easily recognized" and "mutually constituted." By whom? Under what conditions? Out of what behavioral signs? What were the "group's concerted activities" or our own? What "frame of interpretation" did the group "mutually constitute"? Was it building a wall or was it only taking the preexisting wall into account? And what about us? When we construct academic papers either as readers or as authors, do we construct a paper or academia?

Settings can be identified through a careful examination of the activities of participants seen not as effects of external causes but as signs that something is relevant to the analysis. For example, it is analytically interesting to distinguish between matters that are foregrounded and matters assumed or taken for granted. This is what we did in the preceding section. More difficult is another analytic distinction central to our enterprise: Given our insistence that all analyses pay close attention both to cultural constraints and to local agency (at the face-to-face group level and then at the individual level), it is worth identifying within a local performance what is used or taken into account versus what may actually be constructed for future performances to use or take into account. The hunters who in Frost's poem breach the wall are precisely not constructing it, but their breaching activities reveal the reality of the wall in their life. In Dore and McDermott's paper, the phrase "mutually constituted frame of interpretation" harbors a tension at two levels depending on whether we focus on the word "mutual" or on the word "constituted." The tension exists until we are told whether the local collectivity (the group in face-to-face immediate interaction) was revealing in action something that was presented for it to take into account or whether it was actually involved in constructing something that would then become a reality for it (and perhaps for others if the local group is powerful enough). The tension lasts to the extent there is no theoretical reason to limit "mutuality" to a face-to-face collectivity. In a classroom, a teacher also constitutes/takes into account the School, along with the other teachers and administrators, first at the local level of the individual school and then at levels including more and more actors, however dim the teacher's awareness of their existence and contribution.

Let us try to sort these things out. When watching a tape of recorded interaction, our stance is that any observer sees people take into account what has been done for them. Our stance is also that no observer is free from conditions structurally equivalent to those of the people observed. All observers are particular kinds of observers doing observation under specific constraints. When examining published materials, one can also see observers performing signs revealing they are doing such things as recognizing for us a "reading group," particularly a "bottom-track reading group," in a tracked "classroom" in a "school" within "American education" within a "liberal democracy" and so on. Because the original participants did actually perform these signs, "we," particular observers operating within a particular institution, can "easily recognize" what they are doing—thereby revealing ourselves to be comembers of the collectivity of which Rosa, Perry, and the others were also members.[12]

In the tape we can also see the participants at work reproducing something particular—something that never happened before, something McDermott had to teach us to see: It appears that the particular group under observation uses Rosa's "I could read it" as a signal that somebody else has been selected and that it is time for that person to read. If this was the only occurrence, if it could be shown that it was not simply ignored—if, for example, it could be shown that it was the *first* occurrence of a series—then we might have solid grounds for the argument that Rosa, along with the group that accepted the innovation, "constructed" something that then became a fact in the life of the group. But the occurrence analyzed by Dore and McDermott is but one of many instances of such a sequence. Rosa is often ignored when it is time to read. In the video record, we can only say we are seeing the signs of a local institution—"ignoring Rosa (who cannot read)"—a custom that is the product of an older local construction. This institution reveals the cultural particularity of this classroom, but it does not reveal much about the knowledge of any participant or the consensus they may have achieved—at least not in the usual sense of these words: There is no evidence Rosa agreed to being ignored or that the teacher would not have been embarrassed if it had been pointed out to her that she systematically ignored Rosa. There is no reason to assume that Rosa fully participated in her own degradation. She may not have been able to escape the position the group had constructed for her, and there is evidence that the position she inhabited was not a comfortable one. Her "I could read it" could be seen as resistance to the overarching rule of this classroom (ROSA CANNOT READ/ROSA MAY NOT READ/ROSA SAYING "I could read it" IS A SIGN THAT SOMEONE ELSE HAS BEEN SELECTED FOR READING) and possibly as a *de*construction of the class. Still, the pattern existed as something that could be used, abused, and "taken into account" as a practical, consequential reality. To that extent at least, and for the group, this locally produced pattern belonged to the same realm as the School, as something that had become an altogether external "fact."

One could also see the participants at work practically using this fact of their social life together to conduct the moment. We showed that at one point, they were unsure—as one can imagine Frost's hunters when their dogs were stopped by the wall. One could see the teacher, Rosa, and her peers picking up the stones, mending the interactional wall, and proceeding to do what they were accountable for doing. In the sense that they organized their bodies to perform the task, we could talk of "incorporation"—which is not the same as "internalization"—to deal with the fact that Rosa, actually (behaviorally), did perform her own exclusion as she raised a hand to call for a turn, averted her eyes, lowered her arm, and so on in a way that made it possible for the teacher to miss her without explicitly realizing that she had done so. But we must leave open the possibility that Rosa's subjective understanding *might have been* different from Perry's or the teacher's. Her "I could read it" may have been the practical sign that allowed the collectivity to proceed as if she had said, "Perry should read it." But she did not say the latter, and we may also read her statement as a personal struggle with a social machinery that was as oppressive for being locally produced as such machineries can be. We do not have much evidence to state what *her* reality might have been, although we know it cannot have been independent of her actual experiences in school and at home. What is sure is that any account of Rosa's own "reality" or "identity" would tell us little about what she actually did in the local conditions she inhabited.

Deconstruction and Local Faction

To frame the discussion more concretely, I look at another moment on McDermott's videotaped record. This is a 145-second segment during which the group moves from getting a turn to read (Positioning II) to reading (Positioning I) to waiting for the teacher (Positioning IV) as she deals with another matter.[13] This progression is mapped in Figure 8.3 and illustrated in Figure 8.4 Each positioning is marked by a fundamental postural organization of the group. Each is performed in a kind of pulsating fashion as other activities intrude and some or all participants briefly move out of the positioning and then return to it. This progression is marked most significantly in the teacher's own movements as she makes disciplinary calls on children in the other reading group that is supposed to be reading quietly while she deals with the group I am focusing on. The movement from getting a turn to read to reading follows the pattern discussed earlier: The teacher starts with a general call: "Raise your hand if you can read page four." After some confusion, Rosa, along with others, says, "I could" in a peculiar manner that seems to ensure that someone else is chosen and all can proceed. Anna is chosen. She starts reading and runs into difficulty with a word; the teacher calls everyone's attention to the board for a brief lesson about the word (Figure 8.5). Anna reaches the end of the page along with many in the group who have started to read along with her. During a minimal (four-second) break from the reading positioning, the teacher asks Maria to read page 4 again. Maria proceeds, again with some of the other students reading along with her, and she finishes. The teacher then points at Jimmy, thereby breaching the turn-taking frame by bypassing Rosa, who should have been selected next given the seating arrangement and the formal rule that Jimmy and Rosa now proceed to repeat (see Figures 8.6 and 8.7).

The reading rule is that each child must read in order, starting with the child sitting at the right of the teacher and proceeding around "the circle." By jumping over Rosa, the teacher has broken the rule; this is picked up by Jimmy and expanded by Rosa. Rosa, however, does not claim the turn. Rather, she resets the turn-taking

196

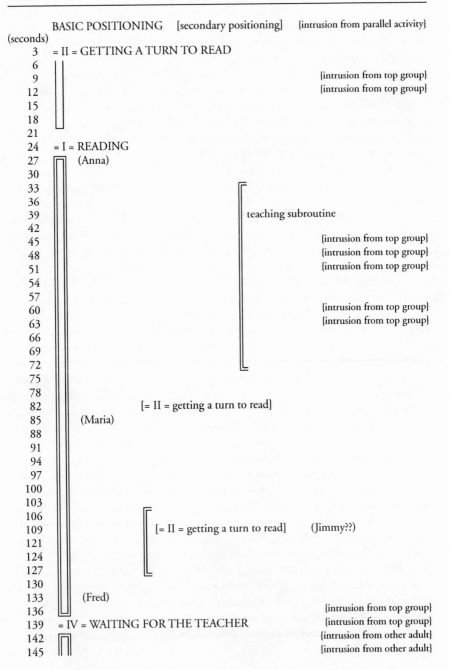

FIGURE 8.3
Sequencing of Positioning

FIGURE 8.4
Major Positionings

II - GETTING A TURN TO READ

A moment in a multi-voiced chorus of children saying "I could" with their hands raised.

(frame number on image can be used to cross-reference it with the transcript; sec. 14 on Fig. 2)

I - READING

All the children are down into their books; several of them have read words in echo with the designated reader.

(sec. 31 on Fig. 2)

IV - WAITING FOR THE TEACHER

The teacher is talking to an adult to the right of the camera; the children look in various different directions (in this instance of the positioning, Jimmy looks at the adult with the teacher; Rosa does not appear focused on anything; Anna and Fred look at something on Fred's book)

(sec. 142 on Fig. 2)

FIGURE 8.5
Major Subsequences

While the students stay
READING, the teacher turns
around and writes on the
blackboard. The co-occurrent
talk has the canonical form for
TEACHING LESSONS iden-
tified by Mehan (1979)

(sec. 40 on Fig. 2)

One of the rare moments
when turn taking within
READING is accomplished
without trouble. Anna has finished the page, the teacher
points at the person next to
her, Maria, who then starts
reading.

(sec. 82 on Fig. 2)

round by calling for Fred to read. Fred is indeed seated at the right of the teacher; at
his right is Anna and then Maria and then Rosa. Interestingly, the teacher and everyone else in the group accept this plan, and Fred starts reading.

What was the nature of Rosa's agency in this sequence? By our account, she was
not determined by either the context, her cognition, or her personal identity to do
what she can be shown to have done. She was not specifically cowed by the "hegemonic power" of the teacher to perform what the teacher specifically required. At the
moment of action, Rosa, like all other participants, was radically free in the world
she inhabited. This is how one should think of her: as an existential "I," affirming
herself in spite of the costs, and not as an identified "me" taking the position others
made for her. At the same time, what she did do, and what she did earlier when she
claimed she "could" read, reveals the structural properties of the institution that had
caught her. Her act was not greeted by astonishment and radical misunderstanding.

FIGURE 8.6
Transcript

		Teacher	Jimmy	Rosa	Fred
110	35230	Alright, let's see you			
111	35260	do it.			
112	35290		What about		
113	35320		Rosa?		
114	35350				
115	35380		- She-she don't		
116	35410		get a turn!		
117	35440				
118	35470			Go around	
119	35500	- - Jimmy			
120	35530	- You seem very very unhappy.		Back to Fred	- Yeh, let's go
121	35560	Perhaps you should go		then back to me.	around.
122	35590	back to your seat.		No. Back to Fred,	
123	35620			back to Anna, and	
124	35650			Maria and back to me	
125	35680				
126	35710	- Alright Fred, can			
127	35740	you read page four.			

FIGURE 8.7
Jimmy and Rosa Protest

"What about Rosa? She don't get a turn!"

(sec. 112–116 on Fig. 2)

Jimmy withdraws from the reading position, turning his head away from the teacher.

As Jimmy completes his withdrawal, Rosa makes a circle with her hand that starts with Fred and ends with her as if to state the rule that reading is done as turns around the table.

(sec. 117 on Fig. 2)

For the second time, Rosa makes a circle with her hand as she declares:

"Back to Fred, back to Anna, and Maria and back to me."

(sec. 118–125 on Fig. 2)

It was fully sensitive to its place. It was an eminently "possible," meaningful act or, better, "fact" in the evolving history of the group. Rosa made something that all others had to take into account. Her work was not simply reproductive even if the next fact interpreted her fact as if it had been.

Given a recognition of the sensitive freedom of her act, we can then wonder about the nature of Rosa's fact. What did she do? Locally, she reaffirmed the rule. Together with Jimmy and Fred, she participated in a challenge to the teacher—revealing in the process the power students always have over their teachers.[14] The effective challenge invokes the responsibility of the teacher as authoritative legislator. In popular language, one might say that Rosa was working "through the system." It is also the case that one feature of the system in this classroom was the fact that rules were not continually restated. The restatement of the rule was both a signal of trouble and constitutive of trouble, since it derailed the current activity (reading) and called for a different conversation (perhaps an explanation of why the teacher was making an exception by not calling on Rosa). We might even say that Rosa deconstructed the reading lesson both by focusing attention on the acts that constituted the reading lesson and by preventing the lesson from actually occurring. The teacher scuttled this revolt by giving the signal (which only she could legitimately perform) to Fred that he should start reading (sec. 126 in Figure 8.6). But Rosa's challenge had already had the effect of getting her off the hook one more time from having to read. It also had the effect of cutting into the time that this "bottom" group of kids could give to reading. It probably also contributed to the impression that this group was so much more difficult to teach than the top group.

We could look at every single act by any of the participants as relatively deconstructive of the most routinized version of what "should" have happened next if all the participants had been machines programmed to perform particular acts in sequence with other acts. For example, one rule of the reading group was not explicitly mentioned, was resisted and ignored during the sequence: the rule that only one specified child should be reading while the others followed silently in their book. Instead, many read aloud, sometimes echoing, sometimes challenging, the reading by the designated reader. Even the teacher could have, in effect, deconstructed something the students had begun to build.[15] For example, at the beginning of the sequence, she asked the group to "raise your hand if you can read page four" (sec. 5–6, Figure C.1 in Appendix C). The students started raising their hands. The teacher looked up toward the other reading group and disciplined one child. As she did, the hands of the bottom-group children moved down. When she came back to them, their hands were down, and she asked rhetorically, "Nobody can read page four?" (sec. 18–19, Figure C.1). In an earlier piece, McDermott (1977a; McDermott and Aron 1978) emphasized that the repetition of such sequences limited the time the bottom group had on task and reconstructed the group as failing to learn to read or as unable to follow directions. In the long run, such acts established the systematic character of the whole pattern. Still, the fact that all the teacher's acts were always sensitively attuned to what was occurring around her and to the nature of her position does not mean that they were the result of a simple programming founded on her "knowledge" of the proper organization of the classroom. Each act, rather, was slightly off from where it "should" have been and thus required extra work from all participants to reconstitute it.

The "I" in the Cultural Machine

When G. H. Mead (1934: 173–178) distinguished the active "I" from the interpreted "me," he did it within the context of a search for a better understanding of the "me," the self as knowable. After close to a century of reflection, the human sciences have reached a rich understanding of the processes that constitute a particular "me" out of experiences with others. Our dispute has been with the generalization of this understanding of the self into matters of social interaction. Mead himself says quite explicitly that at the moment of action, the "I" is in charge and the "me" is left in abeyance. At the moment of action, the actor does not have an explicit knowledge of that which he will be known as having done. This explicit knowledge is possible only a posteriori, through the mediation of a self that is precisely never quite the actor's own self given it is always constructed in concert with others. Thus knowledge cannot be said to determine action, since self-knowledge is always temporarily distanced from the act. Analytically, the self has to do with interpretation, not action. When looking at a prototypical, peaceful, and altogether inconsequential me-you conversation, the problem of interpretation does not impose itself. When looking at action in educational settings where students and also teachers, administrators, schools, and so on are failing, and often with dramatic consequences, the issue becomes a pressing one. A child like Rosa does not fail because she "knows" how to fail, having been taught how to fail either by failing parents (with a culture of poverty) or by failing teachers (who cannot respond to the cultural particularities of the child). Whatever Rosa's self may have been like, at the moment when the teacher passed over her and Jimmy protested, it was her "I" that took over and produced something unexpected and meaningful. The meaningfulness did not refer to her understanding or to an understanding of her act that anyone else in the room had but to the fact that her act contributed to the progression of the scene. It kept the classroom alive in its particular pattern.

How we are to account for these patterns has been our concern. As joint constructions in history, these patterns become realities, social facts, a "culture," for all those who are caught within their walls. They are not simply vague constraints or determining conditions on behavior. They are actually performed in the behavior of the local groups made accountable to them. The work these groups do is necessary for the patterns of accountability, what we call a culture, to remain "alive." A live culture, the system of symbolic, signifying boundaries that place any action as a token of a particular type of action, cannot be said to be *literally*, and we mean literally, the constructed product of the action of those whose action has been so identified. If Rosa's "I could read it" can be properly identified as a meaningful move within the bottom group of a classroom with a particular history within a school with a particular history, all within the American School, it is not because of anything *she* did, it is because of what *we* must do with what she did. Again, she actually did work to produce the sentence. To do it, and to do it in a way appropriate to her motivation—whatever that was in the real time of her performance—she had to take into account her concrete position as one who was made a member of a classroom, a bottom reading group, a group in the "getting a turn to read" positioning. She did all this in such a way that her performance was not marked by her coparticipants as in any way "alien." To that extent she may be said to have been a fully competent member of her culture, or, more accurately, since it should not be possible to say that a "culture" has "members," to have been as competent culturally as she was linguistically.

Her competence, however and again, is not the issue. The reading group would have proceeded equally well even if one of the members had been at a complete cultural loss. It would have proceeded equally well if, as happens regularly in many higher grades (or in such schools as West Side High), some or even most of the students had successfully resisted any effort by the teacher to organize the classroom into the basic positioning. It is possible to do with culture what poets and foreigners do with language when they produce sequences that are recognizable both as relevant to a regularity and as a significant departure from it. When Frost writes, "Something there is that doesn't love a wall," he is breaking certain rules of word order in English and is still considered a great poet. Had we produced the same sentence and not framed it as a quote, any self-respecting editor would have suggested or required that the line be rewritten as "There is something that doesn't love a wall," thereby demonstrating once again that linguistic propriety, meaning, and knowledge in their practical accomplishment are not grammatical but rather social, we would say "cultural," matters.

And yet in the difference between the two possible English versions of Frost's line, an "I" has imposed itself on the world and on the consciousness of all those who have been given ears to hear Frost. This "I" must remain as unutterable as the Chinese 我 is for all the human beings who do not have the ears and eyes that would make sense of the character. Like the child Maxine Hong Kingston staring at "I," unable to speak it and yet fascinated by it, the Chinese 我 is a puzzle, a possibility, a danger. Frost's "I," like Rosa's, is a reality all must confront. But it is not quite a fact. Rather it is an act that can be made into a fact as one attempts to represent it (successful poet, failing child) and co-opt it into a social world of literary genres or educational categories. These genres and categories, the whole historical structure that was constructed in older struggles, are neither more nor less real that the table that supports the keyboard on which "I" (an indexical pointer to Hervé Varenne) am typing this. Once, 我 constructed the table. Some engineers once constructed the keyboard. But at the moment of writing, 我 is not constructing either the table or the keyboard—though 我 is taking them into account. 我 and we, the authors of this book, have also not constructed the rhetorical tools we are using to mark "this is a scholarly work." We have also not constructed all the markers that have been saying "this is a book about education in the United States," and we have been using them even as we have been resisting them for all the ways they make the analysis of educating tasks, and the educating tasks themselves, more difficult for all involved. Our very resistance is inscribed within long traditions of such resistance. But, we hope, this analysis is not simply a restatement of what has been said by earlier critics. We have tried to say more even as we recognize the limitations that our position and our tools place upon us. Like Rosa, Adam, and all the others, we are caught. But not fully.

NOTES

This chapter builds on McDermott's work on "Rosa" (1977, 1978 (with J. Aron), 1978 (with K. Gospodinoff and J. Aron), 1979 (with K. Gospodinoff), 1982 (Dore and McDermott), 1983 (with H. Tylbor). See Appendix C for more details about the video sequences, transcripts, and frame grabs from the videotape that are used in this chapter.

1. Think, for example, of all the settings when School seems to be relevant even as many would wonder about the "educational value" of the activities (e.g., schools with inexperienced teachers or with stereotypically tough kids or, again, schools where all that is done is rote learning of sacred texts). Conversely, think of all the settings where "education" is relevant but the organization of the people is not accountable to the School (e.g., familial outings to a museum of natural history, adult classes in flower arrangement, people reading books in the library with no guidance from teacher or curriculum, etc.).

2. There is a major distinction here between jural injunctions and the historical unfolding of an interaction framed by such injunctions. Bourdieu discussed this distinction in the context of honor exchanges and more generally as he developed the sociology of giving and receiving (1966, [1972] 1977). Varenne recently expanded on this in the context of discourse analysis and turn-taking (1992).

3. This is the title of the collection within which "Mending Wall" appears, a collection that can be read fruitfully as an ethnographic account of that mysterious land "north of Boston."

4. Although we have not found good ethnographies of walls in Europe and the Americas, it is quite clear from the literature on early New England land-tenure systems that they were a major source of tension among the colonists. The practical tasks of deciding whose cows could graze where, when, and under what conditions were always politically charged (Powell 1963; Lockridge 1970). Local agreements were always tenuous and temporary. Consensus could never be assumed. For a lovely account of the hedge in the English countryside, see Frake (1996a, 1996b).

5. The prototype of these is the message "This is play" as understood by G. Bateson (1955).

6. As historians regularly remind sociologists, few institutions arise fully formed out of one constructing sequence. More often than not, the institutional construction is more akin to a re-cognition that something already in progress can become an accountable reality for a population. Lawrence Cremin, for example, argued that "the popularization of schooling antedated the public school movement" (1980: 178). The School was the product of a specific construction with already existing material. There was a time when the School did not exist, but there is no escaping it now.

7. Anyone interested in pursuing this case further must look at McDermott's fundamental methodological paper (McDermott, Gospodinoff and Aron 1978). While McDermott talks

there in the language of "consensus" that might lead some to read him in the classical constructivist tradition, a footnote on the term specifies that he is not talking about "what might be going on in any one person's head" (1978: 268). His term "publicly cognitive" should be interpreted as a new version of Durkheim's "collective unconscious"—still inadequate but preserving what the interactionist and Weberian traditions sometimes obscure: the public, collective character of humanity.

8. The proximate sources for this statement are to be found in the work of Garfinkel and Sacks (1970), Scheflen (1973), and Frake (1980). It also echoes things found in Propp ([1927] 1968) and Lévi-Strauss ([1958] 1963a, 1969–1981).

9. He says both "*CA-*" (sec. 4) and "*CAN-*" (sec. 6) with the particular intonation pattern marking "I am hereby reading aloud." The word "can" is also the first word in the passage to be read.

10. This implicit process of gender identification is interesting in itself, since it may have been forced on Dore and McDermott by the structure of the English language that allows for status labels not to take gender into grammatical account. Compare the word "teacher" with the French "*instituteur*." In a French translation of the article, "T" would be labeled "*institutrice*" (the feminine form of the label, used because, through visual cues, it appears that the teacher was a woman). Note further that, in French, until recently, "*instituteur/institutrice*" marked the person as an *elementary* school person: For postprimary teachers, the French word is *professeur* (which has no feminine form). This distinction is not marked in English. Note also that by not using last names, McDermott prevents us from conducting the stereotypical "ethnic" analysis that common sense would indicate if some of these names had been marked.

11. We rely on Voloshinov's metaphor of communicative salience as electrical current ([1929] 1973: 103).

12. In the phrase "easily recognizable," "easily" clearly implies a well-encultured subject. The underlying issue is not the exact nature of the knowledge but the fact that through the marking of boundaries, the specialness of the event is recognizable in the sense that it can be noticed and investigated even if at the onset the subject does not quite know what to make of it. The phrase "easily recognizable" mostly indexes that the analysis is intended for people who would not find this classroom problematic. Clearly, McDermott's analytic responsibilities would have been different if his tape had been of, say, a Brahmanic school in India. There, more time would have had to be given to a careful explanation of the position of the blackboard, the teacher's desk, the relative size of the table and chairs, the rectangular shape of the table and the fact that it is referred to as a "circle" "around" which one reads, and so on. These are social realities for late-twentieth-century Americans. Anthropologists know them as collective constructions, the development of which can be traced historically.

13. McDermott describes this sequence in detail (1977a: 222–229). A full transcript is included at the end of Appendix C.

14. Various critics of interactionist work in the classroom have misunderstood the point of looking at active mutuality even in formally asymmetrical positions. It is a methodological error leading to theoretical confusion to assume that because the relationship between teacher and student is asymmetrical in social structural terms, everything that happens between them must be approached from the point of view of the power of the teacher. Power, as theoreticians from Rousseau to Bourdieu have pointed out, does not explain social organization unless one also brings in an understanding of legitimacy and authority. Once this understanding is combined with a stress on the agency of the actor, one is most likely to observe raw power

plays among those who are structurally weak in a social sense (Scott 1985). The teacher can rely on her authority; the students must resist.

15. On one hand, the teacher was caught by the authority given to her by her position. She could not quite withdraw into a side activity (though the aside with another adult that started at the end of the segment could be taken as such a withdrawal) to the very extent that the students were continually calling for her attention and proposing alternate, and often quite legitimate, courses of action.

9 Conclusion: Beyond Explaining Why

Hervé Varenne and Ray McDermott

Whatever Rosa did when she neatly deconstructed the reading lesson by reciting the rule "back to Fred, back to Anna, and Maria and back to me," she was not passively or mechanically reproducing "her culture" (*habitus*, learning-disabled self, motivational structure, or whatever). She was actively performing something that made sense immediately both locally, within the unfolding of a day in her school, and translocally, at the school-building level and at the national levels where School is affirmed. Her response was an achievement in all the senses of the word. Her statement was not the statement one would necessarily expect, but her peers and her teacher received this difference and acted with it. This acknowledgment demonstrates that she was an active agent who could not be ignored. Rosa's statements highlight the property of all human action: It was more and less than was required, it elaborated possibilities, and it dramatized restrictions. It made culture, or better, it was culture, culture in process, transforming nature (earlier history) and substituting a new fact for the fact that might have been offered to her peers and the teacher. The class was not quite the same afterward: The teacher's headache likely grew worse, Rosa's possible fate as a future special education student was confirmed, and her classmates were spared another moment when they might have been caught not knowing something. Together they made something for each other. They built their current life together and prepared the way for their future life apart. They did not abolish their conditions; nor did they construct them in their full elaboration. Rather, they used what they were given to furnish the rooms in which they had been placed. Through their work, the School and the Class became This school and This class in a temporary particularity. But neither School nor Class originated with them, and the furniture they assembled was disassembled almost as soon as they had finished their work together. The year ended. Rosa and the teacher went their separate ways; the (sub-sub-sub-) culture that they had built together died just as all cultures do sooner or later.

Our analysis deliberately did not seek to explain "why" Rosa, as a particular person, did what she did. Rather, it sought to analyze and understand the world in which it makes sense for her to be identified by all as not knowing how to read. We offered no answer to why Adam had a bad day, why Sheila appeared to be doing better than Joe, why the singers in the choir at the Inn of the Good Shepherd or the students in West Side High School went through complex scenes with little problem and were still placed within institutional failure and the students of Allwin remained successful, sure of themselves and of their future place in society in spite of daily ritual failures on a multitude of tests that remained "fun." We specifically refuse to ask any "why" question of Rosa, Adam, Sheila, or any of the others. We also refuse to ask such questions of the groups in which they can be commonsensically located (child, girl, African American, daughter of poor or working-class parent, involuntary minority, or whatever). There is no gain we can fathom in attempting to answer "why" Sikhs do better than Mexicans somewhere in California in the 1990s.

We refuse to place ourselves within the long tradition of work that has toyed with "why" questions. Answers to these questions make too much common sense to be trusted. Why did this individual fail? Answer: There is something wrong with Adam's wiring (neurology) or programming (negative early childhood experiences). Answer: Sheila's parents are better educators than Joe's. Answer: The young adults in the choir and West Side High are the product of their mothers' bad nutrition in utero, their parents limited education, a neighborhood with gang leaders who devalue formal education while offering other strategies for survival. Why did this individual succeed? These answers are no better. Answer: The children of some recent immigrants, Maxine Hong Kingston, for example, profit from the single-mindedness of their parents. Answer: The children of Allwin have healthy mothers, competent parents pressing them to accept their school's yoke, and neighbors demonstrably prosperous through formal instruction. Their temporary personal difficulties may be alleviated and remediated by tutors, therapists, and the time to mature slowly away from the bureaucratic mechanisms that place children in tracks that cannot be jumped. All these answers make sense, but they are fundamentally misleading because they prevent us from confronting the source of the categories used to explain.

Other answers apparently move us away from an investigation of personal characteristics as the causes of success or failure—but not much. For every "why" question to the perennial wonder about Johnny's not learning to read, there are "because" explanations that start with the observation that in general, members of Johnny's ethnic, class, racial, or gender group do not learn to read in the same numbers as members of other groups. In the particular history of one child or even of one group at a certain moment in its history, the reasons may suggest a historical sequence that, step-by-step, leads to a particular fate. Given this theorizing, it is not surprising to find an all but illiterate student in West Side High School: After all, wasn't Johnny a severely malnourished infant, born to poor parents, and then placed in an inner-city school with a special education bureaucracy that tracked him, expelled him, and eventually gave him another chance to gain a high school diploma that remains worthless in comparison to the diploma a student from Allwin is getting at the same time? It is also not surprising given the history of immigration into the Americas that black and Hispanic children should be the overwhelming majority of those who end up in the West Side Highs of the United States. Slavery, the conditions of the movement of southern blacks into the urban North, and so on—all this "explains" why malnutrition, poverty, getting acquired by special education, and other problems are not distributed randomly across all the groups of the body politic. All these answers make sense, but they are just as misleading if they prevent us from confronting American Education as a cultural system, that is, as institutionalized discourses and rituals. In America, no *particular* person need fail, and failure need not be confined to the children of any *particular* groups. But half the children must fall below average, and therein lies the problem that concerns us.

This problem needs emphasizing: Random distribution of success and failure along all possible groupings would not abolish the success/failure complex. One can imagine an American world in which whites and blacks, men and women, succeed and fail in exactly the same ratio. This world would be "fairer," but it would remain structurally the *same* cultural world. Social scientists who worry about education in the United States must focus directly on the success/failure complex as a historical construct, a culture, something that we must call America. In this particularly structured social field, it makes sense to fail at becoming educated and to have this failure used as justification for one's eventual fate; it is "American" to worry about who is failing and to look for remedies that might make the whole thing more palatable. Above all, America is to be found where these worries, resistances, and struggles have produced massive institutions with profound implications on local and personal everyday life.[1]

To present America as a culture to America is no easy task, for the very vocabulary available for expression makes it difficult to focus directly on its specificity as a liberal, industrial, egalitarian, capitalistic, democratic polity that is concerned with fostering the "best" and demonstrating absolute fairness. The rhetorical forms available to us make it particularly difficult to talk simultaneously about the division of labor in an industrial society, about an ideology that explains how individuals are distributed among the available positions, and about the processes—particularly education—that move human beings into these positions, along with their own more specialized ideological conversations. We must understand simultaneously (1) the distinctions made between workers at McDonald's and their corporate managers, (2) the processes that place human beings in either position, and (3) the conversations that justify their fate. Concretely, we are attempting to make it possible to talk about the implicit proposition underlying all reform rhetoric that in the best of all American worlds, hamburger flippers (and their corporate managers) would come from among those who are best attuned to the position, those whose psychological qualities make them particularly suited to the task and essentially happy with it (even if they need the help of various therapies to convince them that their fate is the best fate they could have achieved and that they should learn to accept "who they really are").

Much sociological reasoning finds it easy to think deterministically about the relationship between all aspects of the problem. For a while it seemed sensible to think that "modernization" or "industrialization" required that industrial labor had to be divided, an educated workforce was necessary, and various means had to be devised to recruit the best people. More recently, the success of Japan has introduced a doubt: The many cogs of a complex industrial whole could be arranged in quite a different fashion and still produce what Euro-American cultures have prided themselves as being particularly good at producing. If one widens a little the comparative grid, one finds more societies with complex divisions of labor that reveal the open nature of so-called organizational necessities. All societies divide labor among human beings, but the exact arrangement of this division varies quite significantly, and the variation can produce different conditions for the people alive in them. In this perspective, India is an interesting case both because it is historically related to Euro-America and because it has kept for a long time an ideological foundation so revolting to America that its dominant category, caste, is repeatedly used to refer to what all agree is worst about America. The work of Louis Dumont (1980) determinedly highlights the contrast between India and Euro-America at the level that concerns us, that is, at the intersection among major institutions, ideology, and local experience. Dumont shows how Hindu philosophers, political leaders, and local people, together and sometimes in long-standing conflict with each other, elaborated both a complex theory justifying specified rankings and an even more complex set of institutions enforcing caste segmentation in interaction and various mechanisms for changing the relative position of castes vis-à-vis each other. For Dumont, all people in India, even many who are not Hindu or the many who are fighting specifically against caste ideology, must take caste into account. It is inescapable. More important for us, Dumont affirms that in India, caste segmentation is a fundamental value inscribed in myth, religion, and everyday practice—including the resistance to caste. In America, by contrast, it is egalitarian individualism that is inscribed in myth, religion, and everyday practice, and this has major consequences. It is only in an egalitarian universe that the worry about inequality makes sense. The vision of equality for all guides all revolts against the status quo, and solutions rebuild both the democratic foundation and the difficulties that are its products. There is, for example, something fascinating about the messianic tone of writings on the value of "multiculturalism" in the United States. It is a movement that bills itself as resisting what it often calls the "conservative mainstream." And yet a powerful voice in that movement claims that multicultural education is working "to create equal educational opportunities for all students" (Banks 1996: 21). What could be more perennial than the worry that after 200 years of political democracy and after 30 years of various wars on poverty and a multitude of experimental programs, books must still be written about "savage inequalities" in American Education (Kozol 1991).

The problem, of course, is not with the hope that something can be done about inequalities. The problem lies in that the worry about inequalities, as stated and debated by authors such as Banks or Kozol, invites a focus on the individuals who remain unequal, as units of analysis as well as units of ethical and political concern. America provides several ready-made ways of talking and arguing about humanity.

In its glory, when the focus was on personal freedom, responsibility, and empowerment, the American discourse helped establish a workable political system, and this discourse continues to drive its transformation. Analytically, it has also given us complex psychologies that have illuminated much about life behind the eyes. The same discourse has a dark side, particularly when used analytically to talk about differential performance by individuals. Given a system well tuned to let individual talents bloom and to allow all individuals to be different, differences in achievement can be directly attributable to individuals: Picasso could paint but not sing; Einstein could advance physics but not write poetry. Individual merit is not distributed equally, and "that's the way the world is," says the discourse. Some people have inherently differentiated capacities and disabilities. This discourse easily drifts into the worst form of racism when it appears that groups can be ranked by the achievements of the people to be identified with it. At its extreme, it can lead to a specific denial of the full humanity of those who failed. It is now easy to see through the early forms of racism. But the discourse process is still very much alive: Books like *The Bell Curve* (Herrnstein and Murray 1994) are still being written, and worse, they are criticized in the same terms as they are written. More difficult to see through are attempts at justifying differential achievement by identifying particular abilities. Picasso and Einstein with their spectacular talents are overly stereotypified cases. Many psychologists continue to try to identify what might make persons particularly suited to flipping hamburgers or managing the corporation. Note that if they succeeded, protests against the differentiated fates of both persons would lose all legitimacy: When democracy as a political system is finally perfectly tuned, each person will be fully responsible for the occupied position, however uncomfortable or degrading. There is a major problem here, for it is unlikely, of course, that those who have been diagnosed as best suited for menial positions, however fair the diagnosis, would not continue to protest.

This is the problem that the privileged discourse of analytic individualism cannot handle even though it is fundamental to what Myrdal once identified as the "American dilemma": "the ever-raging conflict between . . . the 'American Creed' . . . and the valuations . . . of individual and group living" ([1944] 1962: lxxi). But Myrdal did not go as far as one must go. This is why we turned to Dumont, who by way of a comparison between individualistic Euro-America and caste-based India, went much further. The conflict Myrdal talked about is not one between the American ideal and the real as it can be found in the United States. The conflict is not between one's faith and one's actions. Rather, the dramatic evolution of American history is the direct product of the ideal: Racism and its equivalents are the paradoxical product of an ideology dedicated to human equality and freedom, passionately concerned with the individual, and thereby essentially unable to deal with personal differences in constraining social fields (Dumont 1980).

A second discourse developed out of American ideology starts with the premise that human beings are always found at work *together* in groups or, in the word most typical of this tradition, in *community*. This discourse is concerned with social processes, and at its best, it is magnificently sensitive to the efforts all persons put in to make sense of each other. But this very sensitivity, because it privileges the point of view of persons who construct and are constructed by conditions, can easily collapse an intuition about joint construction into a more normal statement about the constitution of individuals. The slide from "people working hard together in poverty" to "individuals who *are* poor" is easy to perform. The rhetorical shift makes it easy to move one more step and to argue that "poverty" or "disabilities" are diseases that are the proximate cause of people's difficulties and that they are in need of one-on-one help designed to cure them of their disease. By this transformation, what people have done in common becomes "theirs" both because they shape it and because they are shaped by it. The conditions and products people find when they are born become "their identity" and "their culture." We are back with individuals with inherent qualities. We are back to a moral phrasing that may eventually be as dangerous in its implications for analysis and institutional practice as the pure psychologism of the first discourse. As the discourse evolves, people are socialized into "their" community, and they internalize the values and orientations of "their" peers. In the best of all democratic worlds, they are consensually responsible for their conditions; they have, so to speak, voted through their act for a particular form of community life and a particular place within it.

If one is concerned with transforming the landscape of institutions in the United States, one must directly confront the implication of the discourse about community, consensus, and social identity when it is used to analyze or, worse, "explain" the fates of particular persons in difficulties, the organization of particular unpleasant conditions, and the relationship between the two. A conversation based on words like "socialization," "identity," "community," "culture" (as in "multi-cultural-ism") leads to an endless search for the conditions that skew achievement: ethnicity, class, race, gender, and so on. This search only appears to move attention away from the victim. Eventually, it brings the analytic attention back to the individual as the unit that was socialized into this or that position and has now paradoxical ownership of that which makes differentiated success. With the mainstreaming of "multicultural-ism," this discourse may have achieved even more ideological power than it ever had. Missing, again, is any theoretical mechanism for understanding the differentiation of positions and confronting, for example, the process that differentiates hamburger flipping from the management of hamburger flipping and then justifies who is found occupying each position.

Twentieth-century American social thought has repeatedly been recaptured by a discourse of individual responsibility and pain. The intention to think socially is not sufficient without a good understanding of the mechanisms that make it difficult to do so. The evolution of early pragmatism into a social psychology, much against the wishes of the mature Dewey and G. H. Mead, and its reintegration into a psychology of personality (identity) is not a matter of historical happenstance. The same processes blunted what was powerful in the work of Benedict or Parsons, and it makes it difficult to develop what is essential in the work of Bateson, Vygotsky, or Bourdieu.

There is something profoundly systematic about this evolution, and we are resisting it. Our goal has been to gain a more determined control of our own discourse by emphasizing the structuring powers of America. As a culture or ideology, individualism does not quite blind people to the cultural facts of their collective making. Individualism does not keep people in America from complaining about individualism. People in America are not necessarily "individualists" as a property of their selves. But neither does the discourse of individualism allow easy or effective talk about these cultural facts. Always already refocusing attention on the person as an analytic unit as well as a moral center impoverishes analyses of social processes by offering new qualities of persons as explanations for their fate. This kind of analysis may appear social, but it hides ever more completely the interactional processes that construct social differentiations in history. Social qualities are not the products of personal choices or inner potentialities but the end results of joint activity over long periods, end results that become the next settings and resources persons use to construct their lives. White and black, upper-class and lower-class, Hamden Heights and Manhattan Valley, Jewish and Italian, Japanese and Chicano, male and female—all these dichotomies are, by their very definition in American culture, dependent on each other or, as we like to say in the technical literature, mutually constructed: No blacks, then no whites; no upper class, then no middle or lower class. If the people on the bottom resist, they make it harder for those on top, who resist further; together, what they resist is the America that has carved out for them the limited world that sets them against each other. Individualism is not a property of people "believing" in it or "valuing" it. It is the current state of an evolutionary process that has made new conditions for persons to live with and remake.

These considerations may seem to take us too far into social theory and away from educational issues. We hope to have shown this is not so. Educational processes are too central to American ideology to be examined solely from within. Our refusal to answer the question "why" Johnny can't read is part of our resistance in this wider context: Our decision is to focus on the question itself, on when, where, and how the "why question" has allowed us to uncover, however partially, the cultural structures that frame questions and answers, ideologically and practically, while hiding themselves. We must face America before we can get to Johnny.

In conclusion, we have taken the position that Rosa, for example, is not so much "Hispanic" as "interpreted as Hispanic"—even perhaps by herself. As an actor, "she" is not on her way to Special Education; her movement in this direction is something that happens to her in the hands of others using what still others constructed. It has little to do with any determining quality of her self. We emphasize these currents that move her around even as we affirm her own resistance and productivity. Rosa is active as what we called a radical 我. She is not drifting, she is swimming, and this can be shown in the detail of her behavior with others. The complexity of our position partially lies in the fact that we are both resisting America, by emphasizing the external facticity of society, and revealing it, by building our argument on the most extreme version of individualism. We do not to seek radically to transform the democratic discourse available to us. As persons we have not the power to do so, and we are not sure it would be a good idea. As political actors, we are quite sure that all human beings are equal, *individuals* in the absolute sense of the term. This is a moral and metaphysical commitment that we share with the rest of America. Our concern is with the next step. We insist that it must become a matter of scientific postulate that individuals are active within structured social fields. Rosa and the teacher, like all the participants in the scenes we have examined, are absolutely equal in that they are both at work in a setting neither one controls. A classroom is not a consensual community; nor is it a group of persons more or less socialized to the same patterns. A classroom is a single divided field that places the teacher and Rosa in different positions that invite activities of various prescribed forms. Similarly, the kids of Manhattan Valley and those of Hamden Heights are equal, though again, they are placed in different positions and are given different resources. It is not surprising that their activity should reveal itself fully sensitive to their respective positions and resources and that they should *appear* unequal in a context organized for the recognition of inequality.

This is where matters get delicate. The relationship between sensitivity and position or resources must not be understood in a correlational or, worse, causal fashion: Activity is not "dependent" on resource. Activity reveals the radical 我 at work, struggling, resisting, transforming, never passive or overwhelmed. This must be the starting point even if every evidence demonstrates that some activity does not produce anything that remains permanently for others to take into account. Rosa's protest may not take her out of special education, but it is a protest, an act of defiance exquisitely sensitive to its conditions. It is not the product of "her" learning disability; nor is it the product of some untapped quality of perception or knowledge that a proper educational psychology, institutionalized into a special program in an enlightened school, could use to inflect her fate. The set of fates that are available to people is not in the hands of any particular person. At the moment when the teacher passed her over, she was alone in the world, alive, moved to act, absolutely equal, even if she did not make, or "fact," anything for anyone—except perhaps for herself.

To speak about a radical 我 is obviously a move within Euro-American individualism even if inscribed in Chinese. We have not sought to escape the culture and traditions that structure our fields. But we are calling for a theory of human activity founded on the analytic acknowledgment of both the collective and the individual as nothing more than different perspectives on the same realities. It may be true there is nothing to society but single actors, but society, as it arises through the interaction of persons in history, is something systematically different from any persons and, to the extent that it is not under the control of any person, can be said to be "greater"—in the sense of both different and infinitely more powerful—than the individuals taken one at a time. It may be true that every personal self is a social construction deeply shaped by early and continuing experiences. Something of one's own personal history must be "internalized." But social interaction is not dependent on internalization. Participation in school is not dependent on understanding schooling. Participation in school is dependent on the existence of specific, legitimate means for acquiring the many actors who together keep the School alive. Labor in complex societies will always be divided, and human beings will be placed within the positions historically developed to reproduce the society. Human beings as actors, however, do not have to accept the way labor was divided or the methods used to place human beings into positions. If our analysis is right, no human being can ever be this acquiescent. All, like Rosa, are alive and at work. Culture as given is not destiny.

Our emphasis on a radical 我 in a historically constructed world is intended to counteract both psychological and sociological determinisms. Human beings do not *adapt to* culture; they *work with* and they *make* culture. They do not create out of nothing, and what they make always exhibits the traces of the materials they borrow and how it was used in earlier interactions. Children from the inner cities of America necessarily exhibit poverty in their activity, and if they are being acquired by Learning Disability as an institutional possibility, they will also exhibit the signs of LD. This recognition must not be mistaken with a diagnosis that the children "are" poor, deprived, or otherwise disabled. More controversially, if children carry on their faces an African phenotype, they will be seen by their parents, neighbors, peers, teachers, and social workers as African American or black depending on the political orientation of each significant other—and they will exhibit African Americanness (or blackness) as a token of the type even if only in their efforts to not play a part all know can be hurtful to all involved. Whether the children "are" (from birth) or "become" (through various processes) African American or black is a secondary matter of personal construction. To use something is not to *be* this thing. And when one is used by something, this something does not become "one's" thing.

We sketch this most controversial implication of our analytic posture to move to a more prescriptive level. If we refuse to give a "because" to the "why" questions put to us, what else can we offer? Defensively, we wish to protect those who are subjected to the School from any further action by the School—particularly from anything that starts with an identification of the child as a person with qualities to be discovered by agents of the School. This could be couched as a concern with the "privacy" of the child—privacy from all who, whatever their intentions, attempt to identify and pigeonhole selves. This could also be phrased as based on a fundamental trust in the power of *individuals*, each and all as a radical 我 in action, to make the best of their human conditions. It is certainly a call for those acquired by positions of authority—teachers, counselors, psychologists, and researchers, among many others—to work at becoming aware of the practical consequences of their actions: What do they *make* for others? Above all, we call for a critique of authoritative intentionality. We suspect, controversially, that the most dangerous moral prescription is the unassailable one that education must "help children one at a time, starting from where each is." Given that this implies an investigation into identifiable qualities of the child, it must involve an invasion of privacy. There is little evidence that the florescence of special educational programs has done much to improve the chances of inner-city children, and there is much evidence that there are systematic reasons for this. This lack of improvement is not due to programs that have been ill conceived by evil people with sinister motives. We assume instead that the programs were well conceived by good people with the most enlightened motives; they may still end up as the tools of the worst that Euro-American forms of industrialization produces. Inevitably, working with individuals must start with an identification of specific persons as somehow in need of charitable help. It must then proceed with the development of specialized bureaucracies peopled by persons with particular qualities (training, expertise, authority). Inevitably such bureaucracies, as social entities different and more powerful than the people who made them or presently occupy them, take a life of their own that is not often in tune with the original moral impulse (Cicourel and Kitsuse 1963; Edelman 1977). The noble Public School envisioned by Horace Mann becomes PS 1000 in New York City, a complex cog in a system of complex cogs. The idealistic progressivism of John Dewey becomes the dumbed-down curriculum of some high schools. Neither Mann nor Dewey are responsible for what others did with their injunctions. In their time, they may not have had the tools necessary to imagine what could be done with them. Practical educational philosophy is now in a different position.

Positively, we would say that a democracy must help all children "starting with the culture that specifies where children are to be placed." By culture, once again, we mean the institutionalized practices inhabited and used by human beings. We do not mean their minds or selves. The reformist impulse must refocus itself on the institutions that America has evolved over the past 200 years and on the often hidden relationships between them. Why does one need a high school diploma to collect garbage in New York City or an MA to teach in its schools (Berg 1969)? Why should education, as a lifelong process of shaping one's very being and character, be linked to getting particular jobs at particular times? Why, even more minimally, should one reach one's place in society through failure: Why should one be recruited into garbage collecting through a process of failing in school (not getting good enough grades at consequential times to be moved to a college-bound track)? Why is it that an interest in the constitution of the self should take the form of a ranking on some scale? Why should anyone ever be tested for intelligence given that almost everyone will be identified eventually as "not as intelligent as" everyone else? Why indeed should it appear liberalizing to identify "new" forms of intelligence and to develop new tests to measure people? The existence of a statistical relationship between IQ (or self-esteem, etc.) and the ability to perform certain tasks must not be the basis of any action making something for a child. At best, the relationship is statistical and thus tells us little about the possible fates of any particular child. At worst, the identification of the child by a score on a test locks the child in position. In either case, it does nothing to change the system of stratification or to alleviate the problems it can make for those in lower rungs. Whether a test is normed on a scale of 1600 (the SAT) or on a scale of 2 (Pass/Fail), the structural properties are the same. The possibility that one will "fail" is there, inescapable. It may be the case that certain jobs require specifiable skills. One can be properly tested for such skills, and whatever pain may come with failure on this test has to be accepted. But the set of these jobs and skills may be much more limited than has been institutionalized, and there is certainly no reason to seek to identify (lack of) "aptitudes" for jobs that one may never be called upon to perform or, worse, as a means of discouraging a person from trying.

We must, with Adam, "try to make it a better day" for those for whom we have a responsibility. As we do try, we must understand why it has been so difficult to make better days. If we are right in the stance we have illustrated throughout this book, we must above all accept that to make it a better day for Adam, the first and perhaps only step is to turn away from him and to trust him to work with us while we examine what all others, including ourselves, are doing around him. We hope we have shown how this must be so.

NOTES

1. As we mentioned, "America" is one form of a larger culture area within which most European cultures, and now most of the world's culture, must be included. America does have quite a distinct "flavor" within this area. Finally, our presentation of "America" is to be understood as a structural model highlighting certain properties of the historical situation (Lévi-Strauss [1958] 1963a).

Appendix A

This appendix is a summary of parts of Chapter 2 in Naddeo (1991). Like the other two, it is intended to give some further methodological background on data collection, to summarize limitations, and to justify the validity of the conclusions given the overall goals.

The research on which Chapter 3 is based was conducted by Merry Naddeo as part of a dissertation sponsored by Hervé Varenne. In the mid-1980s, she organized a choir for the Inn of the Good Shepherd. The research involved a period of informal participant observation that culminated with the videotaping of one rehearsal. Half an hour from this tape became the primary corpus for the research.

The Inn of the Good Shepherd was at the time an institution with a twenty-year history of growth and, by all published and accepted accounts, success at helping some of the young people who drifted onto the meanest streets of Manhattan. It had developed into a national organization with crisis and long-term shelters in several cities and a budget of close to $100 million, mostly raised from private donations. Permission was given on the basis of the fact that the project provided a direct service to the residents, and Naddeo was officially known as an "outside volunteer." Permission did not include access to the administration or the other programs, preventing any systematic exploration of the organization of the institution. She did talk at length with a number of residents as she explained both the nature of the choir and the use she might make of their participation for research purposes. These talks remained informal. She did not take notes during these talks or interviews. These talks are sparsely used in the analysis itself. This analysis focuses solely on the moment-to-moment joint construction of the one rehearsal that was videotaped and has little to say about the institution that housed the rehearsal.

Methodologically, Naddeo's position was halfway between that of a full participant and that of an experimenter. She started the choir as a quasi-experiment and fully participated in its day-to-day running. She set up the videotaping (by asking a friend to do it for her). She is also one of the central participants in the videotaped scene. This made it necessary to analyze her own activity as that of a participant. This was in line with modern understandings of the difficulty of claiming a purely detached "observer" stance in ethnographic investigation. The researcher is always part of the scene and her activity must be accounted for. Given the difficulties of observing and recording oneself, the video camera allowed for the production of a corpus that could then be submitted to analysis.

Video itself is quite limited in various ways. The camera can record only activity within a rather narrow field. On the day of the rehearsal, Naddeo remembers (and noted in her fieldnotes), another group of residents and administrators were setting up a talent show in another part of the auditorium. On the video record, one sees all choir participants from time to time reacting to something done by these people, but there is no detailed record of their activity. This activity could thus not be investigated, and no statement can be made about the total scene that was being constituted within the auditorium. There is every evidence, however, that the camera focused on what may be analyzed as one subscene, the choir rehearsal. This scene was actually constituted by the interactional space that was placed around it, physically and temporally. It remained an accountable event for all involved (including the people setting up the other event in the room and the people who may have drifted in from outside the room). Nothing that happened destroyed the local facticity of the rehearsal as rehearsal.

Several kinds of transcripts were attempted. The only ones used were those that emphasized shifts in the positionings that the rehearsal required (singing, moving from one song to the next, correction, etc.) and movement within these positionings. The videotape itself was not quite adequate to analyze in detail the exact mechanism of the shifts. It seemed likely from a cursory examination that shifts from transition to singing positionings started synchronically—that is, all participants moved together rather than sequentially after a specific direction from Naddeo (Byers 1976). This, however, could not be verified. The timing of the transcripts presented in the chapter should be considered accurate within two or three seconds, which is sufficient for the purpose of the argument.

The first of the transcripts used (Figure 3.2) maps the first sixteen minutes of the rehearsal. Two main positionings constituted the rehearsal: singing and going from one song to the next. Movements from one to the other and back again are indicated as transitions on the figure. A secondary positioning occurred at times within the singing as the singing stopped, participants remained in position, and Naddeo gave them some direction about the singing. The middle column of the table indicates the title of the song sung. One can assume that enough participants were singing to constitute Singing, though any number of individuals may not have actually been singing. The right-hand column is used for brief notations about other matters, such as the minor transitions and the information-seeking and -giving sequences that are analyzed in the chapter.

The second of the transcripts used (Figure 3.3) is a blowup of the first half of Singing Segment #3 in Figure 3.2. The left-hand column indicates the timing in 2.5 second intervals. The third column is a rendering of Naddeo's major head and upper-body movements during the singing. Throughout the song, she sang, played the piano, and scanned the singers by turning her head. The arrows indicate the direction of her face (her body remained in line with the piano). The Z-shaped arrow indicates that she moved her whole upper body forward over the keys as a "directing" gesture. Starting at second 625 one can also see her turn her head completely to look at something behind her and thus away from the choir (she remembers this movement as being prompted by noise from the other group using the auditorium; this noise was not picked up by the camera's microphone). None of these movements broke the progression of the singing. The next column sketches Angie's activity. Mostly, she sang the words to the song, except on the four occasions when she entered into the specific subsequence with Nan, analyzed in Chapter 3. The last column sketches Nan's activity. She started singing with the choir, turned the first page along with the other members, stopped singing, and then began searching her papers, twice leaning over Angie and entering into a subsequence with her and twice opening herself to her as Angie pointed at the place where she should be. Figures 3.1, 3.4, 3.5, 3.6, and 3.7 illustrate the four instances of the Angie-Nan subsequence. The figures are frame grabs from the videotape.

Appendix B

The original research on which Chapter 4 is based was conducted by Rosemarie Rizzo-Tolk over two academic years in the mid-1980s. It was the basis of a dissertation sponsored by Ray McDermott. At the time she was a social studies teacher at West Side High School. This is the actual name of the school, and we use it with the agreement of the principal at the time, Mr. Ed Reynolds, and to honor all those who work there, teachers and students. All other names are pseudonyms. West Side is an "alternative" high school within the New York City public school system. Such schools were officially described in the following terms: "These high schools are in smaller settings . . . and emphasize academic and personal support." A few years after the research was conducted at the school, the *New York Times* reported that it was "considered a last chance for those who do not make it at other schools" (April 27, 1997, p. 33). West Side High School has always been particularly open to innovative programs, and Rizzo-Tolk came to the school to develop such programs. One of those is the one that led eventually to the videorecording that is the basis of Chapter 4. The exact context of the project is described in the body of the chapter. As indicated, the published research focuses on twenty-five minutes of this tape when the students were talking among themselves. This appendix addresses some of the methodological issues raised in Appendix A, particularly issues related to the participation of the observer and to videotaping itself. It also gives further details about the various transcripts and illustrations used in Chapter 4.

To an even greater degree than Naddeo, Rizzo-Tolk was a full participant throughout the data-collection part of the research. She was a licensed teacher in the New York City system and thus privy to everything that a teacher may have access to, including a wide body of contextual material about the school, the administration, the program she had designed, and the students. Her project, though "alternative" and experimental within the canonical instructional forms, was fully sponsored by her school and was done for official credit. She had specific responsibilities to the school and thus could claim the particular forms of legitimate authority that teachers are given. As demonstrated throughout, the aides, the students, and all others involved in the research acknowledged this authority even if, at times, they resisted it. The videotaping itself was a possibility within the commonsense routine of the school in general and of this class in particular given its use of the technology for the preceding six months as the students filmed the documentary for the directly pedagogical aspect of the project. The taping of the final discussion that is the focus of Chapter 4 can thus be taken as a slice of the everyday life of the school. Every participant, Rizzo-Tolk as teacher and all the students, constructed it as such.

The status of full authoritative participantship limits ethnographic research in two systematic ways that are not relevant here. In general one can assume that a participant in a complex bureaucracy, that is, someone who is commonsensically identified as the embodiment of a status (Rizzo-Tolk *was* a Teacher), cannot have access to other statuses within the bureaucracy except through the channels allowed by the status. In other words, it is unlikely that a teacher could talk with her principal "as if" she were not a teacher under her authority. By contrast, ethnographers who come to the school from the outside may have broad leeway to negotiate a role of relevance in each interaction ("I could be one of *you*") and may be able to play "principal" with the principal, teacher with the teacher, and so on. These possible limitations do not apply here, since in this study, Rizzo-Tolk was not required to act in any other role than the one all participants would commonsensically acknowledge for her, that is, as Teacher. It is as such that she participated in the taping.

The other limitation in a full participant attempting to make an ethnographic record of an interaction arises if the research requires the person to take notes on her behavior in the real time when she is also required to perform within her role: A teacher cannot teach and take notes on her teaching at the same time. This obviously is radically mitigated when the class interaction is videotaped. Although videotape has limitations as an ethnographic recording device (see Appendix A), it does allow participants to collect information about their own performance and that of people in interaction with them that cannot be collected in any other way.

Video analyses allow for a detailed look at the intricacies of joint behavior in the real time of its occurrence that traditional ethnography cannot match. A rough transcript of the talk and major positionings was first made. It was then recognized that it would be fruitful to look more carefully at what the students were doing among themselves. Videotape, however, is relatively unwieldy for an analysis that focuses on interactional sequences shorter than a second. One sequence was chosen for transfer to videodisc, since this technology allows for easy frame-by-frame analysis. The choice of the sequence was a theoretical one: The students were on their own, constituting a long moment by themselves and away from immediate teacherly feedback. Several types of transcripts were then made. Two of them were used extensively for the analysis of this sequence: a transcript of positionings and a transcript focusing on lexical content of the talk. The former emphasized gross bodily movements (laughing, moving back and forth in one's chair, etc.); the latter emphasized semantic matters. Both were precisely timed (accuracy to half a second) by putting the sound through a data-acquisition board on a personal computer and analyzing the waveform printout. This analysis demonstrated the exquisite sensitivity of students to each other's behavior and to the constraints of their task, which they constituted through their own actions.

The first figure (4.1) summarizes the major subsequences within a very stable twenty-minute sequence. During the whole time, the students held the same position: They sat in a circle, bodies facing each other. When they spoke, they turned their heads (but not their bodies, which remained almost motionless throughout) toward Rizzo-Tolk. She stayed invisible, on the side of the camera.

The second figure (4.2) maps the complexities of the sequence of major focus within the chapter. It could analyzed into two main subsequences: getting instructions (shorthanded as "Gg") and discussing choices (Dg). Discussing choices was itself subdivided into two sub-subsequences: reading the questions (Rg) and actually discussing. Two other interstitial sequences consisted of laughing together (Lg). They did not appear to be part of the canonical progression within the teacher-prescribed discussion, but they appeared at particular moments that emphasized the canonical progression and somehow commented on it.

Figure B.1 is a transcript of the verbal stream during the discussion sequence. The transcription, including its timing, was made according to the conventions introduced and justified in Varenne (1992). They focus our attention on timing, semantic content, speaker, and participants (as determined by internal evidence, both visual and verbal, that a person is attending to the speaker)

FIGURE B.1

Transcript of Main Sequence

	RM	Chris	Char	Ed	Rob	Dani	Yasm	Jean	Baby
-0	~ we	~	~	~	~	~	~	~	~
-1	have a task	~	~	~	~	~	~	~	~
-2	~ for you	~	~	~	~	~	~	~	~
-3	to do ~	~	~	~	~	~	~	~	~
-4	now maybe Chris	~	~	~	~	~	~	~	~
-5	uuh ~	~	~	~	~	~	~	~	~
-6	can explain	~	~	~	~	~	~	~	~
-7	task ~	~	~	~	~	~	~	~	~
-8	and uhh	~	~	~	~	~	~	~	~
-9	~ ~	~	~	~	~	~	~	~	~
-10	~ ~	~	~	~	~	~	~	~	~
-11	~ ~	~	~	~	~	~	~	~	~Mommy
-12	~ ~	~ ~	~	~	~	~	~	~	~
-13	~ ~	Uh, what this	~	~	~	~	~	~	~
-14	~ ~	is I suppose	~	~	~	~	~	~	~
-15	~ ~	~	~	~	~	~	~	~	~
-16	~ ~	~ we	~	~	~	~	~	~	~
-17	~ ~	want ~	~	~	~	~	~	~	~
-18	~ ~	you to	~	~	~	~	~	~	~
-19	~ ~	~ rank	~	~	~	~	~	~	~
-20	~ ~	options that you	~	~	~	~	~	~	~
-21	~ ~	Would have if	~	~	~	~	~	~	~
-22	~ ~	You were uh	~	~	~	~	~	~	~
-23	~ ~	~	~	~	~	~	~	~	~
-24	~ ~	Faced with being	~ ~	~	~	~	~	~	~
-25	~ ~	~ homeless	~	~	~	~	~	~	~
-26	~ ~	~ what	~	~	~	~	~	~	~
-27	~ ~	type of	~	~	~	~	~	~	~

	RM	Chris	Char	Ed	Rob	Dani	Yasm	Jean	Baby
-28	~	choices you would	~	~	~	~	~	~	~
-29	~	make I mean	~	~	~	~	~	~	~
-30	~	where would you go	~	~	~	~	~	~	Mommy
-31	~	from there where	~	~	~	~	~	~	~
-32	~	would you sleep	~	~	~	~	~	~	~
-33	~	what would you do	~	~	~	~	~	~	~
-34	~	- that kind	~	~	~	~	~	~	Ahhh
-35	~	of thing	~	~	~	~	~	~	~
-36	~	~ so uh on the	~	~	~	~	~	~	~
-37	~	se index cards	~	~	~	~	~	~	~
-38	~	there's nine	~	~	~	~	~	~	~
-39	~	options and	~	~	~	~	~	~	~
-40	~	we just want	~	~	~	~	~	~	~
-41	~	you to rank	~	~	~	~	~	~	~
-42	~	them as a	~	~	~	~	~	~	~
-43	~	group decide in	~	~	~	~	~	~	~
-44	~	what order you	~	~	~	~	~	~	~
-45	~	would do these	~	~	~	~	~	~	Ahhh
-46	~	things if you were	~	~	~	~	~	~	~
-47	~	homeless	~	~	~	~	~	~	Ahhh
-48	~	~	~	~	~	~	~	~	~
-49	~	~	~	~	~	~	~	~	~
-50	~	~	~	~	~	~	~	~	~
-51	- you	~	~	~	~	~	~	~	~
-52	do it as a group	- yeah so	~	~	~	~	~	~	~
-53	we want you	come to a group	~	~	~	~	~	~	~
-54	to come to	decision	~	~	~	~	~	~	~
-55	agreement ~	~	~	~	~	~	~	~	~
-56	- about	~	~	~	~	~	~	~	~
-57	how to do it	~	~	~	~	~	~	~	~
-58	~	and I can even	~	~		~	~	~	~

	RM	Chris	Char	Ed	Rob	Dani	Yasm	Jean	Baby
-59		give you some paper							
-60	I don't I don't								
-61	think they need to	~ no							
-62	write this								
-63									
-64			~ the first						
-65			one is live with						no
-66			a relative who						
-67			you don't like who						
-68			doesn't like you						no like
-69			the second one is						
-70			go to a group home						
-71			~ the th_						
-72			ird one, go to a						
-73			shelter ~						
-74			live in shanty						
-75			town ~						
-76			~ use a park						
-77			as your						
-78			home base						
-79									
-80									
-81			resort to drug						
-82			~ dealing						
-83			to survive						
-84									
-85									
-86			beg on the str_						
-87			eet ~						
-88			live in a building						
-89			boiler room without						

	RM	Chris	Char	Ed	Rob	Dani	Yasm	Jean	Baby
-90	~		permission or leave	~	~	~	~	~	~
-91	~		city town or	~	~	~	~	~	~
-92	~		state ~	~	~	~	~	~	~
-93	~		~ GROUP LAUGHTER BEGINS						
-94	~								~
-95	~		~	~	~	~	~	~	~
-96	~		~	~	~	~	~	~	~
-97	~								
-98	~		~	~	shoot	~	~	~	~
-99	~		~						
-100	~		~~ GROUP LAUGHTER ENDS						

[AFTER THE FIRST SEQUENCE OF LAUGHTER THE TEACHERS WITHDRAW INTO THE BACKGROUND]

	RM	Chris	Char	Ed	Rob	Dani	Yasm	Jean	Baby
-101	~	~	~	~	~	~	with the fir_	~	~
-102	~	~	~	~	~	~	st one ~	~	~
-103	~	~	~	~	NO ~	~	I was thinking how the	~	~
-104	~	~	~	~	~	~	relatives will let you	~	~
-105	~	~	~	~	~	~	live with them when they	~	~
-106	~	~	~	~	~	~cause	don't like you	~	~
-107	~	~	~	~	~	you their relatives	~	~	~
-108	~	~	if you don't like	~	~	~	this says	~	~
-109	~	~	~	~	~	~	and they don't like	~	~
-110	~	~	~	~	~ because	~	you either ~	~	~
-111	~	~	~	~	they let you they'll	~	~	~	~
-112	~	~	~	~	let you ~	~ live with them	~	~	~
-113	~	~	~	~	~	~	~	~	~
-114	~	~	~	~	~	~	~	~	~
-115	~	~	~	~		~	~	~	~
-116	~	~	~ but then	~	~	~	~	~	~

	RM	Chris	Char	Ed	Rob	Dani	Yasm	Jean	Baby
-117	~ (let me ~		~ I						
-118	ask you a question)			would feel more					
-119			comfortable going to a						
-120			group home than dealing						
-121			with people that I don't						
-122			know being that I						
-123			would have to go with						
-124			a relative who don't						
-125			like me that's too im-						
-126			portant ~						
-127									
-128									
-129									
-130			feelin like a						
-131			stepchild ~			right			
-132			~ that has						
-133			to do every-						
-134			thing ~				~ a wicked		
-135							stepmother		
-136						I wouldn't			
-137						go to a shelter			
-138					I wouldn't				
-139					go to no shel-				
-140					ter either and ~				
-141					I wouldn't beg on				
-142					the street				
-143					sell drugs yes ~				
-144						~ no, not me			
-145			That's the last						
-146			resort ~			~ no			
-147					the last resort				

	RM	Chris	Char	Ed	Rob	Dani	Yasm	Jean	Baby
-148	~	~	~	~	is live in	~	~	~	~
-149	~	~	~	~	the street and	~	~	~	~
-150	~	~	~	~	this goes on	~	~	right ~	~
-151	~	~	~	~	to sellin drugs	~	~	~	~
-152	~	~	I think this should	~		~	~	~	~
-153	~	~	be a second ch_	~		~	~	~	~
-154	~	~	oice ~ I would	~		~	yeah ~	~	~
-155	~	~	~ after going	~		~	~	~	~
-156	~	~	to a gr- a group home	~		~	~	~	~
-157	~	~	I would go live	~		~	with a relative	~	~
-158	~	~		~		~		~	~
-159	~	~	a relative	~		~	~	~	~
-160	~	~	~	~	AAA ~	so put goin to a	~	~	~
-161	~	~	~	~		group home first	~	~	~
-162	~	~	~	by the way group	~	~	~	~	~
-163	~	~	~	homes are pretty rough too	~	~	~yeah they are	~	~
-164	~	~	~	~	~	~	~	~	~
-165	~	~	~	if you really look at it	~	~	~	~	~
-166	~	~	not the ones my	~ depends on	~	~	~	~	~
-167	~	~	girlfriends have been	what you not the	~	~	~	~	~
-168	~	~	staying at they been good	one my girlfriend my cousins	~	~	~	~	~
-169	~	~	~	I'm talkin about	~	~	~	~	~
-170	~	~	~	the male group homes	~	~	~	~	~
-171	~	~	~	it's pretty rough for	~	~	~	~	~
-172	~	~	~	some people who might	~	~	~	~	~
-173	~	~	~	be weaker I know	~	~	~	~	~
-174	~	~	~	I'm not weak so	~	~	~	~	~
-175	~	~	~	I'd have no problem	~	~	~ there's	~	~
-176	~	~	~	living there	~	~	no problem with	~	~
-177	~	~	~	~	~	~	group homes ~	~	~
-178	~	~	~	~	~	~		~	~

Line	RM	Chris	Char	Ed	Rob	Dani	Yasm	Jean	Baby
-179					just have to put		there's xxxx		
-180					your hands up				
-181									
-182			or maybe leave						
-183			leave city town						
-184			or state or						
-185			if you have another			– that's			
-186			relative –			gonna be even			
-187				– that would be		harder cause –			
-188				simple –		– first			
-189						I'd sell drugs	– goin to be		
-190			beg on the street				– hungry and maybe you won't		
-191			for the money				– have any money to eat		
-192					this then				
-193						and then I'd			
-194			we all have this			leave the state			
-195									
-196									
-197			– okay sell						
-198			drugs +++++						
-199								yeah	
-200									
-201			but you would have to						
-202			beg on the street and			– no I wouldn't			
-203			sell drugs and			beg on the street			
-204						I would	that would be the		
-205						sell drugs –	last resort		
-206			– really?				– yeah,yeah		
-207							yeah,yeah		
-208						yes –	– yes with the		
-209			– I				shelter		

Line	RM	Chris	Char	Ed	Rob	Dani	Yasm	Jean	Baby
-210	˷˷	˷˷	would ask nicely	˷˷	˷˷	˷˷	˷˷	˷˷	˷˷
-211	˷˷	˷˷	before I sell	˷˷	˷˷	me too I	˷˷	˷˷	˷˷
-212	˷˷	˷˷	drugs ~	˷˷	˷˷	would rather beg	˷˷	˷˷	mommy
-213	˷˷	˷˷	˷˷	˷˷	˷˷	cause sellin	˷˷	˷˷	˷˷
-214	˷˷	˷˷	˷˷	˷˷	˷˷	drugs you rakin	˷˷	˷˷	˷˷
-215	˷˷	˷˷	˷˷	˷˷	˷˷	a chance you	˷˷	˷˷	˷˷
-216	˷˷	˷˷	˷˷	˷˷	˷˷	might just get caught	˷˷	˷˷	˷˷
-217	˷˷	˷˷	may be put in jail	˷˷	˷˷	yeah ~	~but you'd have a	˷˷	˷˷
-218	˷˷	˷˷	˷˷	˷˷	that would be a	˷˷	~place to stay	˷˷	˷˷
-219	˷˷	˷˷	˷˷	~ and then you'd	nice place to	˷˷	˷˷	˷˷	˷˷
-220	˷˷	˷˷	˷˷	get free room and	˷˷	˷˷	˷˷	˷˷	˷˷
-221	˷˷	˷˷	˷˷	board	˷˷	˷˷	˷˷	˷˷	˷˷
-222	˷˷	˷˷	jail is no_	˷˷	˷˷	˷˷	˷˷	˷˷	˷˷
-223	˷˷	˷˷	not no fun	˷˷	˷˷	~ but just	˷˷	˷˷	˷˷
-224	˷˷	˷˷	˷˷	˷˷	˷˷	think of all the time	˷˷	˷˷	˷˷
-225	˷˷	˷˷	˷˷	˷˷	˷˷	that you gonna have to	˷˷	˷˷	˷˷
-226	˷˷	˷˷	~ just cause	˷˷	˷˷	spend just cause	˷˷	˷˷	˷˷
-227	˷˷	˷˷	you chose ~	˷˷	˷˷	you was afraid your	˷˷	˷˷	˷˷
-228	˷˷	˷˷	˷˷	˷˷	˷˷	pride was too big for	˷˷	˷˷	˷˷
-229	˷˷	˷˷	˷˷	˷˷	˷˷	you to beg and you	˷˷	˷˷	˷˷
-230	˷˷	˷˷	˷˷	˷˷	˷˷	just wanted to go	˷˷	˷˷	˷˷
-231	˷˷	˷˷	˷˷	˷˷	~ I'll	sell drugs	˷˷	˷˷	˷˷
-232	˷˷	˷˷	˷˷	˷˷	handle it	~ okay	˷˷	˷˷	˷˷
-233	˷˷	˷˷	gotta have	˷˷	˷˷	˷˷	~ nowadays	˷˷	˷˷
-234	˷˷	˷˷	˷˷	˷˷	˷˷	˷˷	you have	˷˷	˷˷
-235	˷˷	˷˷	˷˷	˷˷	˷˷	˷˷	a job	˷˷	˷˷
-236	˷˷	˷˷	˷˷	˷˷	we talkin about	˷˷	˷˷	˷˷	˷˷
-237	˷˷	˷˷	˷˷	˷˷	okay go ahead	˷˷	˷˷	˷˷	˷˷
-238	˷˷	˷˷	˷˷	˷˷	˷˷	˷˷	˷˷	˷˷	˷˷
-239	˷˷	˷˷	o-okay so we have go to a	˷˷	˷˷	˷˷	˷˷	˷˷	˷˷
-240	˷˷	˷˷	group home live with a	˷˷	˷˷	˷˷	˷˷	˷˷	˷˷

	RM	Chris	Char	Ed	Rob	Dani	Yasm	Jean	Baby
-241	~	~	relative who you don't	~	~	~	~	~	~
-242	~	~	like who it's either	~	~	~	~	~	~
-243	~	~	between resort to	~	~	~	~	~	~
-244	~	~	dealin drugs or	~	~	~	~	~	~
-245	~	~	beg on the	~	~	~	~	~	~
-246	~	~	street	~	~	~ how	~	~	~
-247	~	~	~ beg	~	~	many beg on the	~	~	~
-248	~	~	on the street	~	~	I'm with that	~	~	~
-249	~	~	~	~	~	~	me too	~	~
-250	~	~	~	~	uhhugg	~	~	~	~
-251	~	~	~	~	~	~	~	~	~
-252	~	~	sell drugs	~	~	~	~	~	~
-253	~	~	~	~	~ I'm with	~	~	~	~
-254	~	~	~	~	~	~ what	~ God	~	~
-255	~	~	~	~	~	you want ~	so ~	~	~
-256	~	~	~	~	~	beg or sell		beg on the	~
-257	~	~	~	~	~	drugs ~	~	street 1 right	~
-258	~	~	~	~ I	~	~	~	~	~
-259	~	~	~	would rather beg on	~	~	~ beg on the	~	~
-260	~	~	~	the street	~	~	~ street first	~	~
-261	~	~	~	It might be embarrassing	~	~	~	~	~
-262	~	~	and then resort	at first but after awhile ~	~	~	~	~	~
-263	~	~	to dealin drugs if you	~	~	~	~ yeah	~	~
-264	~	~	can't get enough from	~	~ yeah	~	~	~	~
-265	~	~	beggin on the street and	~ yeah	~	~	~	~	~
-266	~	~	then you would leave	~	~	~	~ yeah	~	~
-267	~	~	city or town or	~ yes	~	~	~	~	~
-268	~	~	try and stay with	~	~	~	~	~ if	~
-269	~	~	a relative	~	~	~	~	they let you	~
-270	~	~	~	~	~	~	~	~	~
-271	~	~	~ And	~	~	~	~	~	~

Line	RM	Chris	Char	Ed	Rob	Dani	Yasm	Jean	Baby
272	~	~	then ~	~	~I'd live	~	~	~	~
273	~	~	~	~	in a building before	~	~	~	~
274	~	~	~	~	I would live in a	~	~	~	~
275	~	~	~	~	shelter	~ yeah	~	~	~
276	~	~	~	~ or live in			~	yeah ~	~
277	~	~	~	A park ~	~ or shanty_	~ yes	~	~	~
278	~	~	~		town I wouldn't		~	~	~
279	~	~	~	I would	live in a park		~	~	~
280	~	~	~	rather live in a			~	~	~
281	~	~	~	boiler room			~live in shantytown	~ at	~
282	~	~	live in a boiler room						~
283	~	~	without permission				~least you got food		~
284	~	~	~					there ~	~
285	~	~	~	I would live			~	~	~
286	~	~	~	in a boiler room		It's on there	~	~	~
287	~	~	~	without permission			~	~	~
288	~	~	~	before I would live		It's on there	~	~	~
289	~	~	~ shantytown	in shantytown	and then		~	~	~
290	~	~	would be the			last one	~	~	~
291	~	~	~		~ no		~	~	~
292	~	~	~		then the shelter		~	~	~
293	~	~	~				~	~	~
294	~	~	~				~	~	~
295	~	~	~				~	~	~
296	~	~	~				~	~	~
297	~	~	~		then use		~	~	~
298	~	~	~		the parkbench		~	~	~
299				BUILDING GROUP LAUGHTER					
300									
301			GROUP LAUGHTER						
302	~	~	~	~	~	~	~	~	~

	RM	Chris	Char	Ed	Rob	Dani	Yasm	Jean	Baby
-303	˘ ˘	˘ ˘	˘ ˘	˘ ˘	˘ ˘	˘ ˘	˘ ˘	˘ ˘	˘ ˘
-304	˘ ˘	˘ ˘	˘ ˘	˘ ˘	˘ ˘	˘ ˘	˘ ˘	˘ ˘	˘ ˘
-305	˘ ˘	˘ ˘	˘ ˘	hang it up right	˘ ˘	˘ ˘	˘ ˘	˘ ˘	˘ ˘
-306	˘ ˘	˘ ˘	˘ ˘	there ~	˘	˘	˘	˘	˘
-307				LAUGHTER TAPERS OFF					
-308	˘ ˘	˘ ˘	˘ ˘	˘ ˘	˘ ˘	˘ ˘	˘ ˘	˘ ˘	˘ ˘
-309	˘ ˘	˘ ˘	˘ ˘	˘ ˘	˘ ˘	˘ ˘	˘ ˘	˘ ˘	˘ ˘
-310	˘ ˘	˘ ˘	˘ ˘	˘ ˘	˘ ˘		˘ ˘		

Appendix C

McDermott has written extensively about the methodological justification for the work with Rosa, her teachers, and her peers, particularly in "Criteria for an Ethnographically Adequate Description of Concerted Activities and Their Contexts" (1978). This appendix deals mostly with the reanalysis by Varenne. In the late 1980s, as part of a broader project, a few minutes of the Rosa videotape were transferred to videodisc, and two and a half minutes were then timed and transcribed via the same methods developed by Varenne (1992) and used in Chapter 4. Figure 8.3 is a development of McDermott's positioning analysis. It emphasizes the complex interplay of a main activity with various subactivities more or less closely tied to the main one. That is, a "bottom group" is at work within a reading lesson during which it would be expected that much reading would get done. McDermott showed that the participants in this class (including the students in the top group), as observable in their own behavior, constituted this lesson as being made of three main activities. McDermott talks of these activities as "positionings" to emphasize that they were inscribed in the very body of the participants as they positioned themselves vis-à-vis each other. These positionings were reading, getting a turn to read, and waiting for the teacher.

The full transcript of the excerpt transferred to videodisc is included as Figure C.1. The following summary is intended to help a reader follow Figure 8.3 and the transcript. The transcript starts at a time when the students are getting a turn to read. This is completed by second 24 as the students install themselves within the reading positioning. In the reading performance that lasted from second 24 to second 136 in the sequence, there are two minimal performances of a getting-a-turn-to-read positioning. The first getting-a-turn sequence (a brief four seconds, 81–85) is led by the students coming up from a focus on their books, and after the teacher says, "Alright, Maria, read page four," everyone returns to a reading positioning.

The second getting-a-turn sequence (sec. 110–127) is a complex act that involves the teacher passing up Rosa and calling on Jimmy (who protests about Rosa being passed over and ends up not reading). Rosa, in turn, suggests a reading order, and the teacher calls on a third child, Fred, at the other end of the reading table. During time in the getting-a-turn positioning, reading, the very activity for which everyone has gathered around the table, the very activity for which they hold each other accountable, is of course suspended, delayed, and made visible for its absence. We can even say that reading, as an activity and a social positioning, is sabotaged by what can be interpreted as an act of resistance to the teacher's and the school's authority even while the protesters specifically use and thereby reconstitute that authority.

Actual reading, in the sense of reading words in the book, is also suspended from second 33 to second 75 as the teacher enters into a teaching routine (in the sense identified by Mehan 1979) and writes on the board the letter that Maria and Anna have misidentified (they said "pammy" when they should have said "patty"). Eventually, she gives them the word (sec. 54) and the reading progresses again. During this time, most of the children in the reading group and even the teacher engage other children in the class. These intrusions do not quite interrupt the currently relevant reading positioning, and it takes only an "uhm uh" from the teacher to move everyone back into an appropriate display of reading.

The illustrations in Figures 8.4, 8.5, and 8.7 are frame grabs from the videodisc. The frame numbers on each image can be used to place it in the transcript in which each line is identified by its timing (each line is a second) and by the frame number at the beginning of the second (video moves at thirty frames a second). For better quality versions of these images and more displays of the original data, see our website at URL http://varenne2.tc.columbia.edu/www/hv/sf/sf.html.

FIGURE C.1
Transcript

sec.	frame #	Teacher	Anna	Jimmy	Rosa	Fred	Maria	P
1	31990	Alright, alright raise your						
2	32020	hand if you can read page						
3	32050	four ~						
4	32080	~	~ page					
5	32110	Raise your hand if you can	four? ~					
6	32140	read page four						
7	32170	~						
8	32200	~						
10	32230	~ Paul						
11	32260	~						
12	32290	~						
13	32320	Eliza you're						
14	32350	wasting your time						
15	32380	~		~ I can't				
16	32410	Alright page four						
17	32440	~		~ Not me				
18	32470	~ Nobody can read						
19	32500	page four?						
20	32530	~		~ Noooo				
21	32560	~ Why not?						
22	32590	~			I could			
23	32620	~	I could.			~ I could	~ I could	
24	32650	~ Alright, what						
25	32680	does it say?						
26	32710	~						
27	32740	~		COME				
28	32770	~						
29	32800	~						GO OUT

sec.	frame #	Teacher	Anna	Jimmy	Rosa	Fred	Maria	P
30	32830	~	GO OUT	~	~	~	GO OUT	~
31	32860	~	~	~	OUT	~	~	OUT DAMMY
32	32890	~	DAMMY	~	~	~	~	~
33	32920	~	~	~	~	~	~	No, PPP
34	32950	~	~	~	~	~	~	~
35	32980	AMMY	~	~	~	~	~	AMMY
36	33010	~	~	~	~	~	~	~
37	33040	Watch, what does	~	PAMMY	~	~	~	~
38	33070	this word say?	~	~	~	~	~	~
39	33100	~	~	~	~	~	~	~
40	33130	~	- PAMMY	- PAMMY	~	~	~	PAMMY
41	33160	~	~	~	~	Nooo	~	~
42	33190	~	~	Nooo	~	~	~	~
43	33220	~	- Bka Bka	~	~	~	~	~
44	33250	~	~	~	~	~	~	~
45	33280	- Excuse me Paul, but	~	~	~	~	~	~
46	33320	I did not give	~	~	~	~	~	~
47	33350	you permission to talk.	~	~	~	~	~	~
48	33380	~	- PAMMY	- PAMMY	~	- PAMMY	~	~
49	33410	~	~	~	~	~	~	~
50	33440	~	PAMMY	PAMMY	~	~	~	~
51	33470	~	~	~	~	~	~	PAMMY
52	33500	~	~	~	~	~	~	PAMMY
53	33530	~	~	~	~	~	~	~
54	33560	- P.P.P. PATTY	~	~	~	~	~	- P.P.P. PATTY
55	33620	~	~	~	~	~	~	~
56	33620	~	~	~	~	~	~	~
57	33650	-- Alright	~	~	~	~	~	~
58	33680	~	~	~	~	~	~	PATTY PATTY
59	33710	~	~	~	~	~	~	~
60	33730	- Alright Jimmy.	~	~	~	~	~	~

sec.	frame #	Teacher	Anna	Jimmy	Rosa	Fred	Maria	P
61	33760	~	~	~	~	~	~	~
62	33790	Alright, what does this word	~	~	~	~	~	~
63	33820	say? ~	~	~	~	~	~	PAT
64	33850		~	~	~	~	~	~
65	33880	~ PAT	~	~	~	GO OUT PATTY ~ PATTY	~	~
66	33910	~						
67	33940	~	~	~	~	~	~	GO OUT PATTY
68	33970	PATTY	~	~	~	~	~	~
69	34000		~	~	~	~	~	~
70	34030	PATTY	~	~	~	~	~	~
71	34060				[chorus]	PATTY		
72	34090	~			[chorus]	GO OUT		
73	34120	~			[chorus]	PATTY AND JUMP		
74	34150	~						
75	34180	~	~	~		~	~	~
76	34210	~	~	~	[Chorus]	GO OUT	~	~
77	34240	~			[Chorus]	PATTY AND JUMP		
78	34270	~			~ GO		~ GO	
79	34300	~	~	~			OUT AND JUMP ~	
80	34330	~	~	~				
81	34360	Alright let's	~	~				~ Now I read
82	34390	Now we're						the next page
83	34420	gonna read page four again.	~	~				
84	34450	Alright, Maria read	~	~				
85	34480	page four.	~	~				
86	34510	~	~	~ Uhhhauhhh				
87	34540	~	~	~				~
88	34570	~	~	~	~ GO			~
89	34600	~	~	~				~ JUMP
90	34630	~ Shhh	~	~	~ GO	~	~	~

sec.	frame #	Teacher	Anna	Jimmy	Rosa	Fred	Maria	P
91	34660	Shhh	~~	~~	~ OUT	~~	~~	~~
92	34690	~~	~~	~~	~~	~~	GO OUT PATTY	~~
93	34720	~~	~~	~~	~~	~~	~~	~~
94	34750	~~	~~	~~	~~	~~	~~	~~
95	34780	~~	~~	~~	~~	~~	~ GO OUT	~~
96	34810	~~	~~	~~	~~	~~	~~	~~
97	34840	~~	~~	~~	~~	~~	~~	~~
98	34870	~~	~~	~~	~~	~~	~~	~~
99	34900	~~	~~	~~	~~	~~	~~	~~
100	34930	~~	~~	~~	~~	~~	~~	AND AND
101	34960	~~	~~	~~	~~	~~	~ AND	~~
102	34990	~~	~~	~~	~~	~~	- JUMP	JUMP
103	35020	~~	~~	~~	~~	~~	~~	~~
104	35050	~~	~~	~~	~~	~~	~ GO	~~
105	35080	~~	~~	- GO	~~	~~	OUT AND JUMP~	~~
106	35110	~~	~~	OUT AND JUMP ~~	OUT AND JUMP ~~	~~	~~	~~
107	35140	~~	~~	~~	~~	~~	~~	~~
108	35170	~~	~~	~~	~~	~~	~~	~~
109	35200	~~	~~	~~	~~	~~	~~	~~
110	35230	Alright, let's see you	~~	~~	~~	~~	~~	~~
111	35260	do it.	~~	~~	~~	~~	~~	~~
112	35290	~~	~~	- What about	Go around	~~	~~	~~
113	35320	~~	~~	Rosa?	~~	~~	~~	~~
114	35350	~~	~~	- She-she don't	~~	~~	~~	~~
115	35380	~~	~~	get a turn!	~~	~~	~~	~~
116	35410	~~	~~	~~	~~	~~	~~	~~
117	35440	~~	~~	Go around	~~	~~	~~	~~
118	35470	~~	~~	~~	~	~~	~~	- You don't
119	35500	-- Jimmy	~~	~~	Back to Fred	~~	~~	get a
120	35530	- You seem very unhappy.	~~	~~	then back to me.	~~	- Yeh, let's go	~~
121	35560	Perhaps you should go	~~	~~	~~	~~	around.	~~

sec.	frame #	Teacher	Anna	Jimmy	Rosa	Fred	Maria	P
122	35590	back to your seat.	~~	~~	No. Back to Fred,	~~	~~	~~
123	35620	--	~~	~~	back to Anna, and	~~	~~	~~
124	35650	--	~~	~~	Maria and back to me	~~	~~	~~
125	35680	--	~~	~~	~~	~~	~~	~~
126	35710	- Alright Fred, can	~~	~~	~~	~~	~~	~~
127	35740	you read page four.	~~	~~	~~	~~	~~	~~
128	35770		~~	~~	~~	- K	~~	~~
129	35800		~~	~~	~~		~~	~~
130	35830		~~	~~	~~	GO OUT	~~	~~
131	35860		~~	~~	~~		~~	~~
132	35890		~~	~~	~~	PATTY	~~	~~
133	35920		~~	~~	~~		~~	~~
134	35950		~~	~~	~~	GO OUT	~~	~~
135	35980		~~	~~	~~		~~	~~
136	36010		~~	~~	~~		~~	~~
137	36040		~~	~~	~~		~~	~~
138	36070		~~	~~	~~		~~	~~
139	36100	Stephen	~~	~~	~~		~~	~~
140	36130	you must do your	~~	~~	~~		~~	~~
141	36160	number paper before you	~~	~~	~~		~~	~~
142	36190	look at the library	~~	~~	~~		~~	~~
143	36220	--	~~	~~	~~		~~	~~
144	36250	--	~~	~~	~~		~~	~~
145	36280	And Paul	~~	~~	~~		~~	~~
146	36310	please go to your seat	~~	~~	~~		~~	~~

References

Amano, Ikuo. 1990. *Education and examination in modern Japan*. Tokyo: University of Tokyo Press.

Arensberg, Conrad. 1982. "Generalizing anthropology." In *Crisis in anthropology*. Ed. E. A. Hoebel, R. Currier, and S. Kaiser. New York: Garland.

Au, Katherine. 1980. "Participation structure in a reading lesson with Hawaiian children." *Anthropology and Education Quarterly* 11:91–115.

Bakhtin, Mikhail. [1940] 1984. *Rabelais and his world*. Tr. H. Iswolsky. Bloomington: Indiana University Press..

Banks, James, ed. 1996. *Multicultural education, transformative knowledge, and action: Historical and contemporary perspectives*. New York: Teachers College Press.

Basso, Keith. 1970. "'To give up on words': Silence in Western Apache culture." *Southwestern Journal of Anthropology* 26:213–230.

_____. 1979. *Portraits of "The Whiteman": Linguistic play and cultural symbols among the Western Apache*. New York: Cambridge University Press.

Bateson, Gregory. 1955. "The message 'This is play.'" In *Group processes: Transactions of the second conference*. Ed. B. Schaffner. New York: Josiah Macy, Jr. Foundation.

_____. *Naven*. [1936] 1958. Stanford, CA: Stanford University Press.

_____. 1972. *Steps to an ecology of mind*. New York: Balantine Books.

Bateson, Mary Catherine. 1975. "Mother-infant exchanges: The epigenesis of conversational interaction." In *Developmental psycholinguistics and communication disorders*. Ed. D. Aaronson and R. Rieber. New York: New York Academy of Sciences.

Becker, A. L., ed. 1989. "Introduction." In *Writing on the tongue*. Ann Arbor, MI: Center for South and Southeast Asian Studies.

Becker, Howard. 1963. *Outsiders*. New York: Free Press.

Benedict, Ruth. 1934. *Patterns of culture*. Boston: Houghton Mifflin.

_____. 1946. *The chrysanthemum and the sword: Patterns of Japanese culture*. Boston: Houghton Mifflin.

Bentley, Arthur. 1926. "Remarks on method in the study of society." *American Journal of Sociology* 32:456–460.

_____. [1908] 1995. *The process of government: A study of social pressures*. New Brunswick, NJ: Transaction Books.

Berg, Ivar. 1969. *Education and jobs: The great training robbery*. New York: Beacon Press.

Berger, Peter, and Thomas Luckmann. 1966. *The social construction of reality*. New York: Doubleday.

Birdwhistell, Ray. 1970. *Kinesics and context: Essays on body motion communication*. Philadelphia: University of Pennsylvania Press.

Blumer, Herbert. 1969. *Symbolic interactionism: Perspective and method*. Englewood Cliffs, NJ: Prentice-Hall.

Boas, Franz. 1928. *Anthropology and modern life*. New York: W. W. Norton.

_____. 1938. *The mind of primitive man*. New York: Free Press.

Bock, Philip. 1980. "Tepoztlán reconsidered." *Journal of Latin American Lore* 6:129–150.

Boggs, Stephen. 1972. "The meaning of questions and narratives to Hawaiian children." In *Functions of language in the classroom*. Ed. C. Cazden, V. John, and D. Hymes. New York: Teachers College Press.

Boon, James. 1982. *Other tribes, other scribes: Symbolic anthropology in the comparative study of cultures, histories, religions, and texts*. New York: Cambridge University Press.

Bourdieu, Pierre. 1966. "The sentiment of honour in Kabyle society." In *Honour and shame*. Ed. J. G. Peristiany. Chicago: University of Chicago Press.

_____. [1972] 1977. *Outline of a theory of practice*. Tr. R. Nice. New York: Cambridge University Press.

_____. [1970] 1990. "The Kabyle house or the world reversed." In *The logic of practice*. Cambridge: Polity Press.

_____. 1994. *Raisons pratiques: Sur la théorie de l'action*. Paris: Seuil.

Bourdieu, Pierre, and Jean-Claude Passeron. [1970] 1977. *Reproduction in education, society and culture*. Tr. R. Nice. Beverly Hills, CA: Sage.

Bourgois, Philippe. 1996. *In search of respect: Selling crack in East Barrio*. New York: Cambridge University Press.

Boyd, Cory. 1993. *The interactional positioning for a literacy related moment during grocery shopping*. Doctoral dissertation, Teachers College, Columbia University.

Byers, Paul. 1976. "Biological rhythms as information channels in interpersonal communication behavior." In *Perspectives in ethology II*. Ed. P. Bateson and P. Klopfer. New York: Plenum Press.

Canaan, Joyce. 1986. "Why a 'slut' is a 'slut': Cautionary tales of middle-class teenage girls' morality." In *Symbolizing America*. Ed. H. Varenne. Lincoln: University of Nebraska Press.

_____. 1990. "Passing notes and telling jokes: Gendered strategies among American middle school teenagers." In *Uncertain terms*. Ed. F. Ginsburg and A. Tsing. Boston: Beacon Press.

Cazden, Courtney. 1988. *Classroom discourse*. Portsmouth, NH: Heinemann.

Cazden, Courtney, Vera John, and Dell Hymes, eds. 1972. *Functions of language in the classroom*. New York: Teachers College Press.

Certeau, Michel de. 1984. *The practice of everyday life*. Berkeley: University of California Press.

Chaiklin, Seth, and Jean Lave, eds. 1993. *Understanding practice: Perspectives on Activity and Context*. New York: Cambridge University Press.

Chomsky, Noam. 1966. *Cartesian linguistics*. New York: Harper & Row.

Cicourel, Aaron. 1974. *Cognitive sociology*. New York: Free Press.

Cicourel, Aaron, and John Kitsuse. 1963. *Educational decision-making*. Indianapolis: Bobbs-Merrill.

Cole, Michael. 1996. *Cultural psychology: A once and future discipline*. Cambridge: Harvard University Press.

Cole, Michael, and Peg Griffin. 1986. "A sociohistorical approach to remediation." In *Literacy, schooling and society*. Ed. S. de Castell et al. New York: Cambridge University Press.

Cole, Michael, and Kenneth Traupmann. 1981. "Comparative cognitive research: Learning from a learning disabled child." In *Aspects of the development of competence*. Ed. W. Collins. Hillsdale, NJ: Lawrence Earlbaum.

Cole, Michael, Lois Hood, and Ray McDermott. 1978. *Ecological niche picking: Ecological invalidity as an axiom of experimental cognitive psychology.* Working paper 14, Laboratory of Comparative Human Cognition. New York: Rockefeller University.

Coles, Gerald. 1987. *The learning mystique.* New York: Pantheon.

Cremin, Lawrence. 1961. *The transformation of the school: Progressivism in American education, 1876–1957.* New York: Random House.

_____. 1980. *American education: The national experience, 1783–1876.* New York: Harper & Row.

_____. 1988. *American education: The metropolitan experience, 1876–1980.* New York: Harper & Row.

Darnton, Robert. 1985. *The great cat massacre and other episodes in French cultural history.* New York: Basic Books.

Dean, Mitchell. 1991. *The constitution of poverty: Toward a genealogy of liberal governance.* London: Routledge.

Deshen, Shlomo. 1992. *Blind people: The private and public life of sightless Israelis.* Albany: State University of New York Press.

Deutsch, Martin, ed. 1967. *The disadvantaged child.* New York: Basic Books.

Dewey, John. 1899. *School and society.* Chicago: University of Chicago Press.

_____. 1922. *Human nature and conduct.* New York: Holt.

_____. 1938. *Experience and education.* New York: Collier Books.

_____. 1939. *Freedom and culture.* New York: G. P. Putnam's Sons.

_____. [1916] 1966. *Democracy and education.* New York: Free Press.

Dore, John, and R. P. McDermott. 1982. "Linguistic indeterminacy and social context in utterance interpretation." *Language* 58:374–398.

Douglas, Mary. 1966. *Purity and danger: An analysis of concepts of pollution and taboo.* London: Routledge & Kegan Paul.

Drake, St. Clair, and Horace Clayton. 1945. *Black metropolis.* 2 vols. New York: Harper & Row.

Drummond, Lee. 1978. "Transatlantic nanny: Notes on a comparative semiotics of the family in English-speaking societies." *American Ethnologist* 5:30–43.

Dumont, Louis. [1966] 1970. "Caste, racism and 'stratification': Reflections of a social anthropologist." In *Homo hierarchicus.* Tr. M. Sainsbury. Chicago: University of Chicago Press.

_____. 1980. *Homo hierarchicus.* Rev. ed. Tr. M. Sainsbury. Chicago: University of Chicago Press.

Dumont, Robert. 1972. "Learning English and how to be silent: Studies in Sioux and Cherokee classrooms." In *Functions of language in the classroom.* Ed. C. Cazden, V. John, and D. Hymes. New York: Teachers College Press.

Duneier, Mitchell. 1992. *Slim's table: Race, respectability, and masculinity.* Chicago: University of Chicago Press.

Durkheim, Émile. [1897] 1951. *Suicide.* Tr. J. Spaulding and G. Simpson. New York: Free Press.

Eckstein, Max, and Harold Noah. 1993. *Secondary school examinations: International perspectives on policies and practice.* New Haven: Yale University Press.

Edelman, Murray. 1977. *Political language: Words that succeed and policies that fail.* New York: Academic Press.

Erikson, Erik. [1950] 1970. *Childhood and society.* 2nd ed. New York: W. W. Norton.

Erickson, Frederick, and Gerald Mohatt. 1982. "Cultural organization of participation structures in two classrooms of Indian students." In *Doing the ethnography of schooling.* Ed. G. Spindler. New York: Holt, Rinehart and Winston.

Erickson, Frederick, and Jeffrey Shultz. 1982. *The counselor as gatekeeper: Social interaction in interviews.* New York: Academic Press.

Feffer, Andrew. 1993. *The Chicago pragmatists and American progressivism.* Ithaca, NY: Cornell University Press.

Fisher, Berenice, and Anselm Strauss. 1979. "G. H. Mead and the Chicago tradition of sociology." *Symbolic Interaction* 2:9–25.

Foley, Douglas. 1990. *Learning capitalist culture: Deep in the heart of Tejas.* Philadelphia: University of Pennsylvania Press.

Frake, Charles. 1980. *Language and cultural description.* Stanford, CA: Stanford University Press.

_____. 1996a. "A church too far near a bridge oddly placed: The cultural construction of the Norfolk countryside." In *Redefining nature.* Ed. R. Ellen and K. Fukui. Washington, DC: Berg.

_____. 1996b. "Pleasant places, past times and sheltered identity in rural East Anglia." In *Senses of place.* Ed. S. Feld and K. Basso. Santa Fe, NM: School of American Research Press.

Fraser, James. 1908. "A new visual illusion of direction." *British Journal of Psychology* 2:307–337.

Frazier, E. Franklin. [1948] 1966. *The Negro family in the United States.* Chicago: University of Chicago Press.

Frost, Robert. 1949. *Complete poems.* New York: Holt, Rinehart and Winston.

Frykman, Jonas, and Orvar Löfgren. [1979] 1987. *Culture builders: A historical anthropology of middle-class life.* Tr. A. Crozier. New Brunswick, NJ: Rutgers University Press.

Garfinkel, Harold. 1946. "Color trouble." In *Primer for white folks.* Ed. B. Moon. Garden City, NY: Doubleday Doran.

_____. 1956. "Conditions for a successful degradation ceremony." *American Journal of Sociology* 61:420–424.

_____. 1967. *Studies in ethnomethodology.* Englewood Cliffs, NJ: Prentice-Hall.

Garfinkel, Harold, and Harvey Sacks. 1970. "On formal structures of practical actions." In *Theoretical sociology: Perspectives and developments.* Ed. J. McKinney and E. Tiryakian. New York: Meredith.

Geertz, Clifford. [1972] 1973a "Deep play: Notes on the Balinese cockfight." In *The interpretation of cultures.* New York: Basic Books.

_____. 1973b. *The interpretation of cultures.* New York: Basic Books.

Gibson, Margaret, and John Ogbu, eds. 1991. *Minority status and schooling: A comparative study of immigrant and involuntary minorities.* New York: Garland.

Gilmore, Perry. 1984. "Research currents: Assessing sub-rosa skills in children's language." *Language Arts* 61, 4:384–391.

_____. 1986. "Subrosa literacy." In *The acquisition of literacy.* Ed. B. P. Gilmore and B. Schieffelin. Norwood, NJ: Ablex.

Giroux, Henry. 1983. *Theory and resistance in education.* South Hadley, MA: Bergin and Garvey.

_____. 1996. *Fugitive cultures: Race, violence, and youth.* New York: Routledge.

Goffman, Erving. 1967. *Interaction ritual: Essays in face-to-face behavior.* Chicago: Aldine.

Goldman, Shelley. 1982. *Sorting out sorting: How stratification is managed in a middle school.* Doctoral dissertation, Teachers College, Columbia University.

Goldman, Shelley, and Ray McDermott. 1987. "The culture of competition in American schools." In *Education and cultural process.* Ed. G. Spindler. Prospect Heights, IL: Waveland Press.

Goodwin, Charles. 1981. *Conversational organization: Interaction between speakers and hearers.* New York: Academic Press.

Goodwin, Charles, and Marjorie Goodwin. 1992. "Assessments and the construction of context." In *Rethinking context.* Ed. A. Duranti and C. Goodwin. New York: Cambridge University Press.

Goodwin, Marjorie. 1990. *He-said-she-said: Talk as social organization among Black children.* Bloomington: Indiana University Press.

Gould, Stephen. 1981. *The mismeasure of man.* New York: W. W. Norton.

Green, Bryan. 1982. *Knowing the poor: A case study in textual reality construction.* Boston: Routledge & Kegan Paul.

Groce, Nora. 1985. *Everyone here spoke sign language.* Cambridge: Harvard University Press.

Hannerz, Ulf. 1969. *Soulside: Inquiries into ghetto culture and community.* New York: Columbia University Press.

Heath, Shirley Brice. 1983. *Ways with words: Language, life, and work in communities and classrooms.* New York: Cambridge University Press.

———. 1990. "The children of Trackton's children: Spoken and written language in social change." In *Cultural psychology.* Ed. J. Stigler, R. Shweder, and G. Herdt. New York: Cambridge University Press.

Heath, Shirley, and Milbrey McLaughlin, eds. 1993. *Identity and inner-city youth: Beyond ethnicity and gender.* New York: Teachers College Press.

Henry, Jules. 1963. *Culture against man.* New York: Random House.

Herrnstein, Richard, and Charles Murray. 1994. *The bell curve: Intelligence and class structure in American life.* New York: Free Press.

Hockett, Charles. 1964. "Scheduling." In *The view of language: Selected essays 1948–1974.* Ed. C. Hockett. Athens: University of Georgia Press.

Holloman, Regina, and Fannie Lewis. 1978. "The 'Clan': Case study of a Black extended family in Chicago." In *The extended family in Black societies.* Ed. D. Shimkin, E. Shimkin, and D. Frate. The Hague: Mouton.

Hood, Lois, R. P. McDermott, and M. Cole. 1980. "'Let's try to make it a good day': Some not so simple ways." *Discourse Processes* 3:155–168.

Hsu, Francis. 1983. *Rugged individualism reconsidered: Essays in psychological anthropology.* Knoxville: University of Tennessee Press.

Humphrey, Frank. 1980. *"Shh!" A sociolinguistic study of teacher's turn-taking sanctions in primary school lessons.* Doctoral dissertation, Georgetown University.

Jackall, Robert. 1988. *Moral mazes.* New York: Oxford University Press.

Jacoby, Russel, and Naomi Glauberman, eds. 1995. *The Bell Curve debate.* New York: Random House.

Joas, Hans. 1985. *G. H. Mead: A contemporary reexamination of the thought.* Cambridge: MIT Press.

Joyce, James. 1939. *Finnegans wake.* New York: Viking Press.

Kendon, Adam. 1982. "The organization of behavior in face-to-face interaction: Observations on the development of methodology." In *Handbook of methods in nonverbal research.* Ed. K. Scherer and P. Ekman. New York: Cambridge University Press.

———. 1990. *Conducting interaction: Patterns of behavior in focused encounters.* New York: Cambridge University Press.

Kingston, Maxine Hong. 1975. *The woman warrior: Memoirs of a girlhood among ghosts.* New York: Vintage Books.

Köhler, Wolfgang. 1947. *Gestalt psychology: An introduction to new concepts in modern psychology*. New York: Liveright.

_____. 1969. *The task of gestalt psychology*. Princeton, NJ: Princeton University Press.

Kozol, Jonathan. 1991. *Savage inequalities: Children in America's schools*. New York: Crown.

Kroeber, A. L., and Clyde Kluckhohn. 1953. *Culture: A critical review of concepts and definitions*. New York: Random House.

Labov, William. 1972. *Language in the inner city*. Philadelphia: University of Pennsylvania Press.

Lacey, Colin. 1970. *Hightown grammar: The school as a social system*. Manchester: Manchester University Press.

Lagemann, Ellen. 1989. "The plural worlds of educational research." *History of Education Quarterly* 29:185–214.

_____. 1992. "Prophecy or profession? George S. Counts and the social study of education." *American Journal of Education* 100:137–165.

Lave, Jean. 1988. *Cognition in practice: Mind, mathematics, and culture in everyday life*. New York: Cambridge University Press.

Lave, Jean, and Étienne Wenger. 1991. *Situated learning: Legitimate peripheral participation*. New York: Cambridge University Press.

Lavine, Thelma. 1995. "Introduction." In A. Bentley, *The process of government*. New Brunswick, NJ: Transaction.

Leacock, Eleanor, ed. 1971. *The culture of poverty: A critique*. New York: Simon and Schuster.

Leichter, Hope. 1985. "Children's response to a literate environment: Literacy before schooling." In *Awakening to literacy*. Ed. F. Smith. Exeter, NH: Heinemann.

Lévi-Strauss, Claude. [1958] 1963a. *Structural Anthropology*. Tr. C. Jacobson and B. Grundfest. New York: Doubleday.

_____. [1962] 1963b. *Totemism*. Tr. R. Needham. Boston: Beacon Press.

_____. [1955] 1963c. *Tristes tropiques*. Tr. J. Russell. New York: Atheneum.

_____. 1964. *Le Cru and le cuit*. Paris: Plon.

_____. [1962] 1966. *The savage mind*. Chicago: University of Chicago Press.

_____. [1949] 1969. *The elementary structures of kinship*. Tr. J. Bell and J. von Sturmer. Boston: Beacon Press.

_____. 1969–1981. *Mythologics*. 4 vols. Tr. J. and D. Weightman. New York: Harper & Row.

_____. [1971] 1981. *The naked man*. Tr. J. Weightman and D. Weightman. New York: Harper & Row.

Lewin, Kurt. 1935. *A dynamic theory of personality*. New York: McGraw Hill.

Lewis, Oscar. 1951. *Life in a Mexican village: Tepoztlán restudied*. Urbana: University of Illinois Press.

_____. 1961. *The children of Sanchez: Autobiography of a Mexican family*. New York: Random House, 1961.

_____. 1965. *La vida: A Puerto Rican family in the culture of poverty—San Juan and New York*. New York: Random House.

_____. 1966. "The culture of poverty." *Scientific American* 5:19–25.

Liebow, Elliot. 1967. *Tally's corner*. Boston: Little, Brown.

Lockridge, Kenneth. 1970. *A New England town: The first hundred years*. New York: W. W. Norton.

Luria, Alexander. 1979. *The making of mind*. Cambridge: Harvard University Press.

Lynd, Robert, and Helen Lynd. [1929] 1956. *Middletown: A study in modern American culture*. New York: Harcourt, Brace and World.

MacLeod, Jay. 1994. *Ain't no making it: Aspirations and attainment in a low-income neighborhood*. Boulder: Westview Press.

Malinowski, Bronislaw. 1923. "The problem of meaning in primitive languages." In *The meaning of meaning*. Ed. C. K. Ogden and I. A. Richards. New York: Harcourt.

Manicas, Peter T. 1987. *A history and philosophy of the social sciences*. New York: Basil Blackwell.

———. 1993. "Naturalizing epistemology: Reconstructing philosophy." In *Philosophy and the reconstruction of culture*. Ed. J. J. Stuhr. Albany: SUNY Press.

McDermott, John. 1973. "Introduction." In *The philosophy of John Dewey*. Ed. J. McDermott. New York: G. P. Putnam.

McDermott, R. P. 1977. "Kids make sense: An ethnographic account of the interactional management of success and failure in one first grade classroom." Unpublished doctoral dissertation, Stanford University.

———. 1980. "Profile: Ray L. Birdwhistell." *Kinesis Report* 2:1–16.

———. 1987. "The explanation of minority school failure, again." *Anthropology and Education Quarterly* 18:361–367.

———. 1988. "Inarticulateness." In *Linguistics in context*. Ed. D. Tannen. Norwood, NJ: Ablex.

———. 1993. "The acquisition of a child by a learning disability." In *Understanding practice*. Ed. S. Chaiklin and J. Lave. New York: Cambridge University Press.

———. 1997. "Achieving school failure, 1972–1997." In *Education and cultural process*. Ed. G. Spindler. 3rd ed. Prospect Heights, IL: Waveland Press.

McDermott, R. P., and Jeffrey Aron. 1978. "Pirandello in the classroom: On the possibility of equal educational opportunity in American culture." In *Futures of education*. Ed. M. Reynolds. Reston, VA: Council on Exceptional Children.

McDermott, R. P., and Shelley Goldman. 1983. "Teaching in multicultural settings." In *Multicultural education: A challenge for teachers*. Ed. L. Berg-Eldering, F. De Rijcke, and L. Zuck. Dordrecht, Holland: Foris.

McDermott, R. P., and K. Gospodinoff. 1979. "Social contexts for ethnic borders and school failure." In *Nonverbal behavior*. Ed. A. Wolfgang. New York: Academic Press.

McDermott, R. P., and Lois Hood. 1982. "Institutionalized psychology and the ethnography of schooling." In *Ethnography and education: Children in and out of school*. Ed. P. Gilmore and A. Glatthorn. Washington, DC: Center for Applied Linguistics.

McDermott, R. P., and Henry Tylbor. 1983. "On the necessity of collusion in conversation." *Text* 3:277–297.

McDermott, R. P., and Hervé Varenne. 1995. "Culture *as* disability." *Anthropology and Education Quarterly* 26:324–348.

———. 1996. "Culture, development, disability." In *Ethnography and human development*. Ed. R. Jessor, A. Colby, and R. Shweder. Chicago: University of Chicago Press, 1996.

McDermott, R. P., Shelley Goldman, and Hervé Varenne. 1984. "When school goes home: Some problems in the organization of homework." *Teachers College Record* 85:391–409.

McDermott, R. P., K. Gospodinoff, and J. Aron. 1978. "Criteria for an ethnographically adequate description of concerted activities and their contexts." *Semiotica* 24:245–275.

Mead, George Herbert. 1934. *Mind, self and society*. Chicago: University of Chicago Press.

———. [1909] 1964. "Social psychology as counterpoint to physiological psychology." In *Selected writings*. Ed. A. Reck. Indianapolis: Bobbs-Merrill.

_____. [1910a] 1964. "Psychology of social consciousness implied in instruction." In *Selected writings*. Ed. A. Reck. Indianapolis: Bobbs-Merrill.

_____. [1910b] 1964. "What social objects must psychology presuppose." In *Selected writings*. Ed. A. Reck. Indianapolis: Bobbs-Merrill..

_____. [1927] 1932. "The objective reality of perspectives." In *The philosophy of the present*. Chicago: University of Chicago Press.

Mead, Margaret. 1928. *Coming of age in Samoa*. New York: W. Morrow.

_____. [1942] 1965. *And keep your powder dry: An anthropologist looks at America*. New York: W. Morrow.

Mehan, Hugh. 1978. "Structuring school structure." *Harvard Educational Review* 48:32–64.

_____. 1979. *Learning lessons: Social organization in the classroom*. Cambridge: Harvard University Press.

_____. 1982. "The structure of classroom events and their consequences for student performance." In *Children in and out of school*. Ed. P. Gilmore and A. Glatthorn. Washington, DC: Center for Applied Linguistics.

Mehan, Hugh, Alma Hertwerk, and J. Lee Meihls. 1986. *Handicapping the handicapped*. Stanford, CA: Stanford University Press.

Miller, David. 1973. *George Herbert Mead: Self, language and the world*. Chicago: University of Chicago Press.

Miller, Robin. 1993. *Chaotic organization: A study of disaster*. Doctoral dissertation, Teachers College, Columbia University.

Mills, C. Wright. 1956. *The power elite*. New York: Oxford University Press.

Miyazaki, Ichisada. 1976. *China's examination hell: Civil service examinations of Imperial China*. Tr. C. Schirokauer. New Haven, CT: Yale University Press.

Moffatt, Michael. 1989. *Coming of age in New Jersey: College and American culture*. New Brunswick: Rutgers University Press.

Moore, Sally. 1975. "Selection for failure in a small social field." In *Symbol and politics in communal ideology*. Ed. S. F. Moore and B. Myerhoff. Ithaca, NY: Cornell University Press.

Morison, Ann. 1982. *Getting reading and writing: Literacy patterns in three urban families*. Doctoral dissertation, Teachers College, Columbia University.

Moynihan, Daniel. [1965] 1967. "The Negro family." In *The Moynihan report and the politics of controversy*. Ed. L. Rainwater and W. Yancey. Cambridge: MIT Press.

Murphy, Robert. 1987. *The body silent*. New York: Henry Holt.

Murphy, Yolanda, and Robert Murphy. 1974. *Women of the forest*. New York: Columbia University Press.

Myrdal, Gunnar. [1944] 1962. *An American dilemma: The Negro problem and modern democracy*. New York: Harper & Row.

Naddeo, Merry. 1991. *The New Life Singers: A discourse analysis of street kids "doing" a choir rehearsal*. Doctoral dissertation, Teachers College, Columbia University.

_____. 1993. "The New Life Singers: A study of street kids 'doing' choir." *Journal of Music Teaching and Learning* 4:24–34.

Newman, Denis, Peg Griffin, and Michael Cole. 1989. *The construction zone: Working for cognitive change in schools*. New York: Cambridge University Press.

Newman, Fred, and Lois Holzman. 1993. *Lev Vygotsky: Revolutionary scientist*. New York: Routledge.

Newman, Katherine. 1988. *Falling from grace: The experience of downward mobility in the American middle class*. New York: Free Press.

Oakes, Jeannie. 1987. *Keeping track.* New Haven, CT: Yale University Press.

Ogbu, John. 1974. *The next generation: An ethnography of education in an urban neighborhood.* New York: Academic Press.

_____. 1978. *Minority education and caste: The American system in cross-cultural perspective.* New York: Academic Press.

_____. 1987. "Opportunity structure, cultural boundaries and literacy." In *Language, literacy and culture.* Ed. J. Langer. Norwood, NJ: Ablex.

_____. 1991a. "Immigrant and involuntary minorities in comparative perspective." In *Minority status and schooling.* Ed. M. Gibson and J. Ogbu. New York: Garland.

_____. 1991b. "Low school performance as an adaptation: The case of Blacks in Stockton, California." In *Minority status and schooling.* Ed. M. Gibson and J. Ogbu. New York: Garland.

Ortner, Sherry. 1993. "Ethnography among the Newark: The class of '58 of Weequakic High School." *Michigan Quarterly Review* 32:411–429.

Padden, Carol, and Tom Humphries. 1988. *Deaf in America: Voices from a culture.* Cambridge: Harvard University Press.

Page, Reba. 1991. *Lower-track classrooms: A curricular and cultural perspective.* New York: Teachers College Press.

Paine, Thomas. [1776] 1976. *Common sense.* With an introduction by I. Kramnick. London: Penguin Books.

Parsons, Talcott, and Edward Shils, eds. 1951. *Toward a general theory of action.* New York: Harper & Row.

Peacock, James. 1986. *The anthropological lens.* New York: Cambridge University Press.

Philips, Susan. 1972. "Participant structures and communicative competence: Warm Springs children in community and classroom." In *Functions of language in the classroom.* Ed. C. Cazden, V. John, and D. Hymes. New York: Teachers College Press.

_____. 1983. *The invisible culture: Communication in classroom and community on the Warm Springs Indian reservation.* New York: Longman.

Pirandello, Luigi. 1922. *Naked masks.* New York: Dutton.

Plath, David. 1980. *Long engagements: Maturity in modern Japan.* Stanford, CA: Stanford University Press.

Plath, David, ed. 1983. *Work and lifecourse in Japan.* Albany: State University of New York Press.

Pollner, Melvin. 1978. "Constitutive and mundane versions of labeling theory." *Human Studies* 1:269–288.

Powell, Sumner. 1963. *Puritan village: The formation of a New England town.* Middletown, CT: Weslesyan University Press.

Propp, Vladimir. [1927] 1968. *Morphology of the folktale.* Tr. L. Scott. Austin: University of Texas Press.

Rawson, Margaret. 1968. *Developmental language disabilities: Adult accomplishments of dyslexic boys.* Baltimore: Johns Hopkins University Press.

Redfield, Robert. 1930. *Tepoztlán, a Mexican village: A study in folk life.* Chicago: University of Chicago Press.

_____. [1956] 1960. *The little community.* Chicago: University of Chicago Press.

Reimer, Joseph. 1977. *A study of moral development on a kibbutz.* Doctoral dissertation, Harvard University.

Rizzo-Tolk, Rosemarie. 1990. *Student interaction and the construction of laughter.* Doctoral dissertation, Teachers College, Columbia University.

Rizzo-Tolk, Rosemarie, and Hervé Varenne. 1992. "Joint action on the wild side of Manhattan: The power of the cultural center on an educational alternative." *Anthropology and Education Quarterly* 23:221–249.

Rohlen, Thomas. 1980. "The Juku phenomenon." *Journal of Japanese Studies* 6:207–242.

_____. 1983. *Japan's high schools.* Berkeley: University of California Press.

_____. 1993. "Learning." In *The political economy of Japan.* Vol. 3, *Socio and cultural dynamics.* Ed. S. Kumon and H. Rosovsky. Stanford: Stanford University Press.

Rohlen, Thomas, and Gerald LeTendre, eds. 1995. *Teaching and learning in Japan.* New York: Cambridge University Press.

Rosenthal, Robert, and Lenore Jacobson. 1968. *Pygmalion in the classroom.* New York: Holt, Rinehart and Winston.

Sacks, Harvey. 1974. "An analysis of the course of a joke's telling in conversation." In *Explorations in the ethnography of speaking.* Ed. R. Bauman and J. Sherzer. New York: Cambridge University Press.

Sacks, Harvey. 1984. "On doing 'being ordinary.'" In *Structures of social action.* Ed. J. M. Atkinson and J. Heritage. New York: Cambridge University Press.

Sarason, Seymour, and John Doris. 1979. *Educational handicap and public policy.* New York: Free Press.

Scheflen, Albert. 1973. *Communicational structure: Analysis of a psychotherapy transaction.* Bloomington: Indiana University Press.

Schegloff, Emanuel. 1984. "On some questions and ambiguities in conversation."" In *Structures of social action.* Ed. J. M. Atkinson and J. Heritage. New York: Cambridge University Press.

Schegloff, Emanuel, G. Jefferson, and H. Sacks. 1977. "The preference for self-correction in the organization of repair in conversation." *Language* 53:361–382.

Schneider, David. [1968] 1980. *American kinship: A cultural account.* Chicago: University of Chicago Press.

Schneider, David, and Raymond Smith. 1973. *Class differences and sex roles in American kinship and family structure.* Englewood Cliffs, NJ: Prentice-Hall.

Schutz, Alfred. 1951. "Making music together." *Social Research* 18:76–97.

Scott, James. 1985. *Weapons of the weak.* New Haven, CT: Yale University Press.

Shimkin, Demitri, G. Louie, and D. Frate. 1978. "The Black extended family: A basic rural institution and a mechanism of urban adaptation." In *The extended family in Black societies.* Ed. D. Shimkin, E. Shimkin, and D. Frate. The Hague: Mouton.

Shuman, Amy. 1986. *Story telling rights.* Philadelphia: University of Pennsylvania Press.

Shweder, Richard. 1991. *Thinking through cultures: Expeditions in cultural psychology.* Cambridge: Harvard University Press.

Shweder, Richard, M. Mahapatra, and J. G. Miller. 1990. "Culture and moral development." In *The emergence of moral concepts in early childhood.* Ed. J. Kagan and S. Lamb. Chicago: University of Chicago Press.

Silverman, Cheryl. 1989. *Jewish emigres and popular images of Jews in Japan.* Doctoral dissertation, Teachers College, Columbia University.

Sinclair, J., and R. Coulthard. 1975. *Towards an analysis of discourse.* New York: Oxford University Press.

Smith, David, Perry Gilmore, Shelley Goldman, and Ray McDermott. 1993. "Failure's failure." In *Minority education.* Ed. E. Jacob and C. Jordan. Norwood, NJ: Ablex.

Spindler, George. 1959. *The transmission of American culture.* Cambridge: Harvard University Press.

Stack, Carol. 1975. *All our kin.* New York: Harper & Row.

Street, Brian. 1984. *Literacy in theory and practice.* New York: Cambridge University Press.

Suchman, Lucy. 1987. *Plans and situated actions: The problem of human machine communication.* New York: Cambridge University Press.

Susser, Ida. 1982. *Norman street: Poverty and politics in an urban neighborhood.* New York: Oxford University Press.

Suttles, Gerald. 1972. *The social construction of communities.* Chicago: University of Chicago Press.

Taylor, Denny. 1983. *Family literacy: Young children learning to read and write.* Portsmouth, NH: Heinemann.

Taylor, Denny, and Catherine Dorsey-Gaines. 1988. *Growing up literate: Learning from inner-city families.* Portsmouth, NH: Heinemann.

Thomas, A., N. Herzog, L. Dryman, and D. Fernandez. 1971. "Examiner effects on IQ testing of Puerto-Rican working class children." *American Journal of Orthopsychiatry* 41:809–821.

Tocqueville, Alexis de. [1848] 1969. *Democracy in America.* Tr. G. Lawrence. Garden City, NY: Doubleday.

Valentine, Betty Lou. 1978. *Hustling and other hard work: Life styles in the ghetto.* New York: Free Press.

Valentine, Charles. 1968. *Culture and poverty: Critique and counter-proposals.* Chicago: University of Chicago Press.

_____. 1969. "Review of 'Culture and Poverty.'" *Current Anthropology* 10:181–201.

Varenne, Hervé. 1977. *Americans together: Structured diversity in a Midwestern town.* New York: Teachers College Press.

_____. 1978. "Culture as rhetoric: The patterning of the verbal interpretation of interaction in an American high school." *American Ethnologist* 5:635–650.

_____. 1983. *American school language: Culturally patterned conflicts in a suburban high school.* New York: Irvington.

_____. 1984. "Collective representation in American anthropological conversations about culture: Culture and the individual." *Current Anthropology* 25:281–300.

_____. 1987. "Talk and real talk: The voices of silence and the voices of power in American family life." *Cultural Anthropology* 2:369–394.

_____. 1992. *Ambiguous harmony.* Norwood, NJ: Ablex.

Varenne, Hervé, ed. 1986. *Symbolizing America.* Lincoln: University of Nebraska Press.

Varenne, Hervé, and R. P. McDermott. 1986. "'Why Sheila can read': Structure and indeterminacy in the reproduction of familial literacy." In *The acquisition of literacy.* Ed. B. Schieffelin and P. Gilmore. Norwood, NJ: Ablex.

Varenne, Hervé, R. P. McDermott, Vera Hamid-Buglione, and Ann Morison. 1982. *"I teach him everything he learns in school": The acquisition of literacy for learning in working class families.* New York: Teachers College, Columbia University, Elbenwood Center for the Study of the Family as Educator.

Voloshinov, V. [1929] 1973. *Marxism and the philosophy of language.* Tr. L. Matejka and I. R. Titunik. New York: Seminar Press.

Vygotsky, Lev. 1978. *Mind in society: The development of higher psychological processes.* Cambridge: Harvard University Press.

_____. 1986. *Thought and language.* Cambridge: MIT Press.

Wells, H. G. 1917. "James Joyce." *New Republic* March 10:158–160.

_____. [1904] 1979. *Selected short stories.* Baltimore: Penguin.

Wieder, D. Lawrence. 1974. *Language and social reality: The case of telling the convict code.* The Hague: Mouton.

Williams, Raymond. 1977. *Marxism and literature.* Oxford: Oxford University Press.

Willis, Paul. 1977. *Learning to labor: How working class kids get working class jobs.* New York: Columbia University Press.

Wong, Sau-ling. 1992. "Autobiography as a guided Chinatown tour: Maxine Hong Kingston's Woman warrior and the Chinese American autobiographical controvery." In *Multicultural autobiography.* Ed. J. Payne. Knoxville: University of Tennessee Press.

_____. 1993. *Reading Asian American literature: From necessity to extravagance.* Princeton: Princeton University Press.

Name Index

Amano, Ikuo, 127(n13)
Arensberg, Conrad, 44(n5)
Aron, Jeffrey, 85(n8), 93, 127(n5), 190, 201, 204(nn) , 204(n7)
Au, Katherine, 21(n6)

Bakhtin, Mikhail, 137
Banks, James, 210
Basso, Keith, 21(n6)
Bateson, Gregory, 21(n8), 32, 85(n8), 112, 179, 204(n5), 212
Bateson, Mary Catherine, 62(n8)
Becker, Alton, 25
Becker, Howard, 29
Benedict, Ruth, 11–12, 32, 146, 150, 158–160, 164–166, 174–175, 181(n2), 181(n4), 212
Bentley, Arthur, 159–160, 162–166, 174, 181(n2)
Berg, Ivar, 216
Berger, Peter, 160–161, 175–177
Birdwhistell, Ray, 11–12, 21(n8)
Blumer, Herbert, 160, 163, 181(n1)
Boas, Franz, 8–9, 146, 181(n4)
Bock, Philip, 156(n3)
Boggs, Stephen, 21(n6)
Boon, James, 155(n1), 156(n1)
Bourdieu, Pierre, 21(n10), 128(n20), 135, 161, 169, 172–174, 176, 204(n2), 205(n14), 212
Bourgois, Philippe, 128(n18)
Boyd, Cory, 62(n8)
Byers, Paul, 105(n6), 220

Canaan, Joyce, 126(nn)
Cayton, Horace, 181(n9)
Cazden, Courtney, 54, 148
Certeau, Michel de, 174
Chaiklen, Seth, 61(n3)

Chomsky, Noam, 160
Cicourel, Aaron, 28–29, 128(n14), 216
Cole, Michael, 16, 41, 43(nn) , 43(n1), 43(n2), 61(n3), 141, 181(n8)
Coles, Gerald, 27, 44(n3)
Coulthard, R., 20(n3)
Cremin, Lawrence, 126(n1), 204(n6)

Darnton, Robert, 32
Dean, Mitchell, 147
Deshen, Shlomo, 138, 156(n2)
Deutsch, Martin, 8
Dewey, John, 7–8, 39, 86, 107–108, 126(n1), 163, 166–167, 181(n4), 212, 216
Dore, John, 186–187, 189, 191–194, 204(nn), 205(n10)
Doris, John, 27
Dorsey-Gaines, Catherine, 61(n2), 126(nn)
Douglas, Mary, 125
Drake, St. Clair, 181(n9)
Drummond, Lee, 156(n5)
Dumont, Louis, 20(n2), 143, 210–211
Dumont, Robert, 21(n6)
Duneier, Mitchell, 181(n9)
Durkheim, Emile, 11, 32, 161, 168–169, 177, 181(n7), 183, 205(n7)

Eckstein, Max, 127(n3), 127(n13)
Edelman, Murray, 216
Einstein, Albert, 211
Erickson, Erik, 135, 144–145, 158, 169, 171
Erickson, Frederick, 21(n6), 128(n14), 141

Feffer, Andrew, 167
Fisher, Berenice, 181(n1)
Foley, Douglas, 127(n8)
Frake, Charles, 57, 204(n4), 205(n8)
Franklin, Benjamin, 2
Fraser, James, 12–13

255

Subject Index

我. *See* I/me
Ability, xiii, 45. *See also* Disability
Accomplishment, 5, 10, 18, 66, 69, 84(n2),
  95, 99, 120, 176. *See also* Achievement;
  Concerted activity
Accountability, 47, 49, 53–54, 57, 67–68, 88,
  90, 92–93, 97, 99, 102, 104(n2),
  109–110, 180–181, 183–186, 193–194,
  202–203, 204(n1), 214, 220
Achievement, 9, 50, 95, 186, 207. *See also*
  Accomplishment; Concerted activity
Action, Chapter 7
  as constitutive of a 'me,' 127, 147–148
  as part of institutionalized sequences, 5, 7,
    15–16, 31, 37, 109, 120, 189
  as product of an 'I,' 61, 63, 104, 198,
    202–204, 215
  as theoretical concern, 1, 19, 88, 124–125,
    151, 207, 211
  with others, 10, 14, 46, 108, 146, 193. *See
    also* Concerted activity
  See also Activity; Consequentiality
Activity, Chapter 7
  as product of action, 7, 73, 152, 183–185,
    189, 193. *See also* Concerted activity
  as property of persons, xiv, 13–15, 19, 38,
    46, 51, 63, 70, 82, 93, 108, 110,
    120–126, 132, 144–146, 148–149,
    152–154, 186, 202–204, 207, 213–214
Adaptation, 153–154, 159
African American, 5, 10, 18, 21, 65, 87, 92,
  97, 141, 150, 152, 156(n9), 163,
  171–172, 181(n9), 208–209, 213, 215
Agency, 20, 131–132, 135, 156(n1), 158, 161,
  165, 174–177, 179, 186, 193, 198,
  205(n14). *See also* Activity
Alienation, 141, 153, 163
America (as culture), xii–xiv, 1–4, 7, 10–11, 15,
  19–20, 25–27, 38–39, 42, 47, 52, 56,
  60, 82, 91, 99, 103–104, 106, 108–110,
  115, 122–123, 126, 127(n4), 131, 133,
  140, 142, 145, 147, 154–155, 158–159,
  161, 163, 167- 168, 170, 209, 211,
  213–214, 216, 217(n1)
Anthropology, 2, 8–9, 11–12, 21(n8), 32, 136,
  138, 148, 158–159, 165, 175, 181(n5)
  of education, 108–109, 135, 139–154. *See
    also* Education, research in
Arbitrary (cultural), 3, 173–174
Authority, 14, 38, 42, 46, 49, 54, 62(n5), 134,
  165, 205(n14), 206(n14), 215, 221–222
Authorization, 6, 132–133, 155
Autism, 140

Behaviorism, 160, 163
Black. *See* African American
Blindness, 134–137, 140, 142–143, 146,
  156(n2). *See also* Disability
Boundary, 68, 72, 92, 100, 178–181,
  182(n13), 184, 189, 191–192, 202,
  205(n12)
Bricolage, 61

Canonical form, 54, 92. *See also* Positioning;
  Structuralism
Caste, 210–211
Chicano. *See* Hispanic
China. *See* Chinese, American
Chinese, 7–10, 21, 27, 133, 176–177, 214
  American, 27
Christianity, 170
Class (as way of classifying people), xii, 2–4, 8,
  15, 17, 39, 47–49, 64–65, 87–88, 92,
  97, 99, 110, 120–121, 123–126,
  128(nn13, 17), 143, 146–147, 149,
  150–153, 170, 172–173, 181(n9), 208,
  212–213
Cognition, 29–30, 38, 63, 141, 163, 175, 185,
  189, 198, 205(n7)
  and learning, 43(n2)

Sequence (of actions), 6–7, 14, 50–61, 66,
    85(n8), 91, 93–95, 100, 105(n7), 112,
    183–185, 189, 194, 198, 201, 203,
    204(n6)
Sequencing (of actions with other actions), 3,
    14–18, 55–57, 67–82, 84(n2), 124, 208,
    222. *See also* Interaction
Sex. *See* Gender
Sharing, 100, 137, 165–168. *See also*
    Consensus; Conformity
Sight, 143. *See also* Blindness
Slavery, 97, 149, 209
Social fact. *See* Fact, cultural
Socialization, 11, 126, 165–166, 170, 212
Sociolinguistics, 8, 10, 141
Sorting, 110, 112–113, 115–118, 128(n19),
    132–133. *See also* Tracking
Special education, 27, 207–209, 213–215. *See
    also* Disability, learning
Strategy, 39, 51, 141, 161, 173
Structuralism, 76, 173, 179, 184
Suburb, 4, 19, 48, 65, 99
Success/failure in school (explanation of), xiii,
    4, 8, 102–103, 133, 139–154, 157–158,
    171–173, 176, Chapter 9. *See also*
    Deprivation theory; Difference theory
Suicide, 181(n7), 183
Symbolic interactionism, 160, 163
Symbolism, 125

Talent, 64, 83–84, 116. *See also* Merit
Television, 57
Test
    as institution, 16, 31–32, 38, 45, 91, 132,
        135, 155, 173 IQ, 28, 33, 38–42, 117
    in schooling, xiii, 5, 17–18, 25, 28, 30, 51,
        102, Chapter 5, 132, 208, 216
    as social setting, 27–31, 39–41
    taking and giving, ix, 2, 6, 45, 108, 110,
        Chapter 5, 150, 181
Therapy, 64, 82, 145, 208
Tracking, 89, 117, 128(n13), 194, 208, 216.
    See also Sorting
Transcription, 220, 222, 235
Turn-taking, 195, 204(n2). *See also* Conversation
    analysis; Interactional analysis

Videodisc, 222, 235
Videotaping, 52, 54, 57, 59–60, 66, 88, 90,
    93, 100, 187, 219–222, 235
Village (as metaphor for society), 45, 107, 143

Work (as productive of cultural facts), xii, 5–6,
    9, 13–16, 18, 27, 33–34, 45, 52, 57, 60,
    69, 84, 86, 108, 110, 117, 121–125,
    131–133, 137, 145, 148, 173–178, 185,
    187, 189, 191–194, 201–202, 211,
    214–215. *See also* Constitution;
    Construction